NICK HILL lives in Devizes, not far from the Ridgeway. As part of the Trailblazer team he is author, illustrator and cartographer, drawing many of the maps for the guides.

After completing a design degree at university, he set off into Asia ostensibly for a short trip; several enthralling years later he had crossed the continent overland four times. He settled temporarily in Thailand, his four years in Bangkok punctuated with periods in Siberia, China, India and Pakistan.

Nick has updated new editions of the *Trans-Siberian Handbook* and the *South Downs Way* and is co-author of the forthcoming *Indian Rail Handbook* and *China Rail Handbook*.

The Ridgeway
First edition: 2006; this second edition 2009

Publisher
Trailblazer Publications
The Old Manse, Tower Rd, Hindhead, Surrey, GU26 6SU, UK
Fax (+44) 01428 607571, info@trailblazer-guides.com
www.trailblazer-guides.com

British Library Cataloguing in Publication Data
A catalogue record for this book is available from the British Library

ISBN 978-1-905864-17-1

© **Trailblazer 2009**
Text and maps

Editor: Anna Jacomb-Hood
Layout: Anna Jacomb-Hood
Proof-reading: Nicky Slade
Illustrations: © Nick Hill (pp62-4); © Rev CA Johns (p67);
Photographs: cover © Dave Collier;
flora section: C4 – Row 1, left; Row 3, middle & right: © Tricia Hayne
all other flora photographs © Bryn Thomas
all other photographs © Nick Hill
Cartography: Nick Hill
Index: Anna Jacomb-Hood

Warning: long-distance walking can be dangerous
Please read the notes on when to go (pp22-4) and health and safety (pp52-4).
Every effort has been made by the author and publisher to ensure that the information
contained herein is as accurate and up to date as possible. However, they are unable
to accept responsibility for any inconvenience, loss or injury sustained by anyone
as a result of the advice and information given in this guide.

Printed on chlorine-free paper by
D2Print (☎ +65-6295 5598), Singapore

The Ridgeway

AVEBURY TO IVINGHOE BEACON
planning, places to stay, places to eat,
includes 53 large-scale walking maps
N I C K   H I L L

TRAILBLAZER PUBLICATIONS

Acknowledgements

Many thanks to Soph for venturing onto the trail with me on several occasions and to Ms Nun for willingly walking some parts of it again. Thanks also to Bill and Jenny Hill for logistical support, Tom the extreme-Ridgeway walker, Rod for the company on the way up to the Beacon, the helpful staff of the tourist information centre in Wendover and all the people who maintain the Ridgeway for the benefit of others. I particularly enjoyed the fleeting conversations with the many friendly walkers whom I met along the path, especially Mr Sparsholt.

At Trailblazer, many thanks to Anna for all her advice and hard work on the text and also for compiling the index, and also to Bryn for giving me this opportunity, again.

A request

The author and publisher have tried to ensure that this guide is as accurate and up to date as possible. Nevertheless things change. If you notice any changes or omissions that should be included in the next edition of this book, please write to Trailblazer (address on p2) or email us at info@trailblazer-guides.com. A free copy of the next edition will be sent to persons making a significant contribution.

Updated information will shortly be available on:
💻 **www.trailblazer-guides.com**

Front cover: Aerial view of the White Horse at Uffington (Photo © Dave Collier)

CONTENTS

INTRODUCTION

The Ridgeway stretches 87 miles (139km) across five counties, starting at Overton Hill near Avebury in Wiltshire and passing through Oxfordshire, Berkshire and Hertfordshire and ending at Ivinghoe Beacon in Buckinghamshire. Part of a network of tracks that from time immemorial naturally evolved all over the country, the Ridgeway was used by travellers, traders and drovers. Nowadays it is used only by travellers, most of them walking for pleasure. It is easily accessible from major cities such as Swindon, Oxford, Reading and London making it an ideal place to ramble, yet few seem to take the opportunity.

From its starting point in Wiltshire, the trail immediately takes you up onto high ground with views of the countryside which change with the light and stretch endlessly to the horizon. Walking up here can be isolated and it is open to the elements but it is exhilarating; on sunny days the air is wonderful, filling you with energy and physical well-being. You're unlikely to meet many people. The path descends as it gets closer to the River Thames and its character changes completely. You'll pass through a number of attractive villages as the trail runs parallel to the banks of the river before turning eastwards to start the next distinctive stage. Woodland is now the principal feature as you walk through the undulating landscape, passing through market towns and villages before finishing back out on high, exposed terrain.

Overton Hill in Wiltshire marks the present-day start of the trail but you are soon back in the distant past with the huge Iron Age forts of Barbury Castle and Liddington Castle. More ancient remains are at Wayland's Smithy, a Neolithic long barrow, before you reach the magnificent Uffington White Horse. From here on you are likely to be treading a solitary path for some miles, open to all weathers. This is one of the most enjoyable sections of the Ridgeway: in blissful solitude you can look down at the towns and villages far below.

After reaching the village of East Ilsley you'll note the environment starting to change. Human habitation becomes more frequent, and you continue downhill. You'll arrive at the village of Streatley, on the banks of the Thames, before crossing the bridge into the neighbouring town of Goring. From here an easy trail runs along the tranquil banks of the Thames for several miles, passing through the attractive villages of South Stoke and North Stoke, then turns eastwards just before the towns of Wallingford and Crowmarsh Gifford.

The path now follows an ancient earthwork, Grim's Ditch, for several miles until it reaches Nuffield where the Ridgeway crosses a golf course. From here on the woodlands become a frequent companion with many ascents and descents before you can visit some of the old market towns just off the official route, such as Watlington, Chinnor and Princes Risborough. The trail continues through some fine beech woods; from the occasional clearings you look down on the landscape far below. The route then goes through the Chequers Estate, traditional country home of the prime minister. Later it passes close to small, picturesque villages such as Wigginton and Aldbury, after which it climbs steadily as it enters the final section of woodland. When the trees thin out you can see your goal up ahead in the distance, several more hills away. At the end of the path, at Ivinghoe Beacon, you may be tired but you'll be rewarded by some spectacular, panoramic views of the countryside below.

Walking the Ridgeway is not difficult. It can be done in five days but this won't leave much time for relaxation or for enjoying the countryside you are walking through. You should also allow time to explore some of the towns along the way.

About this book

This guidebook is as practically useful, comprehensive and up to date as humanly possible. It is the **only** book you need; no phoning around for tourist brochures. You can find here everything for planning your trip including:

- All standards of accommodation from campsites to luxurious hotels
- Walking companies' details if you want an organised tour
- Suggested itineraries for all types of walkers
- Answers to all your questions: when to go, degree of difficulty, what to pack and the approximate cost of the whole walking holiday

We also give comprehensive information to get you to and from the Ridgeway and 53 detailed maps (1:20,000) and 24 town plans to help you find your way along it. The route guide section includes:

- Walking times in both directions
- Reviews of campsites, hostels, pubs, B&Bs, guesthouses and hotels
- Cafés, pubs, teashops, takeaways and restaurants as well as shops for supplies
- Rail, bus and taxi information for all the villages and towns along the path
- Street plans of the main towns and villages along the route
- Historical, cultural and geographical background information.

Minimum impact for maximum insight

Nature's peace will flow into you as the sunshine flows into trees. The winds will blow their freshness into you and storms their energy, while cares will drop off like autumn leaves.
John Muir (one of the world's earliest and most influential environmentalists, born in 1838)

It is no surprise that, since the time of John Muir, walkers and adventurers have been concerned about the natural environment; this book seeks to continue that tradition. By developing a deeper ecological awareness through a better understanding of nature and by supporting rural economies, local businesses, sensitive forms of transport and low-impact methods of farming and land-use we can all do our bit for a brighter future.

As we work harder and live our lives at an ever faster pace a walking holiday is a chance to escape from the daily grind and the natural pace gives us time to think and relax. This can have a positive impact not only on our own well being but also on that of the area we pass through. There can be few activities as 'environmentally friendly' as walking.

About the Ridgeway

HISTORY

The Ridgeway is very ancient. It's often described as 'the oldest road in Britain' and it's clear that parts of the route were in use as long as 5000 years ago. The Ridgeway, as we know it today, is in fact the middle section of the Greater Ridgeway (see p184), an ancient system of tracks that stretches from Lyme Regis on the Dorset coast up to Hunstanton on the Norfolk coast. These tracks evolved over centuries as people chose the driest and most suitable paths across the countryside for themselves and their animals.

During your walk you will still be able to see and touch stone structures dating back to the prehistoric days of the Ridgeway; the burial mound known as Wayland's Smithy (see box p110) dates back to around 4000BC.

There are also Bronze Age stone structures still standing, with the Avebury stone circle (see box pp96-7) and West Kennet Avenue (see box p78) being by far the most famous and accessible of these. Additionally, you can see numerous Bronze Age burial mounds dotted along the Ridgeway.

From the Iron Age there are several important hill forts along the route to investigate including Barbury Castle (see p96) and Uffington Castle (see p112) plus earthworks such as Grim's Ditch (see box p142) also dating from this time.

During the Dark Ages the Ridgeway was used as a major transport route for invading Danish Viking armies. By the late 9th century they had conquered most of Saxon England and had turned their attention to the kingdom of Wessex. In 871 they marched west along the Ridgeway from their base by the Thames at Reading only to be defeated by King Alfred at the Battle of Ashdown which some think took place in the area around White Horse Hill.

Up until the 18th century the Ridgeway still consisted of a broad network of routes across the country but then the Enclosures Acts were passed by parliament and these initiated the division of previously communal open land into privately owned fields. These fields were then hedged in to protect them from passing livestock and as a result the Ridgeway was forced to follow a single, defined route.

As coaching routes to London developed they avoided the actual course of the Ridgeway so it was left largely neglected – although several towns on the path, such as Marlborough and Wendover, were important rest-stops. The main users of the path, therefore, for several hundred years were drovers transporting their sheep from the West Country, and even Wales, to the large sheep fairs at East Ilsley (see p124). The width of the Ridgeway in this area, sometimes up to

20 metres, gives an idea of just how much livestock was transported on this route. At their peak the fairs held auctions for up to 80,000 sheep a day though by the early 20th century these fairs were in decline: the last one was held in 1934. From then on the path was used mainly by farmers for access to their land.

This was especially the case during the Second World War when many of the hillsides around the Ridgeway saw a change in use from sheep-grazed areas to cultivated fields. This was a result of a government-initiated effort to provide sufficient food for the population as imports were threatened owing to the fighting. This not only changed the visual landscape of many areas of the Ridgeway but also damaged the indigenous wildlife as powerful chemical fertilisers were used to improve the poor soil.

The first calls for the Ridgeway to be recognised as a long-distance walking trail were made in 1947 by the National Parks Committee and in the 1950s the Ramblers' Association (see box p36) joined the appeal. However, it wasn't until 1973 that it was officially opened as a National Trail, since when, the most common use for the path has been for recreation. Only minor alterations have been made to its course since then which enables people like ourselves to make our way along the 87-mile (139km) trail in the footsteps of the first Ridgeway pioneers from thousands of years ago.

HOW DIFFICULT IS THE RIDGEWAY?

If you are reasonably fit you won't encounter any problems walking the Ridgeway. There are no sections that are technically difficult and despite having a couple of steep climbs during each day's walking, it's nothing like as demanding as many other National Trails. The most important thing to do is plan your walking based on your own abilities. If you try to walk too far in one day, not only will you lose the chance to really enjoy the countryside you are walking through, but you will end up exhausted and won't feel much like walking the next day.

If anything, the western section of the Ridgeway, up to Streatley, could be considered more difficult than the eastern section owing to its remote and exposed conditions that become very apparent during bad weather. From Streatley onwards the Ridgeway is often in woodland or passing through fields and goes through, or near to, numerous towns and villages.

Route finding
You shouldn't have any problems staying on the Ridgeway. At nearly all the junctions there are special 'Ridgeway' signposts clearly showing the direction of the trail and other branching paths. For many stretches you barely even need these signposts as the path is clear and well-trodden. However, it is always worth checking them as at

some junctions the Ridgeway does veer off from what you'd consider is the 'obvious' path. All path junctions are included on the maps in this book along with relevant notes.

GPS waypoints

If you have a handheld **GPS receiver** you will be able to take advantage of the waypoints marked on the maps, and listed in the appendix on p185 of this book.

Essentially a GPS will calculate your position on the earth using a number of satellites and this will be accurate to a few metres. You might wonder that if this is possible, what is the point of taking paper maps and a compass with you. The answer is that if the batteries go flat, or the machine malfunctions, you'll be left with only your sense of direction. Depending on how good that is, you might, or might not, be left wondering exactly where you are.

Having said this, it is **by no means compulsory** that you use a GPS in conjunction with this guide and you should be able to get by with simply the signposts on the trail and the maps in this book. However, a GPS can be useful if for some reason you do get lost, or if you decide to explore off the trail and can't find your way back. It can also prove handy if you find yourself on the trail after dark when you can't see further than your torch beam.

If you do decide to use a GPS unit in conjunction with this book don't feel you need to be ticking off every waypoint as you reach it; you'll soon get bored and should get by without turning on your GPS for most of the trail. But if at any point you are **unsure of your position**, or wonder which way you should be headed, your GPS can give a quick and reassuring answer.

You can either manually key the nearest presumed waypoint from the list in this book into your unit as and when the need arises. Or, much less laboriously and with less margin for keystroke error, download the complete list (but not the descriptions) for free as a GPS-readable file from the Trailblazer website. You'll need the right cable and adequate memory in your unit (typically the ability to store 500 waypoints or more). This file, as well as instructions on how to interpret an OS grid reference, can be found in the updates section of the Ridgeway text on the Trailblazer website (💻 www.trailblazer-guides.com).

HOW LONG DO YOU NEED?

This depends on your fitness and experience. Do not try to do too much in one day if you are new to long-distance walking. Most people find that eight days is enough to complete the walk and still have time to look around the villages and enjoy the views along the way. Alternatively the entire path can be done in five days if you are fit enough, but you won't see much of the surrounding countryside.

If you're camping don't underestimate how much a heavy pack laden with camping gear will slow you down. It is also worth bearing in mind that those who take it easy on the Ridgeway see a lot more than those who sweat out long days and tend to only ever see the path in front of them. If you are walking on your own you can dictate the pace, but when walking with someone else you need to take their abilities into account and take time to enjoy their company – this will inevitably slow you down. If you don't take time to do this, you might as well be walking separately and simply meeting up at the end of the day.

On all sections, but particularly the western section, you'll also need to consider how far off the path your accommodation is and build that distance into your daily total. Although some B&Bs will collect you from the Ridgeway and drop you back the next morning not all offer this service, so you do need to check when reserving a room. On p26 there are some suggested itineraries covering different walking speeds that will give you an idea of what you can expect to achieve each day.

If you only have a few days it makes sense to concentrate on the 'best' parts of the Ridgeway; there is a list of recommended day and weekend walks on p27.

Practical information for the walker

ACCOMMODATION

There is plenty of accommodation along the Ridgeway and if you plan ahead you shouldn't encounter any problems finding somewhere to stay. However, most accommodation falls into the B&B category: there are a number of campsites but only one youth hostel and one bunkhouse on/near the path.

On the western section, up to Streatley, there is virtually no accommodation on the Ridgeway itself and the nearest place to stay might be a mile or two off the path: for this reason, you really should book ahead otherwise you might find yourself very tired and without a bed for the night.

Camping

Wild camping (see also p49) is not strictly allowed on the Ridgeway: it's private land and although it's a public right of way this does not entitle you to stop and camp. However, if you pitch your tent on the path and move on the next morning leaving no trace of yourself, you shouldn't have any problems. In many places the path is plenty wide enough to pitch a tent and leave room for anyone else passing by. Unless you have personally asked permission from the landowner, do not pitch your tent in fields or woods next to the Ridgeway.

There are a number of official campsites with basic facilities such as toilets and the all-important showers with prices around £2-5 per person which makes this the cheapest accommodation option. The campsites aren't usually open in the winter (October to March), which is a strong hint that camping at this time of year really isn't much fun.

There simply aren't enough official campsites along the Ridgeway for you to stay at one every night of your walk so sometimes you'll have to engage in a spot of wild camping or splash out on a B&B.

Youth Hostels and bunkhouses

Youth Hostels and bunkhouses are cheap and allow you to travel on a budget without having to carry cumbersome camping equipment. They are also good places to meet fellow walkers and in many cases are just as comfortable as B&Bs. However, there is now only one Youth Hostel actually on the Ridgeway – at Streatley – and one bunkhouse, at Court Hill (formerly Ridgeway Youth Hostel).

Both Streatley (see p130) and Court Hill (see p119) provide bedding (unless you plan to stay in one of Court Hill's tipis) so there is no need to carry a sleeping bag if you are expecting to be in B&Bs most other nights. Additionally both have a self-catering kitchen and provide meals.

Youth Hostels are, despite their name, for anyone of any age as long as you are a member. You can join the **Youth Hostels Association of England and Wales** (YHA; ☎ 01629 529700, 🖳 www.yha.org.uk) on arrival at any hostel, or over the phone or on the internet, for £15.95 per year. However, if you are not a member and are only planning to stay in Streatley for one night it is cheaper to pay the non-member rate.

Bed and breakfast

Anyone who has not stayed in a bed and breakfast (B&B) has missed out on something very British. They usually consist of a bed in someone's house and a big cooked breakfast in the morning. For visitors from outside Britain it can provide an interesting insight into the way of life here as you often feel like a guest of the family.

What to expect B&Bs have been included in this guide primarily owing to their location close to the Ridgeway. They basically all offer the same thing but can vary greatly in terms of quality, style and price.

Many B&Bs offer en suite rooms but often this can mean a shower and toilet have been squeezed into a corner of the room. For a few pounds less you can usually get a standard room and it's rarely far to the bathroom, which may have the choice of a bath or a shower, though admittedly you would have to share with the other guests. At the end of a long day's walking you may prefer to stretch out in a bath rather than squash into a shower.

A **single** room has one bed in it, though not all B&Bs have a single room so if you are walking alone you might have to book a twin or double room and pay a supplement (see p14). **Twin** rooms and **double** rooms are often confused but a twin room comprises two single beds (which may be pushed together or left separate) while a double room has one double bed. **Family** rooms are for three or more people: they often have one double bed and one or two single beds; sometimes these are bunk beds.

Most B&Bs provide **breakfast** (see p14) as part of the room price and some will make a **packed lunch** as long as you request it the night before. If you think you would like an **evening meal** ask when you are booking as most B&Bs require advance warning. Often B&Bs are within walking distance of a pub or restaurant but, if not, the owner may give you a lift to and from the nearest eating place.

B&B owners may also provide a **pick-up service** from the Ridgeway and drop you off there the next morning, which can be a great help; offering to pay something towards the petrol would definitely be appreciated.

Rates B&Bs in this guide vary from around £50 for two people sharing a double/twin room for the most basic accommodation to over £200 for the most luxurious en suite places. Most charge around £60 for a double/twin room. Rates can be substantially less during the winter months and if you are planning to stay for three or more nights. If you are on a budget you could always ask to go without breakfast which will usually result in a lower price. Remember that many places do not have single rooms and usually charge a single occupancy rate of around three-quarters of the price of a double/twin room.

Booking You should always book your accommodation in advance. In summer, at weekends and on public holidays there can be stiff competition for beds and in winter there's the distinct possibility that the place could be closed.

Some B&Bs have their own website and offer online booking. Most places ask for a deposit which is generally non-refundable. Always let the owner know if you have to cancel your booking so they can offer the bed to someone else.

Guesthouses, pubs, inns and hotels
Guesthouses are usually more sophisticated than B&Bs and offer evening meals and a lounge for guests. **Pubs and inns** offer bed and breakfast of a medium to high standard and have the added advantage of having a bar downstairs, so it's not far to stagger up to bed. However, the noise from tipsy punters might prove a nuisance if you want an early night. Prices usually range from £50 to £70 per night for a double room.

Hotels are usually aimed more at the motoring tourist rather than the muddy walker and the prices are likely to put off the budget traveller. You'll probably arrive there in the late afternoon and leave fairly early the next morning so it's hard to justify the price. However, if you want a few more luxuries in your room, or room service, it may be worth considering a hotel.

FOOD AND DRINK

Breakfast and lunch
Almost everywhere you stay, other than if camping, you'll be offered a full English cooked **breakfast**. A cooked breakfast includes some or all of the following: fried bacon, eggs, sausages, tomatoes, mushrooms, baked beans and fried bread – in addition to cereal and toast, washed down with a fruit juice and tea or coffee. This will certainly be enough to set you up for a day's walking – if you are thinking about calories, you'll probably want to spend the day trying to walk it off – but it may be more than you are used to or even want. If so, ask for a continental breakfast. If you want an early start or would prefer to skip breakfast it might be worth asking if you could have a packed lunch instead.

Many places to stay can also provide you with a packed **lunch** at an additional cost. Alternatively, packed lunches (and indeed breakfast) can be bought

❏ **Farmers' markets along the Ridgeway**

If you happen to be in town when a farmers' market is on you should definitely try to have a look at what's for sale. The general rule of these types of markets is that whatever is being sold must have been produced locally and by the people selling it. Not only do these markets offer an outlet for farmers to sell their produce direct to the public but you will also see many other small producers of high-quality niche foods selling too. Although these markets are becoming more commercial, the vendors are still usually from around the surrounding area, so you should get to try some local specialities.

Products that you are likely to find are seasonal fruit and vegetables; meat and game birds; dairy products such as local cheeses and yoghurt; eggs from hens, ducks and geese; sausages and pies; soups; farmed fish such as trout and preserves like chutney and jam. Many of these are likely to be organic.

Few markets are held weekly or throughout the year owing to a current lack of demand and the stallholders need time to work their way round the other markets in the area too. Below is a list of farmers' markets in towns along the Ridgeway, though more are likely to be established as their popularity grows. The markets are usually open in the mornings only.

- **Marlborough** (see p70) Second Saturday of every month, High St
- **Wallingford** (see p139) Third Tuesday of every month, Market Place
- **Princes Risborough** (see p161) Third Thursday of every month, High St
- **Wendover** (see p168) Third Saturday of every month, off the High St
- **Tring** (see p176) Every other Saturday, in the Market Place on Brook St.

and made yourself. In most towns and villages you should be able to find at least one shop selling sandwiches and usually a café. If you are lucky you may be in town when there is a farmers' market (see box above). Remember that certain stretches of the walk are devoid of anywhere to eat so look at the town and village facilities table (pp28-9) and check the information in Part 4 to make sure you don't go hungry.

Evening meals

There are some lovely **pubs** and **inns** on the Ridgeway but nearly all are from Streatley eastwards. Before then there is precisely one pub directly on the path – the Shepherds Rest (though it was closed at the time of writing) at Fox Hill, just after you cross the M4 motorway. Although there are fewer freehouses than there used to be you can still sample some excellent beers (see box pp16-17) during or after a day's walking. Most pubs also serve food (at lunchtime and in the evenings, though not always daily) and this ranges from standard 'pub grub' to restaurant quality fare. There will usually be at least one vegetarian option. A popular lunchtime option in a pub is a 'ploughman's lunch'. This is a cold meal traditionally comprising a thick slice of cheese, bread and butter, salad, some pickles and possibly an apple though there are many variations.

There are some quality **restaurants** in the larger towns. Additionally, most towns and some of the larger villages are riddled with cheap **takeaway** joints offering kebabs, pizzas, Chinese, Indian and fish 'n' chips; they can come in

❏ **Real ales along the Ridgeway**

Among the many pleasures of strolling on the Ridgeway is coming across country pubs and inns that you would never otherwise have visited. As you'll discover, they all have their own character and you'll end up with some very fond memories of your time spent at some of them. You'll usually have the chance to try some real ales that you might not have tried before. There are too many ales to list here and many pubs change their beers on a regular basis, but below is a selection of real ales that you are almost guaranteed to see in the course of your walk.

● **Ridgeway Brewing** Perhaps the most apt beers for Ridgeway walkers are those produced by Ridgeway Brewing, based in South Stoke in Oxfordshire. Their ales have only been brewed under contract by other breweries since 2003 but already have a good reputation. **Ridgeway Bitter**, 4.0%, is their standard brew, but if you have time to linger you might like to try their stronger premium bitter, **Ridgeway Blue**, 5.0%. Stronger still is their **Ridgeway IPA** at 5.5% and there is also **Ridgeway Ivanhoe**, 5.2%. These are all available in bottles and sometimes on draught, though from personal experience they can be quite elusive; if you do see any of them, grab the opportunity!

● **Wadworth** Mainly around the beginning of the Ridgeway, but even as far as Tring, you will find **Wadworth** ales. The most famous of these is **6X** which has an ABV of 4.3%. (ABV means 'alcohol by volume' and is expressed as a percentage of how much alcohol a drink contains.) 6X has been brewed in Wadworth's Devizes brewery since 1921 and has a fruity, malty taste and a copper colour. Among several seasonal ales that they produce, you are most likely to see the light **Summersault**, 4%, which is brewed for the summer and served cool. Heading further east, **Arkell's** brewery in Swindon produces mainly **2B** and **3B**, which you'll see in any of the pubs they own. The 3B is 4%, compared to the 3.2% of the 2B.

handy if you finish your walk late in the day, since they usually stay open until at least 11pm.

Buying camping supplies

If you are camping, fuel for your stove, outdoor equipment and food supplies are important considerations. Plan your journey carefully as particularly on the first half of the Ridgeway, there aren't many opportunities to stock up without embarking on a fair trek to the nearest shop and back.

Drinking water

Depending on the weather you will need to drink as much as two to four litres of water a day. If you're feeling lethargic it may well be that you haven't drunk enough, even if you're not feeling particularly thirsty.

Drinking directly from streams and rivers is tempting, but is not a good idea. Streams that cross the path tend to have flowed across farmland where you can be pretty sure any number of farm animals have relieved themselves. Combined with the probable presence of farm pesticides and other delights it is best to avoid drinking from these streams. There are drinking **water taps** at some points along the Ridgeway and these are marked on the maps. Where these are thin on the ground you can usually ask a friendly shopkeeper or pub barman to fill your bot-

● **Brakspear** You'll certainly come across Brakspear ales, especially during the middle sections. The most common is **Brakspear Bitter** which is easy enough for anyone to drink, being only 3.4%. It has an amber colour and a mild taste. It's a good beer
for more prolonged rest stops and has won many national awards. You'll also see
Brakspear Special which at 4.3% is more like it for a quick lunchtime stop-off. This
pint is a golden brown colour with more bitterness than the normal Brakspear Bitter.
Brakspear also produce a whole range of seasonal beers that you might get the chance
to sample, depending on what time of year you are walking. These include **Brass
Monkeys** and **Fire Dog** in the winter, **Ploughman's** in the spring and **Downpour** in
the summer. On the whole, seasonal ales are stronger than their full-time counterparts.

● **Greene King** There are plenty of Greene King pubs on the east of the Ridgeway.
The beers are all produced in its brewery in Bury St Edmunds, Suffolk, with **Abbott
Ale** and **Greene King IPA** the most common sights on bars along the Ridgeway.
Abbott Ale is fairly strong at 5% and has a very full flavour. It has been brewed since
the 1950s and is one of the most esteemed ales in the country. Greene King IPA isn't
quite as strong (3.6%) and its more subdued flavours make it popular as a session beer.

● **Timothy Taylor** Another real ale that you are likely to see is the famous
Landlord, 4.3%, brewed in West Yorkshire by Timothy Taylor. At the time of writing it had won CAMRA's Beer of the year award four times.

● **Hop Back Brewery** This brewery is in Downton, near Salisbury. Among the range
of ales they produce is one that could be of particular interest to Ridgeway walkers,
namely Crop Circle. Its ABV of 4.2% accompanied by its crisp and thirst-quenching
qualities make it an ideal mid-walk drink. You might find this pint hard to find on the
Ridgeway but it's available in pubs around the south-west of England.

For more information about real ales look at the website for **CAMRA**
(Campaign for Real Ale) at ⌨ www.camra.org.uk.

tle or pouch for you, from a tap of course. When you are filling your bottle have
a good drink from it then fill it again so you leave the tap with a full bottle and
don't feel like drinking half of it 100 metres down the path.

MONEY

As there are no banks and few post offices on the first half of the Ridgeway, you
should take plenty of **cash** with you when you set out. You'll find banks and
ATMs in Streatley and Goring but after that, unless you leave the Ridgeway,
you'll have to wait until Princes Risborough. Increasingly in towns where there
is no bank there will be an ATM in a garage or at a newsagent but be aware that
many of these charge £1.25-1.85 whatever amount you withdraw.

Small independent shops rarely accept payment by card and will require
you to pay in cash, as will most B&Bs and campsites. Shops that do take cards,
such as supermarkets, will sometimes advance cash against a card (cashback) as
long as you buy something at the same time, but these are few and far between
on the Ridgeway. **Travellers' cheques** can only be cashed at banks, foreign
exchanges and at some large hotels. See also p35 and the town and village facilities table, pp28-9.

❏ Information for foreign visitors

● **Currency** The British pound (£) comes in notes of £100, £50, £20, £10 and £5, and coins of £2 and £1. The pound is divided into 100 pence (usually referred to as 'p', pronounced pee) which comes in silver coins of 50p, 20p, 10p and 5p and copper coins of 2p and 1p.

● **Rates of exchange** Up-to-date exchange rates can be found at 🖵 www.xe.com/ucc.

● **Business hours** Most **shops** and main **post offices** are open at least from Monday to Friday 9am-5pm and Saturday 9am-12.30pm. Many shops choose longer hours and some open on Sundays as well. However, some also close early one day a week, often on Wednesday or Thursday. **Banks** are usually open 10am-4pm Monday to Friday. **Pub** opening hours are more flexible. As a general rule, pubs in towns are open daily from 11am to 11pm, though some open earlier and many close later at weekends. In villages it's more normal for pubs to open daily from 11am to 2 or 3pm and then again from 6 or 7pm to 11pm, but often from 11am to 11pm at weekends.

● **National (bank) holidays** Most businesses are shut on 1 January, Good Friday (March/April), Easter Monday (March/April), the first and last Monday in May, the last Monday in August, 25 December and 26 December.

● **School holidays** School holiday periods in England are generally as follows: a one-week break late October, two weeks around Christmas and the New Year, a week mid-February, two weeks around Easter, one week around the end of May/early June and about five or six weeks from late July to early September.

● **Travel insurance** The European Health Insurance Card (EHIC) entitles EU nationals (on production of the EHIC card) to necessary medical treatment under the UK's National Health Service while on a temporary visit here. However, this is not a substitute for proper medical cover on your travel insurance for unforeseen bills and for getting you home should that be necessary. Also consider cover for loss and theft of personal belongings, especially if you are camping or staying in hostels, as there will be times when you'll have to leave your luggage unattended.

● **Smoking** Smoking in enclosed public places is banned. The ban relates not only to pubs and restaurants, but also to B&Bs, hostels and hotels. These latter have the right to designate one or more bedrooms where the occupants can smoke, but you should check whether there are any such rooms when you book. Should you be foolhardy enough to light up in a no-smoking area, which includes pretty well any indoor public place, you could be fined £50, but it's the owners of the premises who suffer most if they fail to stop you, with a potential fine of £2500.

● **Weights and measures** In 2007 the European Commission announced they would no longer attempt to ban the pint or the mile: milk can be sold in pints (560ml), as can beer in pubs, and road distances will continue to be given in miles (1.6km). Most food is now sold in metric weights (g and kg) but the imperial weights of pounds (lb) and ounces (oz) can also be displayed. However, the population remains split between those who are happy with centigrade, kilograms and metres and those who still use fahrenheit, pounds, and feet and inches.

● **British Summer Time (BST)** BST starts the last Sunday in March, ie the clocks go forward one hour, and ends the last Sunday in October ie the clocks go back one hour.

● **Telephone** The international access code for Britain is +44, followed by the area code minus the first 0, and then the number you require. To call a number with the same area code as the phone you are calling from you can omit the code. It is cheaper to phone at weekends and after 6pm and before 8am on weekdays. Mobile phone reception is quite reliable along the Ridgeway.

● **Emergency services** For police, ambulance, fire or mountain rescue dial ☎ 999.

Using the Post Office for banking Several banks in Britain have agreements with the Post Office allowing customers to make cash withdrawals using debit cards (with a PIN number), or cheque books (with a debit card), at branches throughout the country. As many villages along the Ridgeway have a Post Office this can be a very useful service.

OTHER SERVICES

Most villages and all the towns have at least one public **telephone**, a small **shop** and a **post office** though a few may be closed as part of the Post Office's closure programme. Apart from getting cash post offices can be used for sending unnecessary equipment home that may be weighing you down.

In Part 4 special mention is given to other services that may be of use to the walker such as: **laundrettes**, **internet access**, **pharmacies** and **tourist information centres** – the latter can be used for finding and booking accommodation among other things.

WALKING COMPANIES & LUGGAGE TRANSFER

Few UK-based companies offer self-guided holidays on the Ridgeway and none, at the time of writing, offered a fully guided walk.

Self-guided holidays
Self-guided holidays usually include detailed advice and notes on itineraries and routes, maps, accommodation including breakfast, daily baggage transfer and transport arrangements at the start and end of your walk.

● **Contours Walking Holidays** (☎ 01768 480451, 🖳 www.contours.co.uk) Offer two itineraries covering the whole route and two walks offering just part of the route: Avebury to Goring and Goring to Ivinghoe Beacon.
● **Explore Britain** (☎ 01740 650900, 🖳 www.xplorebritain.com) Offer two itineraries covering just part of the route and one for the whole route.
● **Freedom Walking Holidays** (☎ 01522 684104, 🖳 www.freedom-walking .co.uk) Will book anything from one night to the whole route starting and finishing wherever the customer requests.

Luggage transfer
At the time of writing no company offered a complete luggage transfer for this route, unless part of a self-guided holiday, but some of the B&Bs listed in this guide (see Part 4) will take your luggage on to your next overnight stop if you are staying with them. Local taxi companies can also provide this service but will be more expensive.

DISABLED ACCESS

There are no officially recognised stretches of the Ridgeway open for wheelchair users, though that doesn't mean it isn't possible to use some stretches of the path. Particularly on the first half there are no stiles and only a few gates, none of which would prove problematic for a wheelchair user. On the downside though, the route on this section often consists of rutted tracks that can also be very muddy after rain. One area on this first half that is accessible is around Barbury Castle (see p96). There is a car park and café here and although the castle itself would prove very difficult for a wheelchair user, the area around it is beautiful and provides excellent views over the surrounding countryside.

The second half of the Ridgeway is less isolated and the route passes through several towns that could make good starting points. The path heading east from Wendover (see p168) is accessible, but not particularly exciting.

Where the Ridgeway crosses a road there is usually a car park and driving to one of these enables you to quickly get into the open countryside with little effort.

There is an ongoing project by the National Trails organisation to remove kissing gates and stiles and install wide gates in their place; this programme has been particularly successful on the first half of the trail. They also improve the surface of the trail in areas where it has become damaged. In 2008 the section of path near to Wayland's Smithy underwent work to improve its drainage capability and the surface was regraded.

MOUNTAIN BIKING

The Ridgeway and trails leading off it are very popular with mountain bikers. However, not all of it is open to them. The western section from Avebury to Streatley is totally open and has only a short section of road and relatively few gates compared to the eastern section. The paths along this portion are generally wide and fairly smooth. From Streatley heading east most sections of the Ridgeway are closed to cyclists except for an eight-mile stretch from Britwell Hill (near Watlington) to Wainhill (near Bledlow). This, of course, doesn't deter some cyclists who do use the designated footpaths despite doing so illegally.

Conditions on the Ridgeway during the summer months are pretty good for cyclists though some sections of heavily rutted path might cause problems. Also be aware of flint on some sections of the path as it can cause punctures.

It's possible to hire mountain bikes to use on the Ridgeway from Ridgeway Cycle Hire (see p70) in Marlborough.

MOTOR VEHICLES

Despite many people's opposition, motor vehicles are allowed to use selected stretches of the Ridgeway. However, since May 2006, only five short sections are open to cars and motorcycles. The total length of these sections is about 17 miles and all but one mile of that is before the Thames.

Although you will rarely come across a car or 4x4 on the Ridgeway you are far more likely to be overtaken by motorcyclists, often riding in groups, which you'll hear coming from a long way off.

It's obvious that motor vehicles do serious damage to the Ridgeway tracks that they use and the effects of this damage are most keenly felt by walkers. It's not much fun walking on a deeply rutted, muddy track for several miles.

HORSE RIDERS

The same sections of the Ridgeway that are open to cyclists are also open to horse riders. In practice, most horse riders only use short sections of the path which link into many other bridleways. Deeply rutted tracks can be problematic for horses and you should also be aware of the flinty sections of path that can injure horses' hooves.

TAKING DOGS ALONG THE RIDGEWAY

You are allowed to take your dog on all sections of the Ridgeway. Indeed, the majority of people you meet will be accompanied by at least one dog and will be out for a walk: I never met anyone walking the whole path with their dog.

As the owner, you are fully responsible for your dog's behaviour. Dogs should always be kept on leads while around livestock. Having said this, if you are harassed by cattle because of your dog, some people recommend letting the dog off the lead. Dog excrement should be cleaned up and not left to foul the boots of other walkers. Where there are water taps along the Ridgeway, there is often a trough for your dog to drink from but this is not always the case. You should take a bowl for your dog that you can fill from a water tap.

Remember, if you do plan to walk the whole path, or even a section of it, you will need to phone ahead to check if your dog will be welcome wherever you plan to stay. Some inns and hotels charge extra (up to £7 or £8) for a dog.

Budgeting

The amount of money you need to take with you depends on your accommodation plans and how you're going to eat. If you camp and cook your own meals your expenses can be very low but most people prefer to have at least some of their meals cooked for them and even the hardiest camper may be tempted into the occasional B&B when the rain is falling.

Also, don't forget all those little things that inevitably push up your daily bill: postcards, stamps, cream teas, ice-creams, beer, buses here, buses there and more beer; it all adds up! Budget on an extra £50-100 for your trip.

CAMPING

You can survive on as little as £10 per person if you use the cheapest sites and cook all your own food from staple ingredients. Nevertheless, most people find that the best-laid plans to survive on the bare minimum soon fall flat after a couple of hard days' trekking. Always budget for unforeseen expenses and, of course, the end of day pint of beer which costs around £2.50. Assuming such liquid treats and the occasional takeaway or pub meal a budget of £15-20 per day is far more realistic.

HOSTELS AND BUNKHOUSES

Since (at the time of writing) there is only one hostel and one bunkhouse on/near the path using only this kind of accommodation is not feasible for this walk. Accommodation costs from £17 per night and both places offer meals: breakfast costs about £5 and an evening meal about £9. Both places also have a self-catering kitchen. For further details see p119 and p130.

B&Bs

B&B rates can be as little as £40 per night for a double room (for two people sharing a room) but are often nearly twice this. Add on the price of lunch (though if you have had a cooked breakfast you may not want much), an evening meal, beer and other expenses and you can expect to need around £45-60 per person per day. Remember that if you want single occupancy of a double/twin room you will not simply pay half the cost; you'll often be charged around three-quarters of the full rate.

When to go

SEASONS

The western half of the Ridgeway follows the high ground and is very exposed so if it rains you'll certainly know about it. Likewise, if it is sunny, you'll get very hot. To compound this there is very little in the way of shelter on the western section. The eastern section, on the whole, follows lower ground and is often in sheltered woodland. You are also far closer to human habitation on this section should the weather turn really bad. The **main walking season** is from Easter (March/April) to the end of September.

Spring

The biggest attraction of walking the Ridgeway in the spring is to see the wild flowers in bloom, especially the carpets of bluebells in the woods. You'll also get good walking weather at this time but there will be a risk of showers and thick fog can obscure pretty much everything in the early to mid-morning. Unsurprisingly, the Easter holiday is a busy time.

Summer

Obviously summer is the busiest season for walkers on the Ridgeway owing to the good weather. You probably still won't see many people on the western section, but the eastern section is very popular with dog-walkers and day-trippers. If you are walking on your own it can be nice to stop and chat to other walkers every once in a while. Although summer is your best bet for good weather, we all know how unpredictable the English weather is. Look at the forecast before you go and be prepared.

Autumn

Autumn can be one of the best times of year to walk the Ridgeway. Most walkers have finished their holidays but you can still have good, clear weather and the sections of woodland walking are especially colourful. The western section will be getting less inviting at this time owing to its exposed conditions.

Winter

The cold and often unpredictable weather in the winter makes walking the Ridgeway low on most people's lists of priorities. It certainly wouldn't be much fun on some of the open western sections but there is still plenty of opportunity for some good day walks on other sections if the weather is clear.

TEMPERATURES

The English climate is temperate and walking can be enjoyed at most times of the year. However, there will be plenty of days in the winter where it will be too cold for comfortable walking but equally in the summer it can sometimes be too hot. The air temperature will generally be fine, it's the rain you need to watch out for.

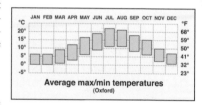

Average max/min temperatures
(Oxford)

RAINFALL

On average it rains on about one day in three in England, though more often in the winter. Rainfall in July can be as much as half that of January in the Ridgeway area, but that's not much consolation if you are caught in a summer downpour.

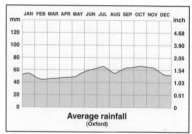

Average rainfall
(Oxford)

DAYLIGHT HOURS

If walking in autumn, winter and early spring, you must take account of how far you can walk in the available light. It may not be possible to cover as many miles as you would in summer. The sunrise and sunset times in the table (see opposite) are based on information for Oxford on the first of each month. This gives a rough picture for the Ridgeway. Also bear in mind that you will get a further 30-45 minutes of usable light before and after sunrise and sunset depending on the weather.

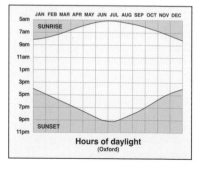

Hours of daylight
(Oxford)

PLANNING YOUR WALK

FESTIVALS AND EVENTS

There are a number of annual events along the Ridgeway. The main ones are listed below:

● **The Ridgeway 40** (🖳 http://ridgeway40.org.uk) This is a 40-mile walk along the Ridgeway from its start at Overton Hill to the Youth Hostel at Streatley. You are expected to complete the walk in one day and there are checkpoints along the route to keep you on track. There is also a separate event for people wishing to run the route. Walkers and runners must register in advance. The Ridgeway 40 is held annually on a weekend in May.

● **Marlborough Jazz** (☎ 01672 515095, 🖳 www.marlboroughjazz.co.uk) This three-day festival features around 60 artists, performing all genres of jazz music, and attracts more than 5000 visitors. The festival takes place early to mid-July.

● **Sarsen Trail** (Wiltshire Wildlife Trust, ☎ 01380 725670, 🖳 www.wiltshire wildlife.org) This sponsored walk in aid of the Wiltshire Wildlife Trust covers a 26-mile route from Avebury to Stonehenge. It's held on the Spring Bank Holiday weekend (late May). The route is dotted with checkpoints and there is a free coach service between the start and finish points. The event attracts more than 2000 walkers and you must register in advance.

● **Uffington White Horse Show** (🖳 www.whitehorseshow.co.uk) This traditional country show, held on ground between Uffington and Kingston Lisle villages, is a well-organised event attracting up to 10,000 visitors. Past attractions have included display flights by WWII aircraft, ferret racing, morris dancing, a heavy horse show and a falconry display. This event is held on the Bank Holiday weekend at the end of August.

● **Goring & Streatley Regatta** (🖳 www.goringgapbc.org.uk) This regatta, held in mid-July, is organised by the Goring Gap Boat Club. The focus is on providing a family day out with a funfair, live entertainment and food and drink stalls in addition to the boat races on the Thames.

● **Canal Festival** (🖳 www.tringcanalfestival.org.uk) Held in Tring to raise money for the restoration of the local canal, this festival features canal boats, live music, food and drink, and children's entertainment. The festival is held on the Spring Bank Holiday weekend (the end of May).

● **Organised events along the Ridgeway** (National Trails Office, ☎ 01865 810224, 🖳 www.nationaltrail.co.uk/ridgeway) The National Trails Office organises walks and activities along the Ridgeway year-round. Most weekends there will be something going on, be it a walk along a particularly interesting section accompanied by a knowledgeable guide, a focus on specific wildlife, or a class in navigating skills. Contact the above office for the full calendar of events.

● **Morris dancing** During the summer months you can see Morris groups performing at festivals and pubs along the first half of the Ridgeway. Most performances are arranged well in advance which allows you to plan your trip to coincide with them if you so desire. See box p113 for more information about the Morris dancing tradition.

Itineraries

This guidebook has not been divided up into rigid daily stages. Instead, it's structured to make it easy for you to plan your own itinerary. If you have a week to spare you can walk the Ridgeway in one go. However, many people decide to walk it in sections over a longer period. Or you might simply want to pick out the best parts for a series of day walks.

To help you plan your walk look at the **planning map** (see opposite inside back cover) and the **table of village & town facilities**, see pp28-9, which gives a rundown on the essential information you need regarding accommodation possibilities and services. Alternatively, you could follow one of the suggested **itineraries**, see p26, that are based on walking speed. There is also a list of recommended linear day and weekend walks (see p27) that cover the best of the Ridgeway. The **public transport map and services table** are on pp42-5.

Once you have an idea of your approach turn to **Part 4** for detailed information on accommodation, places to eat and other services in each village and town on the route. Also in Part 4 you will find summaries of the route to accompany the detailed trail maps.

WHICH DIRECTION?

The generally accepted way to walk the Ridgeway is from west to east though it really doesn't matter. As the two halves are very different you might base your decision on what type of scenery and terrain you'd like to tackle first. Neither section is particularly demanding but the western section is far more isolated and really isn't much fun in bad weather. The eastern section, being in woodlands for much of the time, is far more sheltered and relaxing.

Availability of public transport heading in either direction along the Ridgeway is similar so this shouldn't have much bearing on which direction you choose to walk in.

Although the maps in Part 4 of this book follow the Ridgeway from west to east, there are timings on all the maps for walking in both directions.

SUGGESTED ITINERARIES

The itineraries in the box on p26 are based on different accommodation types: one is for those who prefer to camp; the other is for those who choose to stay in B&B-style accommodation. Each is divided into three alternatives based on walking speeds. They are only suggestions so feel free to adapt them to your needs. **Don't forget** to add your travelling time before and after the walk.

P L A N N I N G   Y O U R   W A L K

SUGGESTED ITINERARIES

CAMPING

Night	Relaxed pace Place	Approx Distance miles/km	Medium pace Place	Approx Distance miles/km	Fast pace Place	Approx Distance miles/km
0	Overton Hill		Overton Hill		Overton Hill	
1	Ogbourne St G	9.5/15.5	Ogbourne St G	9.5/15.5	Ogbourne St G	9.5/15.5
2	Down Brn Frm	14.5/23.5	Down Brn Frm	14.5/23.5	Court Hill	19/30.5
3	Court Hill	4.5/7.5	Court Hill	4.5/7.5	Streatley*	14/22.2
4	Streatley*	14/22.2	Streatley*	14/22.2	Watlington	15/23.8
5	Crowmarsh G	7.3/13.1	Crowmarsh G	7.3/13.1	Princes Risboro'*	11/17.4
6	Watlington	9.6/14.9	Nuffield*	4/6.4	Ivinghoe Beacon	17.5/27.9
7	Princes Risboro'*	11/17.4	Princes Risboro'*	11.4/17.8		
8	Wigginton*	12.4/20	Ivinghoe Beacon	17.5/27.9		
9	Ivinghoe Beacon	3.1/4.9				

*No campsites but alternative accommodation is available

STAYING IN B&B-STYLE ACCOMMODATION

Night	Relaxed pace Place	Approx Distance miles/km	Medium pace Place	Approx Distance miles/km	Fast pace Place	Approx Distance miles/km
0	Overton Hill		Overton Hill		Overton Hill	
1	Ogbourne St G	9.5/15.5	Bishopstone	17.7/28.3	Bishopstone	17.7/28.3
2	Bishopstone	8.7/13.9	Letcombe Rgs	9.9/15.4	East Ilsley	18.7/29.4
3	Letcombe Rgs	9.9/15.4	Goring	14.8/23.7	Nuffield	15.2/24.5
4	Goring	14.8/23.7	Watlington	14.7/23.3	Princes Risboro'	16.5/25.9
5	Nuffield	9.2/14.8	Princes Risboro'	11/17.4	Ivinghoe Beacon	17.5/27.9
6	Chinnor	11.2/17.5	Wigginton	12.4/20		
7	Wendover	11.5/18.4	Ivinghoe Beacon	5.1/7.9		
8	Wigginton	6.2/10				
9	Ivinghoe Beacon					

❏ THE BEST DAY AND WEEKEND WALKS

The desire of most walkers is to tackle the whole Ridgeway in one go but sometimes this isn't possible. Spare time, good weather, transport and money all need to be found at the same time. For this reason many walkers choose to walk the Ridgeway in separate sections, maybe over a series of summer weekends. Other walkers might not be so concerned about walking every inch of the official path and might only want to walk the best bits.

Simply getting out and walking any part of the Ridgeway will be rewarding, but listed below are some especially enjoyable parts. If you're feeling ambitious and the weather is on your side, you could try completing a weekend walk in one day.

For public transport to/from the places listed below, see the public transport map and table, pp42-5.

Day walks
● **Avebury to Ogbourne St George** 9¹/₂ miles/15.5km (see pp89-100) This path starts at Avebury stone circle and walks the quiet high ridge to the Iron Age fort of Barbury Castle where there are magnificent views northwards; it then goes onto Smeathe's Ridge and finally down into the pleasant village of Ogbourne St George where there are a couple of pubs to relax in.
● **Fox Hill to White Horse Hill** 5 miles/8.5km (see pp105-13) Start at the Shepherds Rest pub and quickly climb up onto the open high ground for stunning views, visit the ancient burial site at Wayland's Smithy and finish at White Horse Hill, the site of an Iron Age hill fort, Dragon Hill and the original white horse.
● **White Horse Hill to East Ilsley** 15 miles/24km (see pp113-24) If you fancy a bit of time on your own, this is the most isolated section of the Ridgeway path. It keeps to the high ground with only a few road crossings and a handful of farms on the entire 15-mile stretch. Make sure you choose decent weather for this walk as there is virtually no shelter.
● **Streatley to Wallingford** 7 miles/11km (see pp130-8) Begin in the Thames-side village of Streatley and walk into Goring before following the bank of the Thames northwards through the delightful villages of South and North Stoke. The path then heads into the old town of Wallingford.
● **Wendover to Ivinghoe Beacon** 10 miles/16km (see pp168-83) From the attractive town of Wendover the path takes you through the best woodland walking on the Ridgeway, coming close to the village of Wigginton should you choose to stop off for lunch. The final section takes on Ivinghoe Beacon, a long, steep climb through woodland and finally some excellent open walking with increasingly fantastic views.

Weekend walks
● **Avebury to White Horse Hill** 22 miles/35km (see pp89-113) This walk takes in many of the most interesting ancient sites along the Ridgeway. The walking is mainly along broad, grassy tracks with few steep climbs. There is no accommodation near the middle of this walk so you'll either have a short first day and long second, or vice versa depending on where you decide to stay.
● **East Ilsley to Watlington** 22 miles/35km (see pp124-50) This walk takes in a bit of each of the Ridgeway's main attractions – first, isolated walking, then, the path along the Thames and finally, some fine woodland walking. You can stay in Wallingford to split the journey neatly into two days.

VILLAGE AND

Place name (Places in brackets are a short walk off the Ridgeway)	Distance from previous place approx miles/km (Distances in brackets indicate how far the place is from the nearest point on the Ridgeway)	Cash Machine	Post Office (✔) means limited opening hours	Tourist Information Centre (TIC) Point (TIP)
(Marlborough)		✔	✔	TIP
(Avebury)		✔	(✔)	TIC
(West Overton)				
(East Kennet)				
Overton Hill	0			
Barbury Castle				
(Ogbourne St George)	9/14.4 (+0.6/1)			
(Liddington)	6.5/10.4 (+0.6/1)			
Fox Hill	1/1.5			
(Bishopstone)	1.2/2 (+0.6/1)			
(Ashbury)	1.5/2.4 (+0.6/1)		(✔)	
(Woolstone)	2/3 (+1.2/2)			
(Down Barn Farm)	2.5/4 (+0.6/1)			
(Sparsholt)	0 (+1.5/2.5)			
(Letcombe Regis)	3.9/6 (+1.5/2.5)			
(Court Hill)	0.6/1 (+0.3/0.5)			
(East Ilsley)	8.2/13 (+1/1.5)			
(Compton)	0 (+1.5/2.5)		✔	
(Aldworth)	2.7/4.5 (+1.2/2)			
Streatley	3/4.7			
Goring	0.3/0.5	✔	✔	
South Stoke	1.5/2.4			
North Stoke	2.5/4			
(Wallingford)	1.2/2 (+1.2/2)	✔	✔	TIC
(Crowmarsh Gifford)	0 (+0.7/1.2)			
Nuffield	4/6.4			
(Watlington)	5.5/8.5 (+0.6/1)	✔	✔	
(Lewknor)	2.5/4 (+0.5/0.8)			
(Kingston Blount)	1.7/2.7 (+0.6/1)			
(Chinnor)	1.5/2.4 (+0.3/0.5)	✔	✔	
Princes Risborough	5.3/8.4 (+0.2/0.3)	✔	✔	TIP
Wendover	6.2/10	✔	✔	TIC
Wigginton	6.2/10			
(Tring)	0 (+1/1.5)	✔	✔	TIC
(Aldbury)	2/3 (0.6/1)	✔	✔	
Ivinghoe Beacon	3.1/4.9			
(Ivinghoe)	3.4/5.4 (+1.2/2)		✔	

TOTAL DISTANCE 87 miles/139km

TOWN FACILITIES

Eating Place ✔ = one; ✔✔ = two; ✔✔✔ = 3+	Food Store	Campsite	Hostel/ Bunkhouse	B&B-style accommodation ✔ = one ✔✔ = two; ✔✔✔ = 3+	Place name (places in brackets are a short walk off the Ridgeway: see opposite for distances)
✔✔✔	✔			✔✔✔	(Marlborough)
✔✔	✔		YHA*	✔✔✔	(Avebury)
✔					(West Overton)
				✔	(East Kennet)
					Overton Hill
✔		✔			Barbury Castle
✔		✔		✔✔	(Ogbourne St George)
✔					(Liddington)
✔					Fox Hill
✔✔				✔✔	(Bishopstone)
✔				✔	(Ashbury)
✔				✔	(Woolstone)
		✔		✔	(Down Barn Farm)
✔				✔	(Sparsholt)
✔				✔✔	(Letcombe Regis)
✔		✔	Bunkhouse		Court Hill
✔✔				✔✔	(East Ilsley)
✔	✔			✔	(Compton)
✔				✔	(Aldworth)
✔			YHA	✔✔✔	Streatley
✔✔✔	✔			✔✔✔	Goring
✔				✔✔	South Stoke
				✔	North Stoke
✔✔✔	✔			✔✔✔	(Wallingford)
✔✔	✔	✔		✔	(Crowmarsh Gifford)
✔				✔	Nuffield
✔✔✔	✔	✔		✔✔	(Watlington)
✔				✔	(Lewknor)
✔				✔✔	(Kingston Blount)
✔✔	✔			✔	(Chinnor)
✔✔✔	✔			✔✔✔	Princes Risborough
✔✔	✔			✔✔	Wendover
✔				✔✔	Wigginton
✔✔	✔			✔✔	(Tring)
✔✔	✔			✔✔	(Aldbury)
					Ivinghoe Beacon
✔✔✔	✔	✔		✔✔	(Ivinghoe)

* Clyffe Pypard Youth Hostel is five miles from Avebury

SIDE TRIPS

There are plenty of good circular and linear walks from the Ridgeway. Listed on p27 are just a selection of them, starting from the western end of the trail and heading east. Detailed information about all these routes can be obtained from local tourist information centres (see box p36) or councils (see box p56).

● **Aldbourne Circular Route** This is a 12-mile (19km) route which for several miles uses the Ridgeway. It takes in Aldbourne village, several Bronze Age burial mounds, the deserted village of Snap (see p100), Liddington Castle (see p103) and Sugar Hill. The trail is waymarked with discs and it's also marked on OS Explorer maps 157 and 170.

● **Ashbury Circular Walk** This 10-mile (16km) walk from the village of Ashbury (see p106) takes the walker through some beautiful countryside once the initial steep climb has been completed. The path crosses the Ridgeway and heads to Alfred's Castle, an Iron Age hillfort, before reaching Ashdown House, a 17th-century property owned by the National Trust. From here it returns to the Ridgeway via a different route and takes in Wayland's Smithy (see box p110), before heading back down the hill to Ashbury. The trail is waymarked with discs and although the paths are marked on OS Explorer map 170, they aren't labelled.

● **Lambourn Valley Way** This 20-mile (32km) route starts at the Uffington White Horse and leads down into the valley to reach the village of Lambourn. It then broadly follows the River Lambourn along the valley to its end in Newbury. This is a very peaceful walk passing through several small villages with only the crossing of the M4 to spoil the atmosphere. The route is waymarked with discs and fingerposts and is also marked on OS Explorer maps 170 and 158.

● **East/West Ilsley Circular Route** This 6-mile (10km) walk is best started and finished in one of the pubs in East Ilsley. The path takes a wayward route to West Ilsley before heading up to the Ridgeway and following it for just over a mile before heading back to East Ilsley. Much of this path is on broad tracks that often run close to racehorse gallops. The route is waymarked with discs and the paths are marked on OS Explorer map 170.

● **The Chiltern Link** This 8-mile (13km) linear walk starts on Wendover High St and meanders through woods and open countryside to the town of Chesham where you can pick up the Chess Valley Walk. Several miles into the walk you reach The Lee, a tiny village with a popular pub – The Cock and Rabbit – that is well worth stopping off at. The route is waymarked with discs and fingerposts and is also marked on OS Explorer map 181.

● **Beacon View Walk** This 5-mile (8km) circular walk is usually started and finished at The Greyhound in Wigginton (see p174) and follows the course of the Ridgeway for about two miles from Hastoe Cross to the bridge over the Grand Union Canal. The route then follows the canal to Cow Roast (a village!) before heading back to Wigginton. The paths comprising the route are marked with standard signs and all paths appear on OS Explorer map 181.

● **The Ashridge Drovers' Walk** This 6-mile (10km) circular walk starts and finishes at Tring Station (see Map 47, p179). From there it makes for Aldbury (see p178) then up to the Bridgewater Monument where there is a visitor centre and tea shop. The route then follows the high ground to join the Ridgeway which it follows down to the railway station. The walk often follows wide, sunken lanes used in the past for droving (moving livestock). The paths comprising the route are marked with standard signs and all paths appear on OS Explorer map 181.

● **Two Ridges Link** This 8-mile (13km) linear walk runs from Ivinghoe Beacon, the very end of the Ridgeway, to Leighton Buzzard at the start of the Greensand Ridge Walk. The walk takes you first through the villages of Ivinghoe Aston and Slapton before joining the Grand Union Canal. The trail is fully waymarked with dedicated Two Ridges Walk signs and it's also marked on OS Explorer maps 181 and 192.

● **Ridgeway Link Walk** This 7½-mile (12km) linear walk was officially opened in June 2007. It follows the Icknield Way from the Chilterns Gateway Centre, on Dunstable Downs, to Ivinghoe Beacon (see Map 48, p181). Of course, walking the path in reverse might be more practical for Ridgeway walkers, especially if you are heading to Dunstable for transport connections. The walk passes through Whipsnade and Dagnall, both of which have pubs. The Chilterns Gateway Centre has a café, shop and toilets and there is also a car park there. Although the route is well waymarked with Ridgeway Link discs some of the paths can get rather muddy after rain. The entire route is marked as the Icknield Way on OS Explorer map 181.

What to take

Deciding how much to take with you can be a difficult decision. Experienced walkers know that you really should take only the bare essentials but at the same time you need to ensure you have all the equipment necessary to make the trip safe and comfortable.

KEEP IT LIGHT

Carrying a heavy rucksack really can ruin your enjoyment of a good walk and can also slow you down, turning an easy seven-mile day into an interminable slog. Be ruthless when you pack and leave behind all those little home comforts that you tell yourself don't weigh that much really. This advice is even more pertinent to campers who have added weight to carry.

HOW TO CARRY IT

The size of your **rucksack** depends on where you are planning to stay and how you are planning to eat. If you are camping and cooking for yourself you will probably need a 65- to 75-litre rucksack which can hold the tent, sleeping bag, cooking equipment and food. Make sure your rucksack has a stiffened back and can be adjusted to fit your own back comfortably. This will make carrying the weight much easier.

When packing the rucksack make sure you have all the things you are likely to need during the day near the top or in the side pockets. This includes map, water bottle or pouch, packed lunch, waterproofs and this guidebook, of course. Make sure the hip belt and chest strap (if there is one) are fastened tightly as this helps distribute the weight with most of it being carried on the hips. Rucksacks are decorated with seemingly pointless straps but if you adjust them correctly it can make a big difference to your personal comfort while walking.

If you plan to stay in B&B-style accommodation a 30- to 40-litre pack should be more than enough to carry everything you need.

Consider taking a small **bum bag** or **day pack** for your camera, guidebook and other essentials for when you go sightseeing or for a day walk.

A good habit to get into is to always put things in the same place in your rucksack and memorise where they are. There is nothing more annoying than having to pull everything out of your pack to find that lost banana when you're starving, or scrambling for your camera when there is a rare opportunity to photograph an owl perched on a fencepost. It's also a good idea to keep everything in **canoe bags**, **waterproof rucksack liners** or strong plastic bags. If you don't, it's bound to rain.

FOOTWEAR

Boots
Your boots are the single most important item of gear that can affect the enjoyment of your trek. In summer you could get by with a light pair of trail shoes if you're only carrying a small pack, although this is an invitation for wet, cold feet if there is any rain and they don't offer much support for your ankles.

Although the Ridgeway isn't particularly strenuous, some of the terrain can be quite rough so a good pair of walking boots is a safer bet. They must fit well and be properly broken in. It is no good discovering that your boots are slowly murdering your feet two days into a week-long trek. See p53 for more blister-avoidance advice.

Socks
The traditional wearing of a thin liner sock under a thicker wool sock is no longer necessary if you choose a high-quality sock specially designed for walking. A high proportion of natural fibres makes them much more comfortable. Three pairs are ample.

Extra footwear
Some walkers like to have a second pair of shoes to wear when they are not on the trail. Trainers, sport sandals or flip-flops are all suitable as long as they are light.

CLOTHES

Experienced walkers will know the importance of wearing the right clothes. Especially up on the western part of the Ridgeway the wind, rain and sun can all be fierce and there's often no shelter if you are caught out. Modern technology in outdoor attire can seem baffling but it comes down to: a base layer to transport sweat away from your skin; a mid-layer or two to keep you warm; and an outer layer or 'shell' to protect you from the wind and rain.

Base layer

Cotton absorbs sweat, trapping it next to the skin which will chill you rapidly when you stop exercising. A thin lightweight **thermal top** made from synthetic material is better as it draws moisture away, keeping you dry. It will be cool if worn on its own in hot weather and warm when worn under other clothes in cooler conditions. A spare would be sensible. You may also like to bring a **shirt** for wearing in the evening.

Mid-layers

In the summer a woollen jumper or mid-weight polyester **fleece** will suffice. For the rest of the year you will need an extra layer to keep you warm. Both wool and fleece, unlike cotton, have the ability to stay reasonably warm when wet.

Outer layer

A **waterproof jacket** is essential year-round and will be much more comfortable (but also more expensive) if it's also 'breathable' to prevent the build up of condensation on the inside. This layer can also be worn to keep out the wind.

Leg wear

Whatever you wear on your legs it should be light, quick drying and not restricting. Many British walkers find polyester tracksuit bottoms comfortable. Poly-cotton or microfibre trousers are also excellent. Denim jeans should never be worn; if they get wet they become heavy, cold and bind to your legs. A pair of **shorts** is nice to have on sunny days. Thermal **longjohns** or thick tights are cosy if you're camping but are probably unnecessary even in winter. **Waterproof trousers** are necessary most of the year. In summer a pair of windproof and quick-drying trousers are useful in showery weather. **Gaiters** are not really necessary but may come in useful in wet weather when the vegetation around your legs is dripping wet.

Underwear

Three changes of what you normally wear is fine. Women may find a **sports bra** more comfortable because pack straps can cause bra straps to dig into your shoulders.

Other clothes

A **warm** hat and **gloves** should always be kept in your rucksack, year-round. You never know when you might need them. In summer you should also carry a **sun hat** with you, preferably one that also covers the back of your neck. Also consider a small **towel**, especially if you are camping.

TOILETRIES

Only take the minimum: a small bar of **soap** in a plastic container (unless staying in B&Bs) which can also be used instead of shaving cream and for washing clothes; a tiny tube of **toothpaste** and a **toothbrush**; one roll of **loo paper** in a plastic bag. If you are planning to defecate outdoors you will also need a lightweight **trowel** for burying the evidence (see p48 for further tips). A **razor**, **deodorant**, **tampons/sanitary towels** and a high-factor **sun screen** should cover all your needs.

FIRST-AID KIT

There is a pharmacy in many towns and villages along the route so you only need a small kit to cover common problems and emergencies: pack it in a waterproof container. A basic kit will contain **aspirin** or **paracetamol** for treating mild to moderate pain and fever; **plasters/Band Aids** for minor cuts; **Moleskin**, **Compeed**, or **Second skin** for blisters; a **bandage** for holding dressings, splints or limbs in place and for supporting a sprained ankle or a weak knee; a small selection of different-sized **sterile dressings** for wounds; **porous adhesive tape**, **antiseptic wipes**, **antiseptic cream**, **safety pins**, **tweezers** and **scissors**.

GENERAL ITEMS

Essential

The following should be in everyone's rucksack: a one-litre **water bottle** or **pouch**; a **torch** (flashlight) with spare bulb and batteries in case you end up walking after dark; **emergency food** (see p52) which your body can quickly convert into energy; a **penknife**; a **watch** with an alarm; and a suitable **bag** for packing out any rubbish you accumulate. A **whistle** is also worth taking. It can fit in a pocket and although you are very unlikely to need it you may be grateful for it in the unlikely event of an emergency (see p52).

Although the path is easy to follow, a 'Silva' type **compass** and knowing how to use it is a good idea in case you need to leave the trail when there is heavy fog.

Useful

Many would list a **camera** as essential but it can be liberating to travel without one once in a while; a **notebook** can be a more accurate way of recording your impressions. A **book** helps to pass the time on train and bus journeys and for comfort, particularly in the summer, you may wish to take a pair of **sunglasses**. Also useful are **binoculars** for observing wildlife, a **walking stick** or pole to take the shock off your knees and a **vacuum flask** for carrying hot drinks.

SLEEPING BAG

A sleeping bag is only necessary if you are camping and you should find that a two- to three-season bag is sufficient, but obviously in winter a warmer bag is a good idea.

CAMPING GEAR

Campers will need a **tent** (or bivvy bag if you enjoy travelling light) which is able to withstand wet and windy weather, a **sleeping mat**, a **stove** and **fuel**, a **pan** with a lid that can double as a frying pan/plate (this is fine for two people), a **pan handle**, a **mug**, a **spoon** and a wire/plastic **scrubber** for washing up.

MONEY

There are no banks along the first half of the Ridgeway so you will have to carry most of your money as **cash**. From Streatley onwards most towns have at least one **ATM**. A **debit card** is the easiest way to withdraw money from banks or ATMs and debit/credit cards can be used to pay in larger shops, restaurants and hotels.

A **cheque book** is very useful for walkers with accounts at British banks as a cheque will often be accepted where a card is not, though you will still probably need a debit/cheque card to guarantee the payment.

INSURANCE

Consider having cover for loss and theft of personal belongings, especially if you are camping or staying in a dorm in a hostel/bunkhouse, as there may be times when you have to leave your belongings unattended. Some annual travel insurance policies offer cover in the UK if you are away for more than two nights and if your accommodation is pre-booked. See the box on p18 for information regarding travel and health insurance for non-UK citizens.

MAPS

The hand-drawn maps in this book cover the trail at a scale of 1:20,000; they provide plenty of detail and information to keep you on the right track. If you are only walking on the Ridgeway, you shouldn't need any other maps but for side trips you will need an Ordnance Survey map (☎ 08456 050505, 🖳 www .ordnancesurvey.gov.uk).

The entire Ridgeway route is covered on four OS Explorer/Active maps at a scale of 1:25,000. The numbers of these maps are 157 (Marlborough & Savernake Forest), 170 (Abingdon, Wantage & Vale of White Horse), 171 (Chiltern Hills West, Henley-on-Thames & Wallingford), and 181 (Chiltern Hills North, Aylesbury, Berkhamsted & Chesham). The Explorer maps cost £7.99 each and the Active series (which are covered in laminated plastic) are £13.99 each; these maps are widely available in bookshops or can be ordered from the Ordnance Survey website.

A very useful service which can ease the significant cost of purchasing maps for a walk is provided by the Ramblers' Association (see box p36). Their library allows members to borrow up to ten maps for a period of four weeks at 50p per paper map and £1 per weatherproof map.

❏ SOURCES OF FURTHER INFORMATION

Trail information

The Ridgeway National Trail (☎ 01865 810224, 🖳 www.nationaltrail.co.uk/ridge way) The National Trails Office has a great deal of information about the Ridgeway – history, wildlife, events, future projects etc – and is very helpful if you have any queries. The website has up-to-date information concerning all aspects of the Ridgeway.

Tourist information

● **Tourist Information Centres (TICs)** TICs or tourist information points (TIPs) are based in towns throughout Britain and provide locally specific information; TICs also provide an accommodation-booking service. There are six centres/points relevant to the Ridgeway: **Marlborough** (see p69), **Avebury** (see p74), **Wallingford** (see p138), **Princes Risborough** (see p161), **Wendover** (see p168) and **Tring** (see p176).

● **English Tourist Board** (🖳 www.enjoyengland.com) The tourist board oversees all the local tourist information centres. It's a good place to find general information about the country and information on outdoor activities and local events. They can also help with arranging holidays and accommodation.

Organisations for walkers

● **Backpackers' Club** (🖳 www.backpackersclub.co.uk) A club for people who are involved or interested in lightweight camping through walking, cycling, skiing, canoeing, etc. They produce a quarterly magazine, provide members with a comprehensive advisory and information service on all aspects of backpacking, organise weekend trips and also publish a farm-pitch directory. Membership is £12 per year and £15 for a family.

● **Long Distance Walkers' Association** (🖳 www.ldwa.org.uk) An association of people with the common interest of long-distance walking. Membership includes a journal three times per year giving details of challenge events and local group walks as well as articles on the subject. Information on over 600 Long Distance Paths is presented in the LDWA's Long Distance Walkers' Handbook. Membership is £13 per year or £19.50 for a family.

● **Ramblers' Association** (☎ 020 7339 8500, 🖳 www.ramblers.org.uk) Looks after the interests of walkers throughout Britain. They publish a large amount of useful information including their *Walk Britain* guide (£5.99 to non-members); a full directory of services for walkers published annually. Membership costs £27 per year for an individual and £36 for joint membership.

RECOMMENDED READING

Most of the following books can be found in the tourist information centres. Both Rough Guides and Lonely Planet produce guides to *England*, both priced at £15.99 which would be most useful for foreign visitors.

Those who like to round off the day with a pint may appreciate *Pub Walks Along the Ridgeway* published by Countryside Books with a cover price of £6.95. The National Trails Office publish a *Ridgeway Information Pack* for £3.30, covering the history and natural history of the Ridgeway and also a *Walks Around The Ridgeway Pack* for £4.70 detailing circular walks from the Ridgeway.

Of course if you are a seasoned long-distance walker or even if you are new to the game and like what you see, check out the ever-growing list of titles in the Trailblazer series (see pp191-2).

Flora and fauna field guides

As mentioned above, the National Trails Office publish the *Ridgeway Information Pack* which includes separate leaflets of information on wild flowers, birds and animals you might encounter.

The AA's *Birds of Britain and Europe* at £9.99 is one of many excellent bird guides that can fit inside a rucksack pocket. The extensive but pocket-sized *Wild Flowers* published by Collins is well worth £4.99; they also produce *Butterflies*, for the same price, which could be useful for identifying some of the species you'll see fluttering by on the chalky sections of the path. The Field Studies Council (💻 www.field-studies-council.org) publishes a series of *Identification Guides* (fold out charts) which are also practical.

Getting to and from the Ridgeway

Both the start and finish of the Ridgeway are easily reached by public transport or car and its convenient location in the centre of southern England means that it's one of the most accessible long-distance trails in the country.

The obvious advantages of travelling to the Ridgeway by public transport are that you don't have to go back and collect your car at the end of the walk (in fact, you can't leave your car at the start point of the Ridgeway for more than a day) and you don't need to worry about the safety aspect of leaving your car unattended for a long period of time.

If you are walking the Ridgeway from one end to the other, in one go, you shouldn't need public transport at any point along the trail. If, however, you are just walking one section, or want to skip a certain stretch and move on to the next, you will. For short distances between towns you will be using the bus.

On the whole there are plenty of services throughout the day to most towns and villages. However, getting from one place to another isn't always straightforward; you often need to get a bus to a town from where you can then catch a bus to your destination. This can mean that you might have to finish walking early to ensure you get your bus connections. There are very few services on Sundays and public holidays and in most areas no service at all.

From nearly any given town or village on the Ridgeway it is fairly easy to get to a large town that has connections to the national public transport network. So, if you decide to walk only a certain section, you shouldn't have any problems getting back home, even if it does take some time and a series of buses.

❏ GETTING TO BRITAIN

● **By air** Most airlines serve London Heathrow or London Gatwick. In addition a number of budget companies fly from Europe's major cities to the other London terminals at Stansted and Luton; the latter is the most convenient airport for the end of the walk (or the start if you choose to walk east to west).

These budget companies include easyJet (🖳 www.easyjet.com) who fly from Amsterdam and Barcelona to both Stansted and Luton; they also fly from Paris, Madrid and Berlin to Luton only. Ryanair (🖳 www.ryanair.com) fly from several French and German cities to Stansted; they also fly from Barcelona and Rome to Luton. There are also flights to Bristol from many European cities, including Prague, Berlin, Amsterdam, Rome and Madrid on easyJet and from Brussels with Flybe (🖳 www.flybe.com). Bristol is far closer to the start of the Ridgeway than London Heathrow.

● **From Europe by train** Eurostar (🖳 www.eurostar.com) operates the high-speed passenger service via the Channel Tunnel between Paris/Brussels (and other cities) and London. The Eurostar terminal in London is St Pancras International at St Pancras station; there are connections from Kings Cross St Pancras station on the London Underground to all the other main railway stations in London. Paddington is the main station for trains to Swindon; services to Tring go from London Euston (see box opposite).

For more information about rail services from Europe contact Rail Europe (🖳 www.raileurope.com), or Railteam (🖳 www.railteam.eu).

● **From Europe by coach** Eurolines (🖳 www.eurolines.com) have a huge network of long-distance bus services, connecting over 500 cities in 25 European countries to London. Check carefully, as once expenses, such as food for the journey, are taken into consideration it often does not work out much cheaper than taking a flight, particularly when compared to the prices of some of the budget airlines.

● **From Europe by car** P&O Ferries (🖳 www.poferries.com) has a service from Bilbao to Portsmouth and runs frequent passenger ferries between Calais and Dover; the latter take about 90 minutes. Brittany Ferries (🖳 www.brittanyferries.com) has services from Santander and Roscoff to Plymouth as well as from Cherbourg and Caen to Poole and Portsmouth. Several other ferry operators ply routes between mainland Europe and ports on Britain's eastern coast. Look at 🖳 www.ferry savers.com or 🖳 www.directferries.com for a full list of companies and services.

Eurotunnel (🖳 www.eurotunnel.com) operates a shuttle train service for vehicles via the Channel Tunnel between Calais and Folkestone taking just 35 mins.

NATIONAL TRANSPORT

By rail   [see box opposite]

The most convenient railway station for Overton Hill at the start of the Ridgeway is Swindon (12½ miles/20km away). Swindon is on the main line from London Paddington to Bristol; it takes about an hour from London to Swindon and about half an hour from Bristol to Swindon (services are operated by First Great Western). From Swindon you'll need to take one of the regular local bus services (see box pp142-3) in the direction of Marlborough and get off at the West Kennet stop, just a few hundred metres from Overton Hill.

First Great Western Link has services to Goring & Streatley on the London Paddington to Oxford line via Cholsey and Didcot Parkway (6 miles/10km from the Ridgeway).

The nearest railway station to the other end of the path at Ivinghoe Beacon is at Tring (3¾ miles/6km away). You will already have walked past this station on your way up to the Beacon. Tring is on Silverlink's London Euston to Northampton line via Hemel Hempstead, Berkhamsted and Milton Keynes. Euston to Tring takes about 40 minutes.

Chiltern Railways operate services from London Marylebone to Birmingham – via High Wycombe, Princes Risborough (on the Ridgeway) and Banbury – and to Aylesbury via Wendover (on the Ridgeway). There are also services from London Marylebone to Little Kimble and Saunderton, both of which are fairly close to the Ridgeway.

All timetable and fare information can be found at **National Rail Enquiries** (☎ 08457 484950, 24hrs, 🖥 www.nationalrail.co.uk). You can also purchase tickets over the phone through the relevant train operating company or online at 🖥 www.thetrainline.com and 🖥 www.qjump.co.uk. It is often possible now to

---

❏ RAIL SERVICES

Chiltern Railways (🖥 www.chilternrailways.co.uk)
● London Marylebone to Birmingham via High Wycombe, Princes Risborough, Aylesbury & Banbury, daily 1/hr
● London Marylebone to Aylesbury via Wendover, Mon-Sat 2/hr, Sun 1/hr
● There are also services from London Marylebone to Saunderton, daily 1/hr; plus to Little Kimble and Monks Risborough, Mon-Fri 6/day, Sat 5/day, Sun 1/hr

Silverlink Trains (🖥 www.silverlink-trains.com)
● London Euston to Northampton via Hemel Hempstead, Berkhamsted, Tring & Milton Keynes, Mon-Sat 2/hr, Sun 1/hr

First Great Western (🖥 www.firstgreatwestern.co.uk)
● London Paddington to Swindon via Reading and Didcot Parkway, Mon-Sat 3-4/hr, Sun 1-2/hr
● London Paddington to Oxford via Goring & Streatley, Cholsey & Didcot Parkway, Mon-Sat 1-2/hr, Sun 1/hr
● London Paddington to Reading via Twyford, Mon-Sat 3-4/hr, Sun 2/hr, daily connection to Henley (1/hr)
● London Paddington to Swansea via Reading, Swindon, Bristol Parkway & Cardiff, Mon-Sat 1/hr, Sun 1/hr to Cardiff with a connection to Swansea
● London Paddington to Exeter St David's via Reading, Newbury (not all services), Pewsey (not all services) Mon-Sat 1/hr, Sun 5/day
● Reading to Bedwyn via Newbury & Hungerford, Mon-Sat 1/hr, Sun one every two hours
● Bristol Parkway to Swindon, Mon-Sat 2/hr, Sun 1/hr

Cholsey and Wallingford Railway (recorded message ☎ 01491 835067, 🖥 www.cholsey-wallingford-railway.com) See p138.
Chinnor and Princes Risborough Railway (talking timetable ☎ 01844 353535, 🖥 www.cprra.co.uk) See p156.

PLANNING YOUR WALK

buy a train ticket that includes bus travel at your destination. For further information visit the Plusbus website (🖳 www.plusbus.info).

If you think you may want to book a taxi when you arrive visit 🖳 www.traintaxi.co.uk for details of taxi companies operating at rail stations throughout England.

By coach   [see box below]

National Express is the principal coach (long-distance bus) operator in Britain. Coach travel is generally cheaper but takes longer than travel by train.

Marlborough, which is just 4 miles (7km) from Overton Hill and the start of the Ridgeway, is conveniently located on National Express's NX402 route which runs between London and Frome, in Somerset.

Several National Express services stop in Swindon from where you can take a local bus to Marlborough (see pp42-3). From Marlborough it's a local bus ride (services are frequent and quick) to the West Kennet bus stop, just a few hundred metres from Overton Hill.

Some of the **Oxford Tube** bus services between London and Oxford call at Lewknor, a good starting point for a walk to Princes Risborough or Wendover.

The nearest place to Ivinghoe Beacon at which National Express coaches stop is Hemel Hempstead (10 miles/17km) from where you can get a local

---

❏ **COACH SERVICES**
National Express (☎ 0871 781 8181, lines open 8am-10pm daily, 🖳 www.nationalexpress.com)

NX402 London–Frome via Heathrow, Newbury, Hungerford, Froxfield,
  Marlborough, Beckhampton, Devizes, Sells Green, Melksham &
  Trowbridge, 1/day

NX403 London Victoria–Bath via Heathrow Airport, 10/day: some services
  call at **Swindon**, Calne, Chippenham, Corsham, Rudloe, Box and/or
  Batheaston

NX302 Bristol–Northampton via Bath, Corsham, Chippenham, **Swindon** & Oxford

NX444 London Victoria–Gloucester via Cheltenham, 7/day (4/day call at
  Swindon and/or Cirencester)

NX222 London Heathrow–Gloucester via **Swindon**, Cirencester, Charlton Kings
  and Cheltenham, 1/day

NX335 Poole–Halifax via Bournemouth, Salisbury, **Marlborough**, **Swindon**,
  Cirencester, Gloucester, Cheltenham, Leicester and Huddersfield, 1/day
  (note: not all stops are listed)

JL737 Stansted Airport to Oxford via Hatfield, Luton Airport, **Hemel Hempstead**,
  High Wycombe & Stokenchurch, 6/day

JL787 Heathrow to Cambridge via **Hemel Hempstead**, Luton, Hitchin,
  Letchworth, Baldock, Royston & Harston, 9/day

Green Line (🖳 www.greenline.co.uk)/Arriva (🖳 www.arrivabus.co.uk)
758/768 London to **Hemel Hempstead**, Mon-Fri 17/day, Sat 9/day

Oxford Tube (☎ 01865 772250, 🖳 www.oxfordtube.com)
  London to Oxford via **Lewknor**, daily 4/hr

bus to Tring (see box pp42-3). **Green Line** also operates services to Hemel Hempstead.

By car

The Ridgeway is very easily accessed by car. From junction 15 of the M4 motorway it's a short drive down the A345 to Marlborough, then onto the A4 to the start at Overton Hill. You can't, however, leave your car for more than a day in the small car parking area at Overton Hill so you should find somewhere to leave it in Marlborough or maybe Avebury, though even this could be tricky.

The Ivinghoe Beacon end of the Ridgeway is best reached from junction 11 (Dunstable) of the M40 or via Aylesbury along the A41. There is a National Trust car park for Ivinghoe Beacon about half a mile (1km) south of the B489 on the minor road to Ringshall.

However, overall it's probably easier and cheaper (with the rising petrol prices) and certainly better for the environment to use public transport.

By air

The nearest airport to the start of the path is at Bristol but it is so far from the start of the Ridgeway as to make flying there, particularly for domestic travellers, fairly pointless. At the other end of the path Luton airport is much closer, but in most cases it would still be easier to head into London by train or bus and travel on from there. Air travel really is not the best way to get to the Ridgeway. See 🖥 www.chooseclimate.org for the true costs of flying.

LOCAL TRANSPORT

There are few useful train services along the Ridgeway so you will have to rely on the public bus services. These bus services, although extensive, aren't always frequent, especially at weekends. Buses on the western half of the Ridgeway connect more of the places you might need whereas trying to get from one place to another on the eastern section can involve travelling first to a larger town, then changing buses and continuing from there. Obviously this can be quite time consuming and if you don't want to end up paying out for a taxi this is certainly one aspect of your trip that you will need to plan. Services to smaller towns and villages tend to finish by mid-afternoon.

The public transport map on pp42-5 gives an overview of the most useful bus and train routes, approximate frequency of services in both directions and who you should contact for detailed timetable information. The details given are for summer services, though some of those listed operate year-round. It is essential to check the latest details before travelling: you can pick up bus timetables for free at any of the tourist information centres along the route.

If the contact details in the box on pp42-3 prove unsatisfactory, you can contact **traveline** (☎ 0871 200 2233, daily 7am-9pm; 🖥 www.traveline.org.uk) which has public transport information for the whole of the UK.

❑ LOCAL BUS SERVICES

● **Stagecoach (Swindon ☎ 01793 521415, 🖳 www.stagecoachbus.com/swindon;**
  ☎ 01865 772250, 🖳 www.stagecoachbus.com/oxfordshire)

70	Swindon to Marlborough via Ogbourne St George, Mon-Sat 1/hr
71	Swindon to Marlborough via Ogbourne St George, Sun only 3/day
49	Swindon to Trowbridge (The Trans Wilts Express) via Avebury, Beckhampton & Devizes, Mon-Sat 1/hr
31	Oxford to Wantage, Mon-Sat 2/hr and Sun 1/hr
X30	Oxford to Wantage, Mon-Sat 1/hr

● **Wilts & Dorset Buses (☎ 01722 336855, 🖳 www.wdbus.co.uk)**

95	Swindon to Pewsey via Ogbourne St George & Marlborough, Mon-Sat 5/day, Sun 1/day
96	Swindon to Pewsey via Avebury, West Kennet & Marlborough, Mon-Sat 7/day, Sun 4/day

● **Connect2Wiltshire (☎ 08456 525255, 🖳 www.bookaride.co.uk/c2w)**

Line 4 (43)	Calne to Marlborough via Avebury, Beckhampton, Silbury Hill, West Kennet, East Kennet, West Overton, Mon-Sat 10/day; Avebury to Marlborough only, Mon-Sat 8/day
TaxiBuzz (44)	Devizes to Marlborough via Avebury, Beckhampton, Silbury Hill, West Kennet, East Kennet & West Overton, Mon-Fri 3/day; Devizes to Marlborough direct, Mon-Fri 1/day

Note: Many stops are request only so it is essential to call Connect2Wiltshire (details as above and then choose option 1 for a bus service and option 8 then option 5 for the taxi service) to book a seat: call to book at least 20 minutes before you plan to travel.

● **Thamesdown Transport (☎ 01793 428428, 🖳 www.thamesdown-transport.co.uk)**

46	Swindon to Hungerford via Liddington, Fox Hill, Aldbourne & Ramsbury, Mon-Fri 6/day, Sat 4/day and 2/day Aldbourne to Hungerford
47	Swindon to Lambourn via Bishopstone & Ashbury, Mon-Sat 6/day
48	Swindon to Marlborough via Liddington, Fox Hill, Aldbourne & Ramsbury, Mon-Sat 6/day

● **Heyfordian Travel (☎ 01869 241500, 🖳 www.heyfordian.travel)**

134	Wallingford to Goring via North Stoke & South Stoke, Mon-Fri 3/day; Wallingford to Goring circular route via North Stoke, South Stoke, Goring, Streatley, Moulsford & Cholsey, Mon-Sat 2-3/day
135	Goring to Wallingford via South Stoke & North Stoke, Mon-Fri 2/day; Wallingford to Goring circular route via Cholsey, Moulsford, Streatley, Goring, South Stoke & North Stoke, Mon-Sat 3/day

● **Newbury Buses (☎ 01635 567500, 🖳 www.reading-buses.co.uk)**

4	Newbury to Lambourn, Mon-Fri 9/day
6	Newbury circular route via Chievely, West Ilsley, East Ilsley & Compton, Mon-Sat 4/day
9	Newbury circular route via Compton, East Ilsley, West Ilsley & Chievely, Mon-Sat 4/day
13	Newbury to Hungerford, Mon-Fri 4/day

● **Tourist Coaches (☎ 01722 338359)/AD Rains (☎ 01666 510874)**

X76	Marlborough to Bath via West Kennet, Beckhampton, Calne & Melksham, Mon-Sat 1/day
244/X44	Devizes to Marlborough via Beckhampton & West Kennet, Mon-Fri 1/day
X43	Marlborough to Avebury, Mon-Fri 1/day

RH Transport Services (☎ 01993 869100, ⌨ www.rhtransportservices.co.uk)
67   Wantage to Faringdon via Letcombe Regis, Letcombe Bassett, Sparsholt, Kingston Lisle & Uffington, Mon-Sat 2/day, but only 1/day via Letcombe Regis & Letcombe Bassett
X47   Wantage to Swindon via Letcombe Regis, Letcombe Bassett, Sparsholt, Kingston Lisle, Uffington, Woolstone, Ashbury, Idstone, Bishopstone, Hinton Parva, Fox Hill & Liddington, Sat 3/day

● **Thames Travel (⌨ www.thames-travel.co.uk)**
32   Abingdon to Wantage via Didcot Parkway, Mon-Sat 12/day (at Abingdon there is a connecting service to/from Oxford)
105   Oxford to Wallingford, Mon-Sat 2-3/day
125   Wallingford to Watlington via Crowmarsh Gifford, Mon-Sat 1-2/day
130   Didcot to Wallingford, Mon-Sat 1/hr
132   RAF Benson to Wallingford via Crowmarsh Gifford, Mon-Sat 1/hr, Sun 7/day
132   Goring to Reading via Streatley & Pangborne, Mon-Sat 6/day
136   Wallingford to Cholsey circular route, Mon-Sat 1/hr
139   Henley to Wallingford via Crowmarsh Gifford & Huntercombe (Nuffield), Mon-Sat 1/hr, Sun 5/day
X39   Reading to Oxford via Wallingford & Crowmarsh Gifford, Mon-Sat 1/hr
X40   Reading to Oxford via Woodcote, Wallingford & Crowmarsh Gifford, daily 1/hr
X41   Wallingford to Oxford via Crowmarsh Gifford, Benson Village & RAF Benson, Mon-Sat 4/evening, Sun 2/evening

● **Motts Travel (☎ 01296 398300, ⌨ www.mottstravel.com)**
M1   Stokenchurch to Reading via Lewknor & Watlington, Mon-Sat 1-2/day

● **Red Rose Travel (☎ 01296 747926, ⌨ www.redrosetravel.com)**
124   Watlington to Thame via Lewknor, Tue 2/day, Wed-Sat 4/day
161   Aylesbury to Ivinghoe via Wendover, Tring & Pitstone, Sun & Bank Hol Mon 4/day
387   Tring to Wigginton, Mon-Sat 4/day; Tring to Aldbury, Mon-Fri 8/day, Sat 6/day

● **Carousel (☎ 01494 533436, ⌨ www.carouselbuses.com)**
320   Princes Risborough to Chinnor, Mon-Fri 7/day

● **Walters Limousines (☎ 01865 875222)**
CR   (County Rider) High Wycombe to Princes Risborough via Bledlow Ridge, Bradenham & Saunderton, Mon-Fri 8/day, Sat 4/day

● **Arriva The Shires (☎ 0844 800 4411, ⌨ www.arrivabus.co.uk)**
30   Aldbury to Berkhamsted via Tring, Mon-Sat 3/day
40   High Wycombe to Thame via Kingston Blount & Chinnor, Mon-Sat 1/hr
54   Aylesbury to Wendover, Mon-Sat 2/hr
61   Aylesbury to Luton via Tring, Ivinghoe & Dunstable, Mon-Sat 1/hr (most services go to Luton Airport as well)
300   High Wycombe to Aylesbury via Princes Risborough, Mon-Fri 3/hr, Sat 2/hr
500   Aylesbury to Watford via Tring, Berkhamsted & Hemel Hempstead, Mon-Sat 2/hr

● **Centrebus (☎ 0844 357 6520, ⌨ www.centrebus.co.uk)**
327   Hemel Hempstead circular route (Chiltern Ramblers' Bus) via Berkhamsted, Dunstable, Ivinghoe, Pitstone, Tring, Aldbury & back to Hemel Hempstead, May-Sep only Sun 3/day.

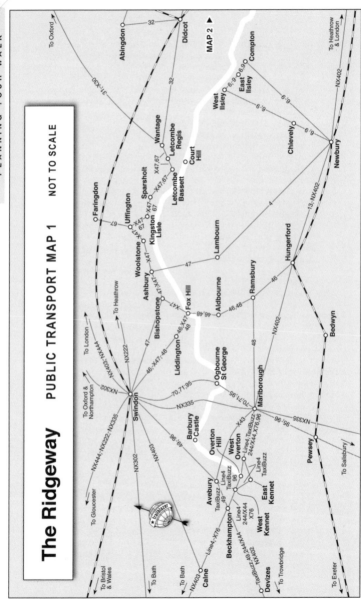

The Ridgeway   PUBLIC TRANSPORT MAP 1   NOT TO SCALE

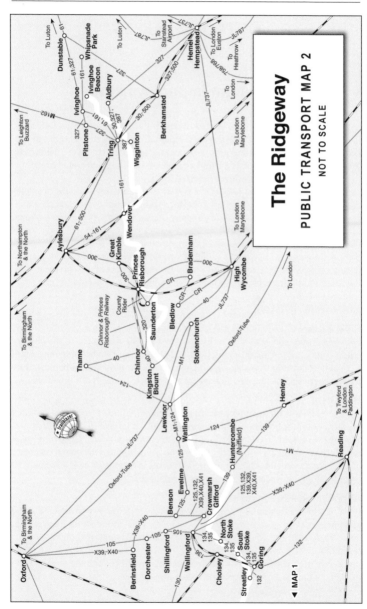

The Ridgeway
PUBLIC TRANSPORT MAP 2
NOT TO SCALE

PLANNING YOUR WALK

▲ MAP 1

Minimum impact walking

In this chaotic world in which people live their lives at an increasingly frenetic pace, many of us living in overcrowded cities and working in jobs that offer little free time, the great outdoors is becoming an essential means of escape. Walking in the countryside is a wonderful means of relaxation and gives people the time to think and re-discover themselves.

Of course. as the popularity of the countryside increases so do the problems that this pressure brings. It is important for visitors to remember that the countryside is the home and workplace of many others. Walkers in particular should be aware of their responsibilities. Indeed a walker who respects and understands the countryside will get far more enjoyment from their trip.

By following a few simple guidelines while walking the Ridgeway you can have a positive impact, not just on your own well-being but also on local communities and the environment, thereby becoming part of the solution.

ECONOMIC IMPACT

Rural businesses and communities in Britain have been hit hard in recent years by a seemingly endless series of crises. Most people are aware of the country code – rules such as not dropping litter and closing the gate behind you are still as pertinent as ever – but in light of the economic pressures experienced by local countryside businesses there is something else you can do: buy local.

Buy local

Seek out and ask for local produce to buy and eat. Not only does this cut down on the amount of pollution and congestion that the transportation of food creates (the so-called 'food miles'), but it also ensures you are supporting local farmers and producers – the very people who have moulded the countryside you have come to see and who are in the best position to protect it. If you can find local food which is also organic so much the better.

Support local businesses

It's a fact of life that money spent at local level – perhaps in a market, or at the greengrocer, or in an independent pub – has a far greater impact for good on that community than the equivalent spent in a branch of a national chain store or restaurant.

While no-one would advocate that walkers should boycott the larger supermarkets, which after all do provide local employment, it's worth remembering that businesses in rural communities rely heavily on visitors for their very existence. If we want to keep these shops and post offices, we need to use them.

The more money that circulates locally and is spent on local labour and materials, the greater the impact on the local economy and the more power the community has to effect the change it wants to see.

Encourage local cultural traditions and skills

No part of the countryside looks the same. Buildings, food, skills and language evolve out of the landscape and are moulded over hundreds of years to suit the locality. Discovering these cultural differences is part of the pleasure of walking in new places. Visitors' enthusiasm for local traditions and skills brings awareness and pride, nurturing a sense of place; this is an increasingly important role in a world where economic globalisation continues to undermine the very things that provide security and a feeling of belonging.

ENVIRONMENTAL IMPACT

A walking holiday in itself is an environmentally friendly approach to tourism. The following are some ideas on how you can go a few steps further in helping to minimise your impact on the natural environment while walking the Ridgeway.

Use public transport whenever possible

By using the local bus you will help to keep it in service. Although the bus routes along the Ridgeway aren't always convenient for walkers, if fewer people use them they are more likely to disappear altogether. Public transport is always preferable to using private cars as it benefits everyone: visitors, locals and the environment.

Never leave litter

Leaving litter shows a total disrespect for the natural world and others coming after you. As well as being unsightly, litter kills wildlife, pollutes the environment and can be dangerous to farm animals. If you've carried everything at the start of the day you can probably carry whatever remains until you reach a rubbish bin. Put all your rubbish in a biodegradable bag so you can dispose of it in a bin in the next village. It would be very helpful if you could pick up litter left by other people too.

Is it OK if it's biodegradable? Not really. Apple cores, banana skins, orange peel and the like are unsightly, encourage flies, ants and wasps and ruin a picnic spot for others. Using the excuse that they are natural and biodegradable just doesn't cut any ice. When was the last time you saw a banana tree in England?

The lasting impact of litter A piece of orange peel left on the ground takes six months to decompose, silver foil takes 18 months, a plastic bag 10 years, clothes 15 years and an aluminium can 85 years.

Erosion

Stay on the main trail The effect of your footsteps may seem minuscule but when they are multiplied by several thousand walkers each year they become rather more significant. Avoid taking shortcuts, widening the trail or taking more than one path; your boots will be followed by many others.

Consider walking out of season Maximum disturbance by walkers coincides with the time of year when nature wants to do most of its growth and repair. In high-use areas, like that along much of the eastern section of the Ridgeway, the trail never recovers. Walking at less busy times eases this pressure while also generating year-round income for the local economy. Not only that, but it may make the walk a more relaxing experience with fewer people on the path and less competition for accommodation.

Respect all wildlife

Care for all wildlife you come across along the Ridgeway: it has as much right to be there as you. Tempting as it may be to pick wild flowers, leave them so the next people who pass can enjoy them too. Don't break branches off or damage trees in any way.

If you come across wildlife, keep your distance and don't watch for too long. Your presence can cause considerable stress, particularly if the adults are with young, or in winter when the weather is harsh and food is scarce. Young animals are rarely abandoned. If you come across young birds keep away so that their mother can return.

The code of the outdoor loo

'Going' in the outdoors is a lost art worth re-learning, for your sake and everyone else's. As more and more people discover the joys of the outdoors this is becoming an important issue.

In some parts of the world where visitor pressure is higher than in Britain walkers and climbers are required to pack out their excrement. This could soon be necessary here. Human excrement is not only offensive to our senses but, more importantly, can infect water sources.

Where to go Wherever possible use a toilet. Public toilets are marked on the trail maps in this guide and you will also find facilities in pubs, cafés and campsites along the Ridgeway.

If you do have to go outdoors choose a site at least 30 metres away from running water. Carry a small trowel and dig a hole about 15cm (6") deep in which to bury your excrement. It decomposes quicker when in contact with the top layer of soil or leaf mould. Use a stick to stir loose soil into your deposit as well as this speeds up decomposition even more. Do not squash it under rocks as this slows down the composting process. If you have to use rocks to cover it make sure they are not in contact with your faeces.

(Opposite) There's no shortage of hostelries to delay your progress along the Ridgeway. The Swan at Streatley (see p130) has an inviting terrace right beside the River Thames.

Toilet paper and tampons Toilet paper takes a long time to decompose whether buried or not. It is easily dug up by animals and may then blow into water sources or onto the path. The best method for dealing with it is to pack it out. Put the used paper inside a paper bag which you then place inside a biodegradable bag (or two). Then simply empty the contents of the paper bag at the next toilet you come across and throw the bag away. You should also pack out tampons and sanitary towels in a similar way: they take years to decompose and may be dug up and scattered about by animals.

Wild camping

Unfortunately, wild camping is not allowed along the Ridgeway, but it is generally tolerated if you leave no trace of yourself on the ground when you leave the next morning. Wild camping is an altogether more fulfilling experience than camping on a designated site. Living in the outdoors without any facilities provides a valuable lesson in simple, sustainable living where the results of all your actions, from going to the loo to washing your plates, can be seen.

If you do insist on wild camping on land off the Ridgeway path always ask the landowner for permission. Follow these suggestions for minimising your impact and encourage others to do likewise.

Be discreet Camp alone or in small groups, spend only one night in each place and pitch your tent late and move off early.

Never light a fire The deep burn caused by camp fires, no matter how small, damages the turf which can take years to recover. Cook on a camp stove instead.

Don't use soap or detergent There is no need to use soap: even biodegradable soaps and detergents pollute streams. You won't be away from a shower for more than a day or so. Wash up without detergent: use a plastic or metal scourer, or failing that, a handful of fine pebbles from the beach or some bracken or grass.

Leave no trace Learn the skill of moving on without leaving any sign of having been there: no moved boulders, ripped up vegetation or dug drainage ditches. Make a final check of your campsite before departing: pick up any litter that you or anyone else has left, so leaving the place in a better state than you found it.

ACCESS

Britain is a crowded cluster of islands with few places where you can wander as you please. Most of the land is a patchwork of fields and agricultural land and the area around the Ridgeway is no different. However, there are countless public rights of way, in addition to the official Ridgeway path, that criss-cross the land; so, what happens if you feel a little more adventurous and want to explore the downs, woodland and hills that can be found around the Ridgeway?

(Opposite) When the weather conditions are right you may see paragliders launching themselves off White Horse Hill (see p113).

Rights of way

As a designated **National Trail** the Ridgeway is a **public right of way**. A public right of way is either a footpath, a bridleway or a byway: the Ridgeway is made up of all three of these.

Rights of way are theoretically established because the owner has dedicated them to public use. However, very few rights of way are formally dedicated in this way. If members of the public have been using a path without interference for 20 years or more the law assumes the owner has intended to dedicate it as a right of way. If a path has been unused for 20 years it does not cease to exist; the guiding principle is 'once a highway, always a highway'.

On a public right of way you have the right to 'pass and repass along the way' which includes stopping to rest or admire the view, or to consume refreshments. You can also take with you a 'natural accompaniment' which includes a dog but obviously could also be a horse on bridleways and byways. All 'natural accompaniments' must be kept under close control (see p21).

Farmers and land managers must ensure that paths are not blocked by crops or other vegetation, or otherwise obstructed, that the route is identifiable and the surface is restored soon after cultivation. If crops are growing over the path you have every right to walk or ride through them, following the line of the right of way as closely as possible. If you find a path blocked or impassable you should report it to the appropriate **highway authority**. Highway authorities are responsible for maintaining public rights of way. Along the Ridgeway the highway authorities are **Wiltshire County Council**, **Swindon Borough Council**, **Oxfordshire County Council**, **West Berkshire Council**, **Buckinghamshire County Council** and **Hertfordshire County Council** (see box p56). The councils are also the surveying authorities with responsibility for maintaining the official definitive maps of the public rights of way.

Right to roam

The Countryside & Rights of Way Act 2000 (CRoW), or 'Right to Roam' as dubbed by walkers, came into effect in full on 31 October 2005 after a long campaign to allow greater public access to areas of countryside, deemed to be uncultivated open country, in England and Wales – this essentially means moorland, heathland, downland and upland areas. Some land is covered by restrictions (ie high-impact activities such as driving a vehicle, cycling, horse-riding are not permitted) and some land is excluded (such as gardens, parks and cultivated land). Full details are given on 🖳 www.countrysideaccess.gov.uk.

With more freedom in the countryside comes a need for more responsibility from the walker. Remember that wild open country is still the workplace of farmers and home to all sorts of wildlife. Have respect for both and avoid disturbing domestic and wild animals.

The Countryside Code

The countryside is a fragile place which every visitor should respect. The Countryside Code (see box opposite) was revised in part because of the changes brought about by the CRoW Act (see above) and was relaunched in July 2004.

It seems like common sense but sadly some people still seem to have no understanding of how to treat the countryside they walk in. Everyone visiting the countryside has a responsibility to minimise the impact of their visit so other people can enjoy the same peaceful landscapes. It does not take much effort; it really is common sense.

Below is an expanded version of the Countryside Code, launched under the logo, 'Respect, Protect and Enjoy':

❏ **The Countryside Code**
● Be safe – plan ahead and follow any signs
● Leave gates and property as you find them
● Protect plants and animals, and take your litter home
● Keep dogs under close control
● Consider other people

● **Be safe – plan ahead and follow any signs** Walking on the Ridgeway is pretty much hazard-free but you're responsible for your own safety so follow the simple guidelines outlined on pp52-4.

● **Leave all gates as you found them** Normally a farmer leaves gates closed to keep livestock in but may sometimes leave them open to allow livestock access to food or water. Leave them as you find them and if there is a sign, follow the instructions.

● **Leave livestock, crops and machinery alone** Help farmers by not interfering with their means of livelihood.

● **Take your litter home** 'Pack it in, pack it out'. Litter is not only ugly but can be harmful to wildlife; small mammals often become trapped in discarded cans and bottles. Many walkers think that orange peel and banana skins do not count as litter, but even biodegradable foodstuffs attract common scavenging species such as crows and gulls to the detriment of less dominant species. See p47.

● **Keep your dog under close control** Across farmland, dogs should be kept on a lead. During lambing time (see box p52) they should not be taken with you at all.

● **Enjoy the countryside and respect its life and work** Access to the countryside depends on being sensitive to the needs and wishes of those who live and work there. Being courteous and friendly to those you meet will ensure a healthy future for all based on partnership and co-operation.

● **Guard against all risk of fire** Accidental fire is a great fear of farmers and foresters. Never make a camp fire and take matches and cigarette butts away with you to dispose of safely.

● **Keep to paths across farmland** Stick to the official Ridgeway path across arable or pasture land. Minimise erosion by not cutting corners or widening the path.

● **Use gates and stiles to cross fences, hedges and walls** The Ridgeway path is well supplied with stiles where it crosses field boundaries. On some of the side trips you may find the paths less accommodating. If you have to climb over a gate because you can't open it always do so at the hinged end.

● **Help keep all water clean** Leaving litter and going to the toilet near a water source can pollute people's water supplies. See pp47-9 for more advice.

MINIMUM IMPACT & OUTDOOR SAFETY

❏ **Lambing**
A great deal of the Ridgeway passes through private farmland some of which is pasture for sheep. Lambing takes place from mid-March to mid-May and dogs should not be taken along the path at this time. Even a dog secured on a lead is liable to disturb a pregnant ewe. If you should see a lamb or ewe that appears to be in distress contact the nearest farmer.

● **Take special care on country roads** Drivers often go dangerously fast on narrow winding lanes. To be safe, walk facing the oncoming traffic and carry a torch or wear highly visible clothing when it's getting dark.
● **Protect wildlife, plants and trees** Care for and respect all wildlife you come across along the Ridgeway path. Don't pick plants, break trees or scare wild animals.
● **Make no unnecessary noise** Enjoy the peace and solitude of the outdoors by staying in small groups and acting unobtrusively.

Outdoor safety

AVOIDANCE OF HAZARDS

With good planning and preparation most hazards can be avoided. This information is just as important for those out on a day walk as for those walking the entire Ridgeway.

Ensure you have **suitable clothes** (see p33) to keep you warm and dry, whatever the conditions and a spare change of inner clothes. A compass, whistle, torch and first-aid kit should be carried and are discussed further on p34. The **emergency signal** is six blasts on the whistle or six flashes with a torch.

Take plenty of **food** with you for the day and at least one litre of **water** although more would be better, especially on the long western stretches. It is a good idea to fill up your bottle whenever you pass a water tap as they aren't very common. You will eat far more walking than you do normally so make sure you have enough for the day, as well as some high-energy snacks (chocolate, dried fruit, biscuits) in the bottom of your pack for an emergency.

Stay alert and **know exactly where you are** throughout the day. The easiest way to do this is to regularly check your position on the map. If visibility suddenly decreases with mist and cloud, or there is an accident, you will be able to make a sensible decision about what action to take based on your location.

If you choose to walk alone you must appreciate and be prepared for the increased risk. It's a good idea to leave word with someone about where you are going and remember to contact them when you have arrived safely.

WEATHER FORECASTS

The western section of the Ridgeway is particularly exposed. The difference in conditions between the villages below the Ridgeway and the path itself can be quite dramatic. You often only notice just how cold and windy it is when you stop for a few minutes.

Try to get the local weather forecast from the internet, newspaper, TV, radio or one of the telephone forecasts before you set off. Plan the day accordingly.

Telephone and internet forecasts

These are frequently updated and generally reliable. **Weather call** (☎ 09068 500414) is useful, but calls are charged at the expensive premium rate (60p per minute).

You can get a localised five-day forecast from 🖥 www.bbc.co.uk/weather if you enter a postcode. Useful postcodes for the Ridgeway are: SN8 (Marlborough); OX12 (Wantage); OX10 (Wallingford); OX39 (Chinnor); HP27 (Princes Risborough) and HP23 (Tring).

HEALTH

Blisters

It is important to break in new boots before embarking on a long walk. Make sure the boots are comfortable and try to avoid getting them wet on the inside. Air your feet at lunchtime, keep them clean and change your socks regularly. If you feel any hot spots stop immediately and apply a few strips of zinc oxide tape and leave them on until the area is pain free or the tape starts to come off.

If you have left it too late and a blister has developed you should surround it with 'moleskin' or any other blister kit to protect it from abrasion. Popping it can lead to infection. If the skin is broken keep the area clean with antiseptic and cover with a non-adhesive dressing material held in place with tape.

Hypothermia

Also known as exposure, this occurs when the body can't generate enough heat to maintain its normal temperature, usually as a result of being wet, cold, unprotected from the wind, tired and hungry. It is usually more of a problem in upland areas. However, even on the Ridgeway in bad weather the body can be exposed to strong winds and driving rain making the risk a real one. The western stretches of the path are particularly exposed and there are few villages making it difficult to get help should it be needed.

MINIMUM IMPACT & OUTDOOR SAFETY

❑ **Dealing with an accident**
● Use basic first aid to treat the injury to the best of your ability.
● Work out exactly where you are. If possible leave someone with the casualty while others go to get help. If there are only two people, you have a dilemma.
● If you decide to get help leave all spare clothing and food with the casualty.
● Telephone ☎ 999 and ask for the ambulance service.

Hypothermia is easily avoided by wearing suitable clothing, carrying and eating enough food and drink, being aware of the weather conditions and checking the morale of your companions. Early signs to watch for are feeling cold and tired with involuntary shivering. If this occurs, find some shelter as soon as possible and warm the person up with a hot drink and some chocolate or other high-energy food. If possible give them another warm layer of clothing and allow them to rest until feeling better.

If the patient's condition deteriorates, strange behaviour, slurring of speech and poor co-ordination will become apparent and they can quickly progress into unconsciousness, followed by coma and death. You should get the patient out of wind and rain quickly, improvising a shelter if necessary. Rapid restoration of bodily warmth is essential and is best achieved by bare-skin contact: someone should get into the same sleeping bag as the patient, both having stripped to their underwear, putting any spare clothing under or over them to build up heat. Send urgently for help.

Hyperthermia

Hyperthermia is the general name given to a variety of heat-related ailments. Not something you would normally associate with England, heatstroke and heat exhaustion are serious problems nonetheless. Symptoms of **heat exhaustion** include thirst, fatigue, giddiness, a rapid pulse, raised body temperature, low urine output and, if not treated, delirium and finally a coma. The best cure is to drink plenty of water.

Heatstroke is another matter altogether, and even more serious. A high body temperature and an absence of sweating are early indications, followed by symptoms similar to hypothermia (see p53) such as a lack of coordination, convulsions and coma. Death will follow if treatment is not instantly given. Sponge the victim down, wrap them in wet towels, fan them, and get help immediately.

Sunburn

It can easily happen even on overcast days and especially if you have a fair complexion. The only surefire way to avoid it is to stay wrapped up, but that's not really an option. What you must do, therefore, is to smother yourself in sunscreen (with a minimum factor of 15) and apply it regularly throughout the day. Don't forget your lips, nose, ears, the back of your neck if wearing a T shirt, and even under your chin to protect against rays reflected up off the ground.

PART 3: THE ENVIRONMENT & NATURE

At first glance, the Ridgeway path doesn't seem to be very distinctive. It doesn't have wide beaches or impressive hills or mountains like many other long-distance trails in the UK. But when you look closer you see a wide variety of terrains and habitats from one end of the path to the other: grasslands, chalk downs, beech woodlands and a section along the banks of the River Thames. These varied environments are home to an equally diverse collection of animals, birds and plants. This book is not designed to be a comprehensive guide to all the wildlife you may encounter, but serves as an introduction to the flora and fauna the walker is likely to find along the Ridgeway.

Making that special effort to look out for wildlife and appreciating what you are seeing will enhance your enjoyment of the walk. To take it a step further is to understand a little more about the species you may encounter, appreciating how they interact with each other and learning a little about the conservation issues that are so pertinent today. At a time when man seems ever more detached from the natural world it is important to remember that we continue to be a part of this complex web and this brings a responsibility to limit our negative influences.

Conservation of the Ridgeway

Like much of the British Isles, the English countryside has had to cope with a great deal of pressure from the activities of an ever-industrialised world. It must have been a fascinating place when the broadleaved forests stretched as far as the eye could see. Today the surviving pockets of forest are still under threat but, thankfully, there is a greater understanding of the value of the natural environment and with it a number of organisations who are actively helping to safeguard what remains of England's natural heritage.

As beautiful as the modern-day countryside may be it is sad to note that almost every acre of land has been altered in some way by man. What we have today are fragments of semi-natural woodland and hedgerows stretched across farmland. This plundering of the countryside has had a major effect on its biodiversity. The wolf, wild boar and a number of other species have been lost and others severely depleted in number so one begins to appreciate the influence that man has had over the years.

There is good news, however. In these enlightened times when environmental issues are quite rightly given more precedence, many endangered species have increased in number thanks to the active work of voluntary conservation bodies.

On the Ridgeway much work has been undertaken to preserve and expand the areas of grassland where chalk-dependent flowers can flourish. In turn this should help to increase the numbers of rare butterflies, such as the Chalkhill Blue, that are reliant on chalkland flowers such as Horseshoe Vetch for their survival. There is also reason to be optimistic: the environment is no longer the least important issue in party politics and this reflects the opinions of everyday people who are concerned about conservation on both a global and local scale. In England there are organisations, both voluntary and government based, dedicated to conserving their local heritage: everything from Norman castles to barn owls.

NATURAL ENGLAND

In October 2006 the Countryside Agency, English Nature and the Rural Development Service merged to become Natural England. This was owing to the National Environment and Rural Communities Bill which became law on 30 March 2006.

The official responsibilities of Natural England are to 'enhance biodiversity and our landscapes and wildlife in rural, urban, coastal and marine areas; promote access, recreation and public well-being, and contribute to the way natural resources are managed, so they can be enjoyed now and for future generations'. Essentially this single organisation has the same powers as the former three bodies and as such gives advice and information, designates **Sites of Special Scientific Interest** (SSSIs), **National Parks**, **Areas of Outstanding Natural Beauty** (AONBs), manages **National Nature Reserves** (NNRs) and enforces existing regulations. Natural England also manages England's National Trails: they provide most of the funding and resources for path maintenance and promote the conservation of wildlife, geology and wild places in England.

❏ **Statutory bodies**
● **Department for Environment, Food and Rural Affairs** (🖳 www.defra.gov.uk) Government department responsible for sustainable development in the countryside.
● **Natural England** (see above; 🖳 www.naturalengland.gov.uk)
● **County/Borough Councils: Wiltshire** (☎ 01225 713000, 🖳 www.wiltshire .gov.uk); **Oxfordshire** (☎ 01865 792422, 🖳 www.oxfordshire.gov.uk); **Buckinghamshire** (☎ 0845 370 8090, 🖳 www.buckscc.gov.uk); **Hertfordshire** (☎ 01438 737555, 🖳 www.hertsdirect.org); **Swindon** (☎ 01793 445500, 🖳 www.swin don.gov.uk); **West Berkshire Council** (☎ 01635 42400, 🖳 www.westberks.gov.uk).
● **English Heritage** (☎ 0870 333 1181, 🖳 www.english-heritage.org.uk) Organisation whose central aim is to make sure that the historic environment of England is properly maintained. It is officially known as the Historic Buildings and Monuments Commission for England. Most of the sites around Avebury (see pp73-81) are English Heritage properties though a number are actually managed by the National Trust (see p58).
● **Forestry Commission** (☎ 0131 334 0303, 🖳 www.forestry.gov.uk) Government department for establishing and managing forests, including Hale Wood (see p171), for a variety of uses.

THE ENVIRONMENT & NATURE

❏ **National Trails**
The Ridgeway is one of 15 National Trails in England and Wales. These are Britain's flagship long-distance paths which grew out of the post-war desire to protect the country's special places, a movement which also gave birth to National Parks and AONBs (see below). The first National Trail was the Pennine Way in 1965. Since then over 2500 miles (4000km) of walking routes have been designated.

Although no part of the Ridgeway is inside a National Park, the route does lie within two pieces of land designated **Areas of Outstanding Natural Beauty** (AONB) which are administered by the relevant local authorities. The western part of the path is in the 1730 sq km **North Wessex Downs AONB** that was created in 1972. It lies within the County Council boundaries of Wiltshire, Hampshire and Oxfordshire.

The eastern part of the trail is included in the 833 sq km **Chilterns AONB** that was created in 1965 and lies within the County Council boundaries of Bedfordshire, Buckinghamshire, Hertfordshire and Oxfordshire.

There are over 220 **NNR**s in England and the course of the Ridgeway includes the Fyfield Down NNR (see p92), just a couple of miles from the beginning of the route and the Aston Rowant NNR (see Map 35, p154) near Watlington. These two areas are also **SSSI**s along with over 4000 others in England. Other SSSIs along the Ridgeway include the White Horse Hill SSSI and the Chinnor Chalk Pit SSSI. **Special Areas of Conservation** (SACs) are designated by the European Union's Habitats Directive and provide an extra tier of protection to the areas that they cover. Along the Ridgeway the Aston Rowant NNR and SSSI is also a SAC along with the Chilterns beechwoods and Hackpen Hill (see p92). More information on NNRs, SSSIs and SACs can be found on 🖳 www.naturalengland.org.uk.

There is no doubt that these designations play a vital role in safeguarding the land they cover for future generations. However, the very fact that we rely on these labels for protecting limited areas begs the question: what are we doing to the vast majority of land that remains relatively unprotected? Surely we should be aiming to protect the natural environment outside protected areas just as much as within them.

Natural England oversees a Management Group that has administered both the Ridgeway and the Thames Path national trails since 1997. This Management Group includes a team of National Trails staff who are responsible for the day-to-day management and running of the Ridgeway. They employ wardens and conservation officers – many of them volunteers – to maintain the trail and they also organise guided events and publish information about the Ridgeway for the public. General maintenance of the trail includes such things as surface repairs, signpost and waymark installation and replacement, converting stiles to gates and installing water taps and troughs.

THE ENVIRONMENT & NATURE

They are also responsible for the protection of endemic species and habitats, as well as geological features, along the Ridgeway. If necessary this may involve access restrictions, especially for motorised vehicles. However, promoting public access and the appreciation of the Ridgeway's natural heritage is also of importance, as is educating locals and visitors about the significance of the environment.

CAMPAIGNING AND CONSERVATION ORGANISATIONS

As its name suggests, the **Friends of the Ridgeway** group focuses specifically on the trail and is particularly vocal on the subject of motorised vehicles using and damaging the tracks. They also have a volunteer scheme for people who wish to get actively involved in preserving the Ridgeway.

The **National Trust** is a charity with over three million members which aims to protect, through ownership, threatened coastline, countryside, historic houses, castles, gardens, and archaeological remains. The Trust manages land and sites along the Ridgeway including the sites in the Avebury area (see pp73-85), the Uffington White Horse area (p112) and the nearby Wayland's Smithy neolithic long barrow (p110). However, all these sites are actually owned by English Heritage (see p56).

The **Wildlife Trust** has several reserves near the Ridgeway including a 70-acre site on Chinnor Hill, just east of Chinnor. It's a mixture of open grassland and woodland comprising oak, ash and beech. Another reserve, Dancersend & Crong Meadow, is between Wendover and Hastoe. The trust undertakes projects to improve conditions for wildlife and promote public awareness; it also acquires land for nature reserves to protect particular species and habitats.

The **Woodland Trust** aims to conserve, restore and re-establish native woodlands throughout the UK: it cares for over a thousand woods around the UK. The Ridgeway passes through one of their woods, namely Tring Park (p173), towards the end of the trail.

❏ **Campaigning and conservation organisations**
● **Friends of the Ridgeway** (🖳 www.ridgewayfriends.org.uk)
● **The Wildlife Trusts** (☎ 01636 677711, 🖳 www.wildlifetrusts.org) is the umbrella organisation for the 47 wildlife trusts in the UK. Regional branches relevant to the Ridgeway are: **Wiltshire Wildlife Trust** (☎ 01380 725670, 🖳 www.wiltshirewildlife.org); **Berks, Bucks & Oxon Wildlife Trust** (☎ 01865 775476, 🖳 www.bbowt.org.uk); **Hertfordshire & Middlesex Wildlife Trust** (☎ 01727 858901, 🖳 www.wildlifetrust.org.uk/herts)
● **National Trust** (☎ 0844 800 1895, 🖳 www.nationaltrust.org.uk)
● **Royal Society for the Protection of Birds** (RSPB; 🖳 www.rspb.org.uk)
● **Woodland Trust** (general enquiries ☎ 01476 581111, specific enquiries ☎ 01476 581135, 🖳 www.woodland-trust.org.uk)
● **Butterfly Conservation** (☎ 01929 400209, 🖳 www.butterfly-conservation.org) Formed to help prevent the declining population of butterflies. The branches relevant to the Ridgeway are Wiltshire branch (🖳 www.wiltshire-butterflies.org.uk) and the Upper Thames (🖳 http://upperthames-butterflies.org.uk).

THE ENVIRONMENT & NATURE

Butterfly Conservation was formed in 1968 by some naturalists who were alarmed at the decline in the number of butterflies, and moths, and who now aim to reverse the situation. They now have 31 branches throughout the British Isles and operate 33 nature reserves and also sites where butterflies are likely to be found.

The **Royal Society for the Protection of Birds (RSPB)** is the largest voluntary conservation body in Europe focusing on providing a healthy environment for birds, with over 150 reserves in the UK.

Although the RSPB doesn't have any reserves directly on the course of the Ridgeway they are running projects on some areas of it. In particular they are involved in a scheme to encourage stone curlew to breed on the Oxfordshire and Berkshire Downs and Chilterns. In 2008 they recorded 103 breeding pairs and aim to have 300 by 2010.

BEYOND CONSERVATION

Pressures on the countryside grow year on year. Western society, whether directly or indirectly, makes constant demands for more oil, more roads, more houses and more cars. At the same time, awareness of environmental issues increases and also the knowledge that our unsustainable approach to life cannot continue. Some governments appear more willing to adopt sustainable ideals, others less so. Yet even the most environmentally friendly of governments are some way off perfect. It's all very well to classify parts of the countryside as National Parks and Areas of Outstanding Natural Beauty but it will be of little use if we continue to pollute the wider environment: the seas and skies. For a brighter future we all need to adopt that sustainable approach to life. It would not be difficult and the rewards would be great.

The individual can play his or her part. Walkers in particular appreciate the value of wild areas and should take this attitude back home with them. This is not just about recycling the odd green bottle or two and walking to the corner shop rather than driving, but about lobbying for more environmentally sensitive policies in local and national government.

The first step to a sustainable way of living is in appreciating and respecting this beautiful complex world we live in and realising that every one of us plays an important role within it. The natural world is not a separate entity. We are all part of it and should strive to safeguard it rather than work against it. So many of us live in a world that seems far removed from the real world, cocooned in centrally heated houses and upholstered cars. Rediscovering our place within the natural world is both uplifting on a personal level and it also positively affects our approach to life.

Walkers are in a great position to appreciate this, yet some people still find it difficult to shake off the chaos of modern life even when they are in the countryside. When you are out on the Ridgeway don't just look at the view. Slow down and use all your senses. Listen, smell and touch everything you see.

Flora and fauna

MAMMALS

You could walk the length of the Ridgeway and come to the conclusion that there isn't much wildlife on the route. Obviously walking in a group and making unnecessary noise will dramatically reduce your chances of seeing anything, but if you take some time to look carefully and become aware of your surroundings you are likely to see much more than just the back end of a rabbit diving into the undergrowth. You can be fairly certain that the wildlife you are looking for will have seen you well before you see it and will often be making its escape by the time you do. You'll have to be either very patient or very quick if you want to get photographs.

As a brief 'checklist', depending on the time of year, you can expect to see the following animals along the Ridgeway: deer, foxes, rabbits, hares, stoats, weasels, grey squirrels and perhaps even a badger.

The biggest wild animal you will see along the Ridgeway is the deer. There are two different species in this region: the **fallow deer** (*Dama dama*) and the **roe deer** (*Capreolus capreolus*). They have basically the same lifestyle, usually living in woodland but sometimes on open land with plenty of hedges and copses for cover. Both species are most likely to be seen in the early morning and early evening when they are feeding. The easiest way to tell them apart, if you are close enough, is their size. The adult roe deer grows to about 60cm high at the shoulder while the fallow deer can be up to 90cm at the shoulder. Male fallow deer have large, flat antlers unlike the roe deer whose antlers are spiky. The rutting season for fallow deer is July and August and this is when the males fight each other both for females and territory. You are most likely to see deer in the open during these months. At other times of year you might be able to spot one or two of them together against a hedge on the edge of a field or at the perimeter of a clearing in the woods.

The much maligned **fox** (*Vulpes vulpes*) inhabits woods and farmland. Despite relentless persecution it is a born survivor, even having adapted to life in cities where they are quite tolerant of human presence. They aren't exclusively nocturnal and in areas where they feel less threatened they are quite likely to be active during the day. Although they can be seen year-round, sightings of foxes are usually brief and at a distance, perhaps as one crosses a field.

Among other denizens of woods and farmland are a number of common but shy mammals. One of the most difficult to see is the **badger** (*Meles meles*), a sociable animal with a distinctive black-and-white-striped muzzle. Badgers live in family groups of around ten in large underground setts, coming out to root for worms on the pastureland after sunset, though they will eat practically anything. Some setts can be in use for well over a hundred years if left undisturbed by humans. They do sometimes emerge during daylight hours and the best time for spotting them is between May and September. Unfortunately the most common sight of badgers is as a bloody mess on the road; they are one of the most frequent animal road casualties.

The animal you are most likely to see on the Ridgeway is the **rabbit** (*Oryctolagus cuniculus*). In fact, at numerous places, especially on the trail near the aptly named Warren Farm just before Streatley, you'll find it hard to miss them. You can see them at all times of year when they come out during the day and at night to find food such as grass and farm crops. Despite the fact that they won't hang around after they have detected your presence, you can still get a good look at them.

Like rabbits, **hares** (*Lepus capensis*) also feed on grass and farm crops and although they live above ground and like open countryside they are far harder to spot. They generally keep well hidden during the day, except for the months of March and April when you might see them dashing around fields or getting involved in 'boxing matches' with other hares. This isn't, as you might presume, an exclusively male preserve as mixed boxing has also been witnessed. If you are hoping to get a photo of a hare be aware that they can run at speeds up to 40mph/65kph!

The carnivorous **stoat** (*Mustela erminea*) and its smaller cousin the **weasel** (*Mustela nivalis*) are common along the Ridgeway and can be seen year-round but just as with the hares you'll have to be quick if you want to see more than the tail-end of one. They can be difficult to tell apart, especially if you only get a glimpse, but the weasel is noticeably smaller than the stoat. Weasels eat mice, shrews and birds' eggs but owing to their size stoats can tackle larger prey such as adult rabbits and farm birds. This has led to their persecution by farmers who lose poultry to them. Weasels and stoats are by nature very inquisitive so just because they dart for cover as you approach doesn't mean they might not poke their head out for another look just after you have passed.

The **grey squirrel** (*Sciurus carolinensis*) was introduced to England from North America in the late 19th century and its outstanding success in colonising Britain is very much to the detriment of other native species including songbirds and, most famously, the red squirrel. Grey squirrels inhabit woodlands, parks and gardens and are a common sight from January to June during their breeding season. You might also see them during the autumn on the woodland floor, burying nuts to keep themselves supplied throughout the winter.

At dusk during the summer months **bats** can be seen hunting for moths and flying insects along hedgerows, over rivers and around street lamps. As the weather gets colder they will hibernate though can sometimes still be seen on warmer evenings. Bats have had a bad press thanks to Dracula and countless other horror stories but anyone who has seen one up close knows them to be harmless and delightful little creatures. As for their blood-sucking fame, the matchbox-sized species in Britain would not even be able to break your skin with their teeth let alone suck your blood. Their reputation is improving all the time thanks to the work of the many bat conservation groups around the coun-

THE ENVIRONMENT & NATURE

try and all fourteen species found in Britain are protected by law. The most common species is the **common pipistrelle bat** (*Pipistrellus pipistrellus*).

Some other small but fairly common species which can be found in the grassland and hedgerows on the Ridgeway include the **hedgehog** (*Erinaceus europaeus*) and a variety of **voles**, **mice** and **shrews**.

BIRDS

The two halves of the Ridgeway provide distinctly different environments for birds. The western half, up to Streatley, is, on the whole, exposed with few trees while the eastern half is mostly wooded. Both sections provide ample opportunity for bird spotting with the western section providing the most variety. Early mornings and early evenings are generally the best times for spotting birds.

SKYLARK
L: 185MM/7.25"

YELLOWHAMMER
L: 160MM/6.25"

LAPWING/PEEWIT
L: 320MM/12.5"

The western half
One of the most common birds on the open downs is the **skylark** (*Alauda arvensis*). Its dull brown plumage with a darker stripe doesn't make it the most distinctive of birds but when in flight you can recognise it by the white edges of the outer tail feathers. It nests on the ground in a hollow and makes little attempt to conceal its eggs.

You are also likely to see some **yellowhammers** (*Emberiza citrinella*) among the hedgerows and bushes along the path. Although the young birds only have a yellow head, as they grow older the entire body takes on a yellow base colour. Their song is a single repetitive note with a higher note to finish.

The **corn bunting** (*Emberiza calandra*) can often be heard singing its sharp jangly song along the path. It doesn't look dissimilar from the skylark though it has no white edging on its tail feathers and its beak is shorter and more rounded. Another common sight on this section is the **meadow pipit** (*Anthus pratensis*). Its light brown plumage, blending into buff on its underside, is marked with darker brown bars all over. You can often see it hopping quickly along the ground where it nests but it conceals its home well with thick brambles.

The **lapwing** (*Vanellus vanellus*) with its long legs, short bill and distinctive long headcrest feeds on arable farmland. Sadly, this attractive bird is declining in numbers. The name comes from its lilting flight, frequently changing direction with its large rounded wings. It's also identified by a white belly, black and white head, black throat patch and distinctive dark green wings.

There are also several larger birds that you might see on the Ridgeway. The **buzzard** (*Buteo buteo*) is the most common and can often be seen hovering in the sky, looking for prey such as mice, rabbits and snakes. It has a deep brown plumage with a rounded black and brown banded tail. The **kestrel** (*Falco tinnunculus*) can also be seen hovering above the ground, hunting for prey. Both the male and female are of a reddish brown colour, though the male has a blueish head. Their wings are broad and flat and widely spread when hovering.

BARN OWL
L: 340MM/13.5"

You might also be lucky enough to see an owl, even in the daytime. The **barn owl** (*Tyto alba*) is normally nocturnal, but when it has young, or if it is desperate for food, it will hunt during the day. The back of the owl is a sandy brown colour with grey spots while the front is white with brown spots. The white face is heart-shaped, set with deep, dark eyes. The legs are covered with dense, short white feathers. If you can see one of these birds perched where you can get a good look at it you really have been fortunate.

Pheasants (*Phasianus colchicus*) are common around hedgerows and bushes; they can often be spotted in open fields when feeding. The male can be seen strutting around, showing off his long brown and black striped tail and colourful neck and head. The females are buff and brown all over with a shorter tail than the males. You can usually get a good look at these birds as they aren't particularly shy which might go some way to explaining why they are also the most popular game bird in England.

Other game birds you may see in the fields along the western part of the Ridgeway include the partridge and the quail. The **partridge** (*Perdix perdix*) is often seen in pairs during the spring and summer. Although there are many colour variations in its plumage, it is often light grey with brown bars and the head is usually brown. This bird feeds mainly on insects and seeds. The **quail** (*Coturnix coturnix*) feeds on similar fare, though it is much smaller than the partridge, at half the size. It is only found in England during the late spring and summer and resembles a partridge but its colouring is reddish-tan with dashes of cream and black. It's not easily spotted as it often hides in grass when disturbed.

If you are very lucky, you might see a **stone curlew**, but realistically, the chances are very low. This long-legged summer visitor nests on the ground and its colouring of light brown with dark brown and cream streaks camouflages it well in such an environment. Their large yellow eyes are ideal for spotting any far-off danger from which they are more inclined to hide rather than take flight.

THE ENVIRONMENT & NATURE

The eastern half

Common birds seen in the woodlands of the eastern section of the Ridgeway include the **nuthatch** (*Sitta europaea*) which can often be seen clinging to tree trunks looking for insects. It's a distinctive small bird with a blue back, white throat and chestnut-coloured underside. The nuthatch nest will often be in a hole in a tree trunk. If the hole is too big, the nuthatch will partially block it with mud, thus making it quite easy to spot.

Various species of tit also live in the woodlands with the **great tit** (*Parus major*) being the largest and one of the most common. It has a black and white head, green back, blue and white wings and a yellow underside. Other tits seen in the woodlands include the **long-tailed tit** (*Aegithalos caudatus*) which is black and white with a long black tail with white edging and the **coal tit** (*Parus ater*), another black and white specimen found in more open areas of woodland.

The numbers of **red kites** in the Chilterns is increasing owing to reintroduction programmes run by English Nature (now Natural England) and the RSPB and there is a good chance that you will see one or more. Their large size – adults have a wingspan of around 1.8m – make them easy to spot and their long forked red tail makes them easy to identify. They have reddish brown bodies with darker wings which also have large patches of white, visible when they are in flight.

You should be able to see woodpeckers during your walk and will certainly hear them hammering away at tree trunks. The most common is the **great-spotted woodpecker** (*Dendrocopos major*) which has mainly black and white plumage enhanced by red patches on the back of its head and on its lower underside. Where the woods are on the edge of open country, you can find **green woodpeckers** (*Picus viridis*). The lifestyle of this bird is similar to that of the great-spotted woodpecker. Its striking green body, white underside and red head with black dashes make this a very attractive bird. The woodpecker bores into trees, not only to find insects and their larvae but also to hollow them out to make a nest. **Blackbirds** (*Turdus merula*) appear all along the Ridgeway and are unmistakable as the males are jet-black with orange beaks. The females are the same size but have brown bodies, graduating to black at the tail; they also have brown beaks.

If you, by chance, spot a **jay** (*Garrulus glandarius*) before it spots you and flies off, you are doing well. They are members of the crow family but are notoriously shy. Their plumage is a brownish-red overall with the top of the head white with black dashes. The tail is black with dark blue flashes.

BUTTERFLIES

The chalk downlands along the Ridgeway provide a habitat in which many species of butterfly can flourish. The most common species seen during the summer is the **meadow brown** (*Maniola jurtina*), overall a dusty brown colour, but with orange patches on its forewings, inside which are black eye-spots. This is one of the most common butterflies in Europe, as well as on the Ridgeway. Also likely to be flitting around at this time is the **small heath** (*Coenonympha*

Peacock
Inachis io

Small Tortoiseshell
Aglais urticae

Common Blue
Polyommatus icarus

Small Garden/Cabbage White
Pieris rapae

Chalkhill Blue
Lysandra coridon

Painted Lady
Cynthia cadui

Large
Garden/
Cabbage White
Pieris brassicae

Small
Copper
*Lycaena
phlaeas*

Small
Heath
*Coenonympha
pamphilus*

Red Admiral *Vanessa atalanta*

White Admiral
Limenitis camilla

Meadow
Brown
*Maniola
jurtina*

Gorse
Ulex europaeus

Common Ragwort
Senecio jacobaea

St John's Wort
Hypericum perforatum

Tormentil
Potentilla erecta

Birdsfoot-trefoil
Lotus corniculatus

Scarlet Pimpernel
Anagallis arvensis

Yarrow
Achillea millefolium

Hogweed
Heracleum sphondylium

Ramsons (Wild Garlic)
Allium ursinum

Common Vetch
Vicia sativa

Old Man's Beard
Clematis vitalba

Germander Speedwell
Veronica chamaedrys

Silverweed
Potentilla anserina

Self-heal
Prunella vulgaris

Violet
Viola riviniana

Meadow Buttercup
Ranunculis acris

Primrose
Primula vulgaris

Cowslip
Primula veris

Dog Rose
Rosa canina

Common Hawthorn
Crataegus monogyna

Ox-eye Daisy
Leucanthemum vulgare

Viper's Bugloss
Echium vulgare

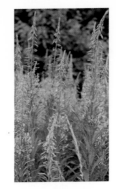

Rosebay Willowherb
Epilobium angustifolium

Foxglove
Digitalis purpurea

Bluebell
Endymion non-scriptus

Red Campion
Silene dioica

Herb-Robert
Geranium robertianum

Early Purple Orchid
Orchis mascula

Spotted Orchid
Dactylorhiza fuchsii

Pyramidal Orchid
Anacamptis pyramidalis

pamphilus), recognisable by its dull-orange wings edged with grey; it has black eye-spots on the underside of its forewings. You'll probably see some **large white** (*Pieris brassicae*) and **small white** (*Pieris rapae*) butterflies too. These are both essentially white with dark-grey wing tips. On the large white, both male and female have two black eye-spots on the underside of the forewings, but only the female has them on the upper side. On the small white, both sexes have two black eye-spots on the underside of their forewings, but on the upper-side, the female has two small spots and the male only a single spot.

There is a collection of blue butterflies that you could also see on the chalk-lands. The most likely is, unsurprisingly, the **common blue** (*Polyommatus icarus*). The male is violet-blue with a fine black edging to its wings; the female is actually brown though has a row of red spots along her wings which are edged with black. Less common is the **chalkhill blue** (*Lysandra coridon*); the male is altogether duller than the common blue but has more extensive black and white edging around the wings. The female is dark brown and has the same wing edging.

There are usually some **small copper** (*Lycaena phlaeas*) butterflies around that are distinctive despite their size. The forewings are bright orange with heavy black spots and black fringing whereas the hindwings are predominantly black with a thick band of bright orange edging at the bottom.

Two common day-flying moths are the **five-spot burnet** (*Zygaena trifolii*) and **six-spot burnet** (*Zygaena filipendulae*). Each has very dark wings, patterned with five or six orange/red spots.

FLOWERS

You'll be walking amongst many different species of wild flowers on the Ridgeway, though unless you keep an eye out it can be easy to miss some of them. Despite the trail being constantly exposed to wind and direct sunlight there will still be a wide selection of common flowers at any time between March and November though the biggest selection appears during the summer months. You'll also have the chance to see some of the more uncommon flowers native to chalk grassland. The best time for spotting these is during the summer months in the areas around Barbury Castle, Uffington Castle, the Pitstone Hills and Ivinghoe Beacon.

There will be plenty of **scentless mayweed** (*Tripleurospermum inodorum*), **common mouse-ear** (*Cerastium glomeratum*) and **common vetch** (*Vicia sativa*) at any time between April and November along most stretches of the Ridgeway. Another common flower is the **red campion** (*Silene dioica*), but this is found mainly in wooded areas and hedgerows. Despite its name, you'll recognise it by the profusion of shocking pink flowers it produces. A common flower with an even more misleading name is the **black medick** (*Medicago lupulina*) that grows mainly on grassland and has yellow flowers. **Herb robert** (*Geranium robertianum*) also flowers throughout the spring, summer and early autumn. It has attractive pink and white flowers and is found in shady, often rocky areas.

THE ENVIRONMENT & NATURE

In the spring, flowers such as **greater stitchwort** (*stellaria holostea*) and **dovesfoot cranesbill** (*Geranium molle*) are common in the hedgerows while the distinctive **cowslip** (*Primula veris*) with its clusters of yellow, funnel-shaped flowers is widespread in more open areas. The **common dog** and **heath dog violets** (*Viola riviniana, V. canina*) can be found in shady, open woodlands during the spring while another violet-coloured flower, the **common field speedwell** (*Veronica persica*), prefers cultivated land.

During the late spring and summer months, the variety of flowers along the Ridgeway is at its best. An aptly named example is the **traveller's joy** or **old man's beard** (*Clematis vitalba*) that climbs over hedgerows and trees and displays dense clumps of white, feathery flowers with a strong scent. Another climber you are likely to see is the large-leafed, white-flowered **white bryony** (*Bryonia dioica*). Summer is also when you can see the striking flowers of the **common mallow** (*Malva sylvestris*) that can grow to 150cm high. The yellow, star-shaped flowers of the medicinal **St John's wort** (*Hypericum perforatum*) can be spotted in wood-ed areas and is so named as it flowers around St John's Day, 24th June.

Upright hedge parsley (*Torilis japonica*) is common along the hedgerows and on the edges of woodland whereas the similar-looking **wild parsnip** (*Pastinaca sativa*) grows mainly on grassland. **Wild carrot** (*Daucus carota*) can sometimes be seen in open grassy areas, distinguished by its large dome-shaped clusters of white flowers. Large **oxeye daisies** (*Leucanthemum vulgare*) are difficult to miss and you should also be able to see **silverweed** (*Potentilla anserina*) along the trail in the summer showing grey/silver sharply toothed leaves and yellow flowers.

Flowers that grow only on chalk grassland areas of the Ridgeway include **devil's-bit scabious** (*Scabiosa pratensis*) that can flower as late as October. This type of chalky ground also plays host to various orchids (see photos opposite p65) including the **common spotted** (*Dactylorhiza fuchsii*) that has pale leaves spotted with crimson and the **fragrant** (*Gymnadenia conopsea*) and **pyramidal** (*Anacamptis pyramidalis*), both with reddish petals but with the pyramidal vari-ety being darker.

TREES

You'll see few trees along the western half of the Ridgeway. Most of the trees you do see have been planted by man over the centuries to serve a specific pur-pose, eg coppices, windbreaks and plantations. Though many of these are no longer maintained you can still see evidence of them if you look. The eastern half of the Ridgeway is often wooded, usually with beech.

Coppices are areas of woodland, usually oak, hazel or elm, managed by man through the periodic cutting of the trees right back to the ground; multiple fast-growing shoots then appear from the cut trees and are harvested.

Many coppices were fenced to keep animals out and often the fence sat on a raised earth ridge that you can still see around many disused coppiced areas. Coppices were an important supply of wood until the mid-1800s after which demand declined. However, most coppices were still maintained and today some are being fully used once more to supply wood for charcoal, greenwood furniture and craft items.

Windbreaks, such as hedges, serve multiple purposes. They give livestock a place to shelter from the wind and also provide shade. They also prevent soil erosion and provide a habitat for varied wildlife such as birds, insects, rabbits and pheasants. With the correct maintenance a hedge can last indefinitely and they are an extremely effective way of containing animals. Despite fences providing none of these benefits, they have often been a more popular choice with farmers who want to maximise their field size or change the layout of their fields. To a small extent, hedges are starting to make a comeback as their full benefits are realised and you'll see some recently planted hedges along parts of the Ridgeway.

Plantations were most common between 1600 and 1900. Popular species included oak, beech, elm and ash, and it was intended that when the trees were mature they would be used for ship-building, furniture-making and other tasks. Many plantations did provide wood for these purposes like the beech plantations on the eastern section of the Ridgeway, but others, especially the oak plantations, which took years to mature, were never used owing to the availability of cheap coal and imported timber being sourced from around the British Empire. These unused plantations form some of what we now consider traditional woodland.

❏ **Oak leaves showing galls**
Oak trees support more kinds of insects than any other tree in Britain and some affect the oak in unusual ways. The eggs of gall-flies cause growths known as galls on the leaves. Each of these contains a single insect. Other kinds of gall-flies lay eggs in stalks or flowers, leading to flower galls, growths the size of currants.

During the First World War there was a timber shortage that led to large conifer plantations being started. However, these weren't ready for cutting during the Second World War and this meant that large tracts of private woodland had to be felled. After the Second World War the increased need for food led to the felling of plantations and removal of hedges to increase the size of available farmland.

Today the creation of new plantations has virtually stopped. Many of the conifer plantations, started between the wars, have matured and been felled though there are still many which are managed for their timber. In a country where so many of the ancient forests have long since disappeared, plantations are now as near as some of us can get to the real thing.

PART 4: ROUTE GUIDE AND MAPS

Using this guide

This route guide has been divided according to logical start and stop points. However, these are not intended to be strict daily stages since people walk at different speeds and have different interests. The maps can be used to plan how far to walk each day. The route summaries below describe the trail between significant places and are written as if walking the path from west to east. To enable you to plan your own itinerary practical information is presented clearly on the trail maps. This includes walking times for both directions, all places to stay, camp and eat, as well as shops where you can buy supplies. Further service details are given in the text under the entry for each place.

For an overview of this information see Itineraries, p25-9.

TRAIL MAPS

Scale and walking times
The trail maps are to a scale of 1:20,000 (1cm = 200m; 3$\frac{1}{8}$ inches = one mile). Walking times are given along the side of each map and the arrow shows the direction to which the time refers. Black triangles indicate the points between which the times have been taken. **See note below on walking times**.

The time-bars are a tool and are not there to judge your walking ability. There are so many variables that affect walking speed, from the weather conditions to how many beers you drank the previous evening. After the first hour or two of walking you will be able to see how your speed relates to the timings on the maps.

Up or down?
Other than when on a track or bridleway the trail is shown as a dotted line. An arrow across the trail indicates the slope; two arrows show that it is steep. Note that the arrow points towards the higher part of the trail. If, for example, you are walking from A (at 80m) to B (at 200m) and the trail between the two is short and steep it would be shown thus: A— — — >> — — — B. Reversed arrow heads indicate downward gradient.

❏ **Important note – walking times**
Unless otherwise specified, **all times in this book refer only to the time spent walking**. You will need to add 20-30% to allow for rests, photography, checking the map, drinking water etc. When planning the day's hike count on 5-7 hours' actual walking.

Accommodation

Apart from in large towns where some selection of places has been necessary, almost everywhere to stay that is within easy reach of the trail is marked. Details of each place are given in the accompanying text. The number and type of rooms is given after each entry: S = single room, T = twin room, D = double room, F = family room sleeping at least three people.

Prices given are per room (usually for two people) and are summer high-season rates unless otherwise stated. See p14 for more details on prices.

Other features

Other features are marked on the map only when they are pertinent to navigation. To avoid clutter, not all features are marked all the time.

Marlborough

Marlborough is the nearest town to the start of the Ridgeway. It has all the shops and services you might need before setting off and boasts a large array of pubs, cafés and restaurants for you to enjoy. Convenient public transport links to the start of the Ridgeway, and its proximity to Avebury, also make this a useful place to base yourself before you start.

Although there is evidence of human activity in the area dating back to around 3700BC, the first mention of the town is in the Domesday Book of 1087. A royal charter was granted by King John in 1204 that allowed the town to hold markets on Wednesdays and Saturdays, a practice that remains to this day. In 1653 a devastating fire destroyed around 250 houses in Marlborough and it was decreed that from then on no house in the town could have a thatched roof. The long-term prosperity of the town was assured by its position on the old coach road between London and Bristol and the town still has an air of affluence, perhaps owing in part to the presence of the exclusive Marlborough College, founded in 1843.

SERVICES

The town's shops and services are concentrated along the High St and include a **post office** (Mon-Fri 9am-5.30pm, Sat 9am-12.30pm) in the **One Stop** convenience store (daily 6am-10pm) and various **banks**, all with **ATMs**. Inside the **library** (☎ 01672 512663; Mon 10am-8pm, Wed & Fri 9.30am-5pm, Thu 9.30am-8pm, Sat 9am-4pm, closed Tue and Sun), at the southern end of the High St, is the **Tourist Information Point**. It's really just several shelves of leaflets and brochures but if you have any questions the library staff should be able to help. There is also free **internet access** but it is limited to half an hour per session. At the other end of the High St **White Horse Bookshop** (☎ 01672 512071; Mon-Sat 9am-5.30pm) has a good selection of books about the local area. There is also a **chemist** (Boots, Mon-Sat 9am-5.30pm) and two **super-**

markets (Waitrose and M&S Simply Food) on the High St. If you're here on the second Saturday of the month visit the **farmers' market** (see box p15).

For outdoor supplies and equipment try **Activ8** (☎ 01672 513414, 🖳 shop @acceler8.biz; Mon-Sat 9am-5.30pm, Sun 10.30am-2.30pm) located in Hilliers Yard, off the High St. They have a good range of outdoor clothing and accessories in case you have forgotten something. Next door is **Ridgeway Cycle Hire** (same details as Activ8) where you can hire bikes for exploring the local area. If you need repairs to your own bike you can try here or possibly head to **Bertie Maffoon's Bicycle Co** (☎ 01672 519119; Mon 10am-5pm, 10am-6pm, Sat 9am-5pm) in Hughenden Yard.

Taxi firms include Arrow (☎ 01672 515567) and Marlborough Taxis (☎ 01672 512786) though the **bus** services are good so you shouldn't need them. There are regular services to: Avebury, Calne and Devizes (Connect2Wiltshire's Line 4 & TaxiBuzz, formerly Nos 43 & 44); some services are operated by Tourist Coaches and AD Rains; Swindon (Wilts & Dorset's Nos 95 & 96, Thamesdown's No 48 and Stagecoach's Nos 70 & 71); Ogbourne St George (Stagecoach's Nos 70 & 71) and one service a day to Calne (AD Rains No X76); see public transport map and table, pp42-5, for more details.

WHERE TO STAY

On the High St the rather grand-looking *Castle & Ball Hotel* (☎ 01672 515201, 🖳 www.castleandball.com; 25D/8T/1F) dates back to the 15th century and has a large range of rooms, all en suite, which start at £80/95 for single/double occupancy. Slightly cheaper, but just as atmospheric, is *Ivy House Hotel* (☎ 01672 515333, 🖳 www.ivyhousemarlborough.co.uk; 25D/5T/3F, all en suite). The rooms in this well-kept Georgian house start from £80-95 for single occupancy and £90-110 for a double, a family room costs £110-115. Just along from here is *The Merlin Hotel* (☎ 01672 512151; 3S/5D/1F). This hotel is in the large, cream-coloured Georgian building, and shares an entrance with the Pizza Express restaurant (see p73). En suite singles/doubles start from £55/70, the family room costs from £85; breakfast costs an extra £5 per person.

Several pubs in town also offer accommodation. *The Bear* (☎ 01672 512134; 6D) charges from £30 per person; two rooms are en suite, the others share a bathroom. Breakfast is not included but an evening meal is which makes this good value. Around the corner from The Bear is *The Lamb Inn* (☎ 01672 512668, 🖳 www.thelambinnmarlborough.com; 4D/1T/1F, all en suite) that has light, airy rooms for £70-80, or £50-55 single occupancy. The family room costs £80 for two, £99 for three and £116 for four sharing.

At the other end of the High St is *The Sun Inn* (☎ 01672 515011, 🖳 www .thesunmarlborough.co.uk; 4D, en suite) offering rather stylish accommodation for £70; £60 for single occupancy.

WHERE TO EAT AND DRINK

A good choice during the day is *Armadillo Café* (☎ 01672 516933; Mon-Fri 8am-4.30pm, Sat 9am-4.30pm) on the High St. They serve hot breakfast baguettes with a sausage (made from locally reared pigs) and bacon filling, sandwiches (fillings include free-range chicken and pesto, and oak-smoked salmon), salads, cakes, ice cream and good coffee.

On the other side of the High St is **Berits and Brown** (☎ 01672 511511, 🖳 www.beritsandbrown.com; Mon-Sat 9am-5.30pm, Sun 10am-4pm, Thu, Fri & Sat 6-10pm), a delicatessen and coffee shop serving rolls and sandwiches from £4.25, tapas from £5.95 and flaked salmon salad for £6.95. Just a couple of doors down is **The Food Gallery** (☎ 01672 514069, sandwich order line ☎ 0800 634 9200, 🖳 www.thefoodgallery.co.uk; Mon-Sat 8.45am-5pm), which takes great pride in the quality of its coffee and produces some excellent eat-in or takeaway sandwiches: goat's cheese and fig relish for £2.90, or crayfish tails and mayo for £3.30, for example.

Located down Hilliers Yard **Bytes Café** (☎ 01672 511377; Mon-Sat 9am-5pm, Sun 10am-4pm) serves toasted panini and homemade soup, amongst other items. There is also WiFi **internet access** here.

In Hughenden Yard you'll find **Azuza** (☎ 01672 513380, 🖳 www.azuza.co.uk; food Sun-Fri 9am-5pm, Sat 8.30am-5pm) which is a café/bar

ROUTE GUIDE AND MAPS

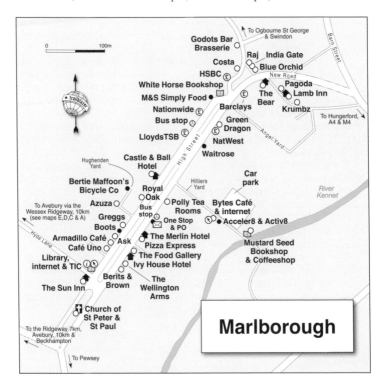

Marlborough

(licensed all day). After 5pm it changes to a Sports bar; the night club upstairs is open until 3am at weekends. Their Big Breakfast (£5.85) will certainly set you up for a full day of walking.

Also good for breakfast are the *Polly Tea Rooms* (☎ 01672 512146; Mon-Fri 8.30am-5pm, Sat 8am-5pm, Sun 9am-5pm) which have been here since 1932. Apart from cooked breakfasts (£4-7) they also have plenty of home-made lunches, such as quiche and salad (£7.45) and cream teas for £5.25.

Most of the pubs on the High St serve food both at lunchtime and in the evening and are open for drinks all day. You could head to *The Wellington Arms* (☎ 01672 512954; food Mon-Sat 11am-2.30pm & 6-9pm, Sun noon-2.30pm & 6-8.30pm) for a hearty three sausages and mash at £6.95, or the 15th-century *Sun Inn* (see p70; food Tue-Fri 12-3pm & 6-9pm, Sat 12-6pm, Sun 12-2.30pm) where steaks cost from £8.95 to £10.95.

The *Royal Oak* (☎ 01672 512064; food Mon-Thu 11am-8.30pm, Fri & Sat 11am-5pm, Sun noon-8.30pm) has Greene King ales to go with a wide selection of lunchtime baguettes and wraps, or in the evening a curry of the day for £6.95. They have a quiz on Tuesday evenings. The *Castle & Ball Hotel* (see p70; food Mon-Fri 7am-9.30pm, Sat & Sun 8am-9.30pm) serves breakfasts and pastries in the morning. From lunchtime onwards they have choices such as duck and plum sauce wrap (£4.75) or, in the evening, seafood, chicken and chorizo paella (£9.95).

Continuing on the pub crawl you might like to visit *The Bear* (see p70, food daily noon-3pm, Mon-Sat 6-9pm) for Arkell's beers and pub grub such as ham, egg and chips (£5.95) or the *Green Dragon* (☎ 01672 512366; food Mon-Fri 9am-2pm & 6-9pm, Sat 10am-2pm & 6-9pm, Sun noon-3pm) for breakfast and, later on, to try some locally brewed 6X from the Wadworth brewery. Not to be left out, the *Lamb Inn* (see p70; food Mon-Thu noon-2.30pm & 6.30-9pm, Fri, Sat & Sun noon-2.30pm) also serves food. A rather tasty salt pork with lentils will set you back £9.

For a non-alcoholic lunch you could head to the compact *Mustard Seed Bookshop and Coffeeshop* (☎ 01672 511611, 🖥 www.mustardseedbooks.com; Mon-Sat 9am-5pm) overlooking the river where sandwiches are £3.20-5.95 and home-made soup with a roll is £3.95. For a quick takeaway lunch try *Krumbz* (☎ 01672 516333; Mon-Sat 7.30am-3pm) which charges £2.30-3.10 for its sandwiches: they have a good range of vegetarian fillings. On the High St, *Greggs* (☎ 01672 516681; Mon-Sat 8am-5.30pm) also serves sandwiches.

There is a *coffee shop* in the redundant church of St Peter and St Paul at the end of the High St. It shares the ex-church with a craft shop and art exhibition and is open Mon-Sat 10am-5pm and 11am-4pm on Sundays during the summer. It's well worth a visit to sample a generous wedge of homemade cake with a nice cup of tea. They also serve simple but tasty lunches costing from £3 to £6.25.

Costa (☎ 01672 516302; Mon-Sat 7am-7pm, Sun 9am-5pm) serves up pretty much exactly the coffees, teas and light lunches you would expect from a coffeeshop chain.

Of course, there is an Indian restaurant here, too: it's called *Raj* (☎ 01672 515661; daily noon-2pm, Sun-Thu 5.30-11.30pm, Fri & Sat 5.30pm-midnight) and is always busy. On the extensive menu is a good *shorisha sylheti* (hot mustard sauce with herbs and chicken) for £7.50. If you just want a takeaway you should head down the steps next to Raj for the *India Gate* (☎ 01672 514044; daily 5.30-11.30pm, closed on Tuesday). Just next door is the *Blue Orchid* (☎ 01672 513353, 🖳 www.blueorchidthai.co.uk; Mon-Sat noon-2pm & 5.30-11pm) serving Thai food. They have an extensive menu and serve a delicious *goong pad khing pak* (tiger prawns fried with ginger and vegetables) for £10.50 (£8.50 for takeaway).

A minute or so away is the *Pagoda Peking Restaurant* (☎ 01672 512886; Mon-Sat 6-11pm) that also does takeaways. This is a pretty standard Chinese restaurant with a lengthy menu and reasonable prices: £5.30 for *kung po* chilli chicken. They close for the first two weeks of November.

There is also a scattering of eateries serving Italian food. They are all chain restaurants and are on the High St. *Pizza Express* (☎ 01672 519229; Sun-Thu noon-10pm, Fri noon-10.30pm, Sat noon-11pm), at The Merlin Hotel (see p70), has a sunny courtyard and the usual selection of pizza and pasta.

Café Uno (☎ 01672 511181; Mon-Sat 9am-9pm, Sun 10am-9pm), near the library, is located in one of the oldest buildings in town. There are plenty of pasta dishes (£7.95-8.95) to choose from. Perhaps the best Italian in town is *Ask* (☎ 01672 515797; daily noon-11pm) only a few doors away from Café Uno. It's always busy and has an easy-going atmosphere. Pizzas go for £5.95-8.65 and pasta dishes are £6.45-8.95. They are also open for coffee and pastries from 10am.

For something a little more stylish there is *Godots Bar Brasserie* (☎ 01672 514776, 🖳 www.godotsrestaurant.co.uk; Tue-Sat noon-2.30pm & 7-10pm, last orders 9pm), a short walk from the High St. Reservations are necessary. Expect to pay £12-16 for a main course such as crayfish risotto with dill.

Avebury and around

AVEBURY
[See map p75]

This small village, spread around one of the most important Neolithic sites (see box pp76-7) in Europe, attracts thousands of tourists every year, but for all that, it's still essentially a quiet and unassuming place. Most tourists are here for just a couple of hours on a whistle-stop coach tour and those day trippers who arrive by car are usually gone by mid-afternoon, too. It's remarkable how you can walk just a few minutes away from the throngs of visitors around the stone circle and be on your own in the countryside. Another remarkable thing about this place, that's impossible to miss, is how the busy A4361 road from Beckhampton to Swindon zig-zags straight through the stone circle itself. It really couldn't be any less subtle.

It is well-worth spending as much time as you can in and around Avebury. There is so much to see and the walking is easy – an ideal warm-up for the Ridgeway proper. Not only is there the stone circle, but the Great Barn and museums, West Kennet Avenue, Silbury Hill, West Kennet Long Barrow, the Sanctuary and Windmill Hill. And if you're really lucky you might even see a crop circle (see box p80)! A useful website for information about all these is 🖳 www.avebury-web.co.uk.

The **Alexander Keiller Museum** (☎ 01672 539250, 🖳 www.nationaltrust .org.uk; daily Easter-Oct 10am-6pm, Nov-Easter 10am-4pm) is spread over two locations: the **Barn Gallery**, in the magnificent late 17th-century **Great Barn** and the **Stables Gallery**, a few minutes' walk away. This museum was started in 1935 to gather together archaeological finds from Avebury and the surrounding area dating back 6000 years. A visit is recommended as it really helps to put the surviving monuments in and around the village in context. Entry is £4.70/2.35 for adults/children, £3.70/1.85 for cyclists or people arriving by public transport (on production of a bus ticket). Walkers can also take advantage of the reduced rate, but this is discretionary owing to the difficulty of proving they are genuine walkers.

Close to the Stables Gallery is **Avebury Manor and Gardens** (☎ 01672 539250, 🖳 www.nationaltrust.org.uk). There was originally a Benedictine Priory on this site dating back to the 13th century, but the current buildings date from the 16th century with renovations made by a Colonel Jenner in the early 20th century. The immaculate gardens, with their box hedges and medieval walls, are open to the public (Easter-Oct, Fri-Tue 11am-5pm; £3/1.50 adults/children. The manor house itself is still lived in and only part of it is open to the public (Easter-Oct, Sun-Tue 2-4.40pm; £4/2 adults/children including entry to the garden). Guided tours are compulsory and leave every 40 minutes; numbers are limited so it's worth getting there early.

Entry is free for National Trust and English Heritage members as well as for holders of the Great British Heritage pass. One ticket admits you to both galleries.

Services

The **post office** closed in 2008 though a limited service is still provided (Mon 9am-noon, Wed-Fri 2-5pm) on the High St; the village shop has now closed completely. The **tourist information centre** (TIC; ☎ 01380 734669 or ☎ 01672 539179, 🖳 www.kennet.gov.uk/tourism) is in the 17th-century chapel at the beginning of Green St. This place has a very good selection of leaflets, books and maps and the staff are always helpful. At the time of writing the centre was open Tue-Sun 9.30am-5pm and Wed-Sun from the end of October to the end of March; however, this may change so contact them to check.

There's also an information centre close to the Great Barn in the **National Trust Shop** (NT; ☎ 01672 539384; daily Easter-Sep 10am-6pm, Mar & Oct 10am-5pm, Nov-Feb 11am-4pm). They have plenty of postcards and souvenirs. If you need cash you should head to the Red Lion pub where there is an **ATM**. There is a large souvenir shop, **The Henge Shop** (daily 9am-5.30pm) that sells some interesting Avebury paraphernalia and shelf upon shelf of generic tourist tat.

There are frequent **bus** services to Marlborough (Connect2Wiltshire's Line 4 & TaxiBuzz, formerly Nos 43 & 44, and Wilts & Dorset's No 96) and to Swindon (Stagecoach's No 49 and Wilts & Dorset's No 96); see pp42-5 for further details. For a **taxi**, call one of the firms in Marlborough, see p70.

Where to stay

The cheapest accommodation in the area is ***Clyffe Pypard*** (☎ 01793 731386, 🖳 clyffepypard@yha.org.uk; 14 beds), a YHA bunkhouse: it is five miles from Avebury and 7¹/₂ miles from the start of the Ridgeway so is not really ideal for Ridgeway walkers. However, it charges £12, is part of a pub, *The Goddard Arms*, and has the usual YHA facilities so keen hostellers may want to consider it.

B&B options in Avebury village are expensive and even if you can afford to stay here you should book well ahead to secure a room.

There is, however, one slightly cheaper option just outside the village at *No 6 Beckhampton Road* (☎ 01672 539588; 1D/1T, shared bathroom). It's run by the friendly Mrs Dixon who has rooms for £60, or £40 if you are on your own. A packed lunch is available for £3 if requested in advance. You could walk here from the village as it's only about half a mile (1km) along the A4361 towards Beckhampton though there isn't a pavement all the way. The B&B is in the line of cottages on the main road at the top of the hill. A quieter and safer but less straightforward route would be to follow the High St to its western end then take the series of paths to Trusloe village and cut through to the B&B. Alternatively, you could get a bus here: the first bus stop out of Avebury village is more or less opposite the B&B.

Manor Farm (☎/🖳 01672 539294; 1D/1T) is a large red-brick farmhouse offering B&B for two sharing from £80, or £65 if you are on your own. The two rooms share a bathroom but only one room is let out at a time, unless a group of four book, so effectively the bathroom is private. Note: this is a different Manor Farm from the one on Green St (see map p79).   *(cont'd on p78)*

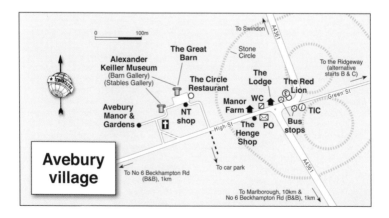

Avebury village

❑ Avebury Stone Circle

A visit to the Neolithic stone circle complex at Avebury is undoubtedly one of the highlights of the Ridgeway. This is one of the largest stone circles in the world though

it's often overshadowed by the more famous Stonehenge, about 24 miles away. Although most tourists are here for just a couple of hours, it would be easy to spend a day or two investigating Avebury and the surrounding monuments.

The immense task of constructing this site spanned about 500 years, starting around 2500BC. The irregular-ly shaped stones come from the Marlborough Downs, a few miles from where they were set up in the henge, and were transported here with great effort though it's still unclear why. There are several clear solar alignments within the formation but an overall theory about the purpose and usage of the stone circle remains elusive. If you are in need of an answer, you'll find plenty of ideas out there, with many entering the realms of fantasy, but none of which can comprehensively explain this huge site.

Starting from the outside and working in there is a roughly circular earth bank about 400 metres in diameter immediately dropping down into a deep ditch. Lining the other side of this ditch is the main stone circle. It is highly significant that the earth bank is on the outside of the ditch as this means that the site cannot have been defensive in nature, unlike all the later hill forts which have the ditch outside the bank and are defensive. The alignment of outer bank and inner ditch is what defines a 'henge', though there is one exception to this of course – Stonehenge itself!

The main stone circle once consisted of nearly 100 stones, but today just 30 are standing. There are two main reasons for the disappearance of the stones: some were pulled over and buried in pits during the 14th century and others were broken up and used as building materials for houses in the village in the late 17th and 18th centuries. Most of the stones you see standing today were unearthed during excavations and re-erected. Within the outer circle are two smaller circles, both about 100 metres in diameter. Like the outer circle, many of the stones that once formed these circles are now missing and have been replaced by concrete markers.

Two of the most famous stones in the outer circle are the 'Swindon Stone' and the 'Barber Surgeon Stone'. The **'Swindon Stone'**, roughly square in shape, is one of the largest and marks the northern entrance to the circle. It weighs in at an estimated 60 tonnes and is one of the only stones never to have fallen. The **'Barber Surgeon Stone'**, towards the south of the outer circle, is so named because a skeleton was found under it during excavations in the 1930s. The story goes that, during the 14th century when many of the stones were pulled over and buried one unfortunate man happened to be in the wrong place and was squashed. When Alexander Keiller excavated this stone the man's skeleton was found underneath it, along with a pouch containing scissors and some coins. Research indicated this unfortunate individual was probably an itinerant craftsman who performed many roles including that of a barber and a surgeon.

What you can see today is the result of immense excavation work and restoration projects, mainly led by Alexander Keiller during the 1920s and 1930s; up till then, the site had suffered centuries of deliberate damage and neglect. *(cont'd opposite)*

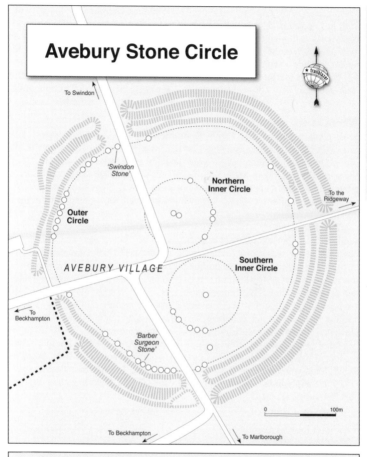

Avebury Stone Circle

To Swindon

'Swindon Stone'

Northern Inner Circle

To the Ridgeway

Outer Circle

AVEBURY VILLAGE

Southern Inner Circle

To Beckhampton

'Barber Surgeon Stone'

0   100m

To Beckhampton

To Marlborough

(cont'd from p76) Keiller relied heavily on the previous work of two antiquarians, John Aubrey and William Stukeley, to interpret the remains of the stone circle. Aubrey was the first person to study Avebury in detail and record what he found. His main findings were written up in 1690 and proved an invaluable resource for William Stukeley who in the 18th century drew maps of the entire complex of stones and also wrote extensively about his findings. As the period following Aubrey's and Stukeley's work was one of the most destructive in Avebury's history, had it not been for their surviving records much of Keiller's work, and indeed even modern archaeology in the Avebury area, would have proved an impossible task.

There is no entrance fee to the circle, mainly because it would be impractical to enforce such a scheme; hence it is open for visitors all day, every day.

(cont'd from p75) **The Lodge** (☎ 01672 539023, 🖥 www.aveburylodge.co.uk;
2D), just up the High St, charges from £150 to £225 per room (single occupancy £90-120), though they sometimes have special offers. One room has an en
suite shower and the other has a private bathroom. The food is vegetarian and,
where possible, organic.

Next door to The Lodge, and the best-known building in the village, is *The
Red Lion* (see below). However, at the time of writing they were not offering B&B
because the rooms were due to be refurbished; contact them for further details.

Where to eat and drink

Most people head to **The Circle Restaurant** (☎ 01672 539514; open daily
Easter-Oct 10am-5.30pm, Nov-Jan 11am-3.30pm, Feb & Mar 10am-5pm, lunch
served noon-2pm) which is in a great location next to the Great Barn. They
serve vegetarian, vegan and gluten-free food. Home-made soup and bread is
around £3.95 and a cheese ploughman's about £6.95. They also serve various
cakes, tea and coffee; if you want something stronger, you could try one of their
organic beers, ciders or wines.

The Red Lion (☎ 01672 539266, 🖥 www.redlion-avebury.com); food in
summer Sun-Thu noon-8pm, Fri & Sat noon-9pm, in winter Tue-Thu noon-
6pm, Fri & Sat noon-8pm) is right in the centre of the stone circle and is also
the only pub in the village. The building dates back to the early 17th century but
it was only in the early 18th that it became a pub. Since then the original building has been enlarged. Naturally, the place has its own ghost – a murdered lady
– who might or might not put in an appearance depending on how long you've
spent at the bar. The pub is always busy with passing trade and is open all day.
However, lunchtimes can be crowded with long waiting times for food. There
is a large restaurant area at the back of the pub serving a wide variety of dishes: lunches such as ham, egg and chips or a ploughman's cost from £6.45 to
£8.95. Main courses in the evening include seafood, chorizo and chicken paella (£9.95) and gammon steak, chips and peas (£7.95). Note that the pub's car
park is pay and display (!).

❑ **West Kennet Avenue**   **[see map opposite]**
West Kennet Avenue dates from about 2400BC and runs south from the henge at
Avebury to The Sanctuary, a distance of about one and a half miles (2.5km). The course
of the avenue was originally marked by two parallel rows of around one hundred
sarsen stones, though today only the first 750 metres of the avenue is lined with them.

These stones were excavated and re-erected by Maud Cunnington in 1912 and
by Alexander Keiller in the 1930s. As with the henge at Avebury, concrete markers
replace stones that have disappeared or been destroyed. Despite various sources of
evidence – the 18th-century records of William Stukeley and excavations in both the
20th century and in 2002 – the exact course of the avenue is still a subject of debate.

There is a second avenue of stones at Avebury, leading away from the henge to the
west. This was first noticed by William Stukeley in the 18th century, but no longer shows
above ground and was only rediscovered following excavations in 1999. It is called the
Beckhampton Avenue because it heads out towards the long stones at Beckhampton.

WEST OVERTON   [see map below]

This village is about one mile/1.6km from the start of the Ridgeway. On the A4 at the main turning for the village is the ***Bell Inn*** (☎ 01672 861663; food daily noon-8.30pm), which is open all day and is a laidback and friendly place serving Greene King and Wadworth beers. They also produce substantial meals including sirloin steaks, gammon steaks and a variety of fish dishes for £7-14. There are usually a couple of vegetarian choices but the focus here is on meat.

Buses (Connect2Wiltshire's Line 4 & TaxiBuzz) stop here en route between Calne/Devizes, Avebury and Marlborough; see pp42-5 for further details.

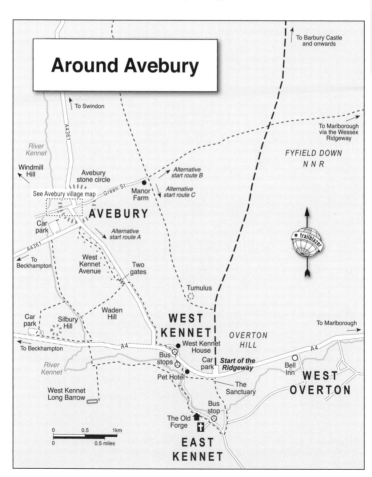

WEST KENNET & EAST KENNET [see map p79]

The hamlet of **West Kennet** consists of a pet hotel and a small number of houses spread out along the main A4 road. Apart from the bus stops, there is nothing of practical use to the traveller. **East Kennet**, a very picturesque village, provides the closest accommodation to the Ridgeway, though very little else.

The Old Forge (☎ 01672 861686; 1T/2D/1F, 🖳 www.theoldforge-avebury.co.uk) does B&B: and one double and the twin room have an en suite shower and the other double has a private bathroom. They charge £60-65 (£55 for single occupancy) and the en suite family room with two double beds costs £70 (for two) and £100 (for four). This place is often busy so book as far in advance as possible. For food *The Bell Inn* (see p79) at West Overton is about ten minutes' walk down the road.

From East Kennet the start of the path is only about half a mile/750m away. Should you need a shop, it's a straightforward half-hour stroll along West Kennet Avenue to Avebury.

❏ **Crop circles**

If you are in the Wiltshire area, particularly around Avebury, during the summer months you have a good chance of seeing a crop circle. It's usually free to go into the field to have a look inside the formation but as you'll be just one of many doing this they get damaged very quickly. It's not often easy to get good photographs of crop circles because although they are generally on hillsides, the gradient isn't steep enough to present a clear view of the pattern.

However, nearly every formation that appears in Wiltshire will have an aerial photograph taken of it and these are easily found on the internet. Websites such as 🖳 www.cropcircleconnector.com often have photos of crop circles within a day of them first being reported.

The appearance of crop circles in Wiltshire certainly dates back as far as the early 1980s and some farmers say they noticed them earlier than that. In the 1990s, when the more elaborate designs started to appear, the media became interested. However, within a few years much of the media interest faded, though the circles continue to appear, getting more elaborate every year. In 2008 there were 77 reported crop circles in the UK.

Theories abound as to how the circles are created. There is no doubt that some are man-made and people have comprehensively demonstrated how to make complex designs in just a few hours. But that still leaves some designs which appear simply too intricate to be created in a few hours in the middle of the night. You can take your pick of the theories out there, some more 'out there' than others. Are they created by a 'plasma vortex', UFOs, the presence of ley lines, or something completely different that no one has even thought of yet?

If it all gets a bit confusing, you might like to unwind with a pint of Crop Circle, a beer produced by the Hop Back Brewery (see pp16-17) in Downton, near Salisbury, and available in some local pubs.

(Opposite) Top: Constructed between 2500BC and 2000BC, Avebury Stone Circle (see pp76-7) originally consisted of 100 massive stones; only 30 remain in place today. **Bottom**: Crop circles near Overton Hill.

Buses (Connect2Wiltshire's Line 4 & TaxiBuzz, formerly Nos 43 & 44) go along the A4 to/from Calne and Devizes to Marlborough stopping both here and at West Kennet. However, if you want to board the bus at East Kennet, you must phone in advance. The Wilts & Dorset No 96 from Marlborough to Swindon and AD Rains's X76 from Calne to Marlborough stop only at West Kennet; see pp42-5 for further details.

A WALK AROUND AVEBURY [See Map A p82; Map B p83]

If you have some spare time before starting the Ridgeway, you might like to take a few walks in the area around Avebury. Detailed below is a walk designed to take in the main attractions outside the village. As this walk is circular and starts from the centre of Avebury, you can walk it in either direction. It will take between 2½ and 4 hours. The general theme of this walk is Avebury–West Kennet Avenue–Silbury Hill–West Kennet Long Barrow–East Kennet village–The Sanctuary–Ridgeway–Green St–Avebury. It's about 6 miles/10km and the walking is generally easy going with just a couple of mildly tiring uphill stints.

Starting from **The Red Lion** follow the main road south through the stone circle then enter the field and follow **West Kennet Avenue** (see box p78). When you reach the gates at the end of the field follow the fence line up **Waden Hill** from the top of which you get very good views of Silbury Hill. At the bottom of the hill you should turn right and follow the stream to the junction where you need to take the left turn and go over the bridge – straight ahead leads back to Avebury, if you are already tired. After turning left you will skirt around **Silbury Hill** (see box p84), eventually arriving at a car park. Here you can get a closer view of the Hill from a special viewing area. You are not allowed to walk any nearer than this though the road does in fact pass much closer.

From the car park, follow the busy and fast A4 road towards and then past Silbury Hill. You must then look for a turning on the other side of the road which leads up to **West Kennet Long Barrow** (see box below). *(cont'd on p84)*

❏ **West Kennet Long Barrow**
Even if you don't plan to do the whole walk described here you should make the effort to walk up to West Kennet Long Barrow, located on a ridge about a mile from Silbury Hill. At 100 metres long it's one of the largest Neolithic burial mounds in the country and dates back to 3600BC, nearly a thousand years before Wayland's Smithy (see box p110). It's thought that this long barrow was used for around a thousand years before it was filled in with earth and sealed with the huge sarsen stones that currently stand across the entrance. During several excavations, the last in 1955-6, the remains of 45 people of all ages were discovered in the various chambers.

The main advantage that this site has over Wayland's Smithy is that you can actually enter this long barrow and walk into all five of the burial chambers, but don't expect the underground passage to take you along the entire length of the long barrow – it only extends about ten metres into the mound. There is no entrance fee for the long barrow and it is open all the time. Take a torch though.

(Opposite) West Kennet Long Barrow.

ROUTE GUIDE AND MAPS

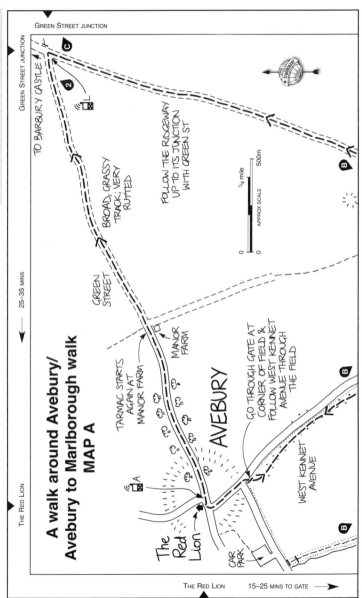

A walk around Avebury/
Avebury to Marlborough walk
MAP A

GREEN STREET JUNCTION

GREEN STREET JUNCTION

TO BARBURY CASTLE

BROAD, GRASSY TRACK; VERY RUTTED

FOLLOW THE RIDGEWAY UP TO ITS JUNCTION WITH GREEN ST

¼ mile

500m

APPROX SCALE

GREEN STREET

TARMAC STARTS AGAIN AT MANOR FARM

MANOR FARM

AVEBURY

GO THROUGH GATE AT CORNER OF FIELD & FOLLOW WEST KENNET AVENUE THROUGH THE FIELD

WEST KENNET AVENUE

The Red Lion

CAR PARK

The Red Lion

25–35 MINS

THE RED LION   15–25 MINS TO GATE ⟶

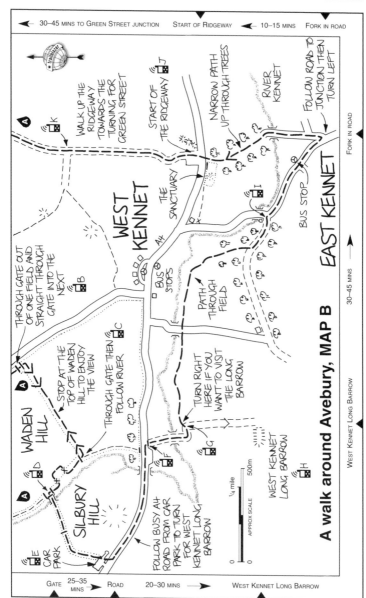

← 30–45 MINS TO GREEN STREET JUNCTION   START OF RIDGEWAY   ← 10–15 MINS   FORK IN ROAD

A walk around Avebury, MAP B

WEST KENNET   WALK UP THE RIDGEWAY TOWARDS THE TURNING FOR GREEN STREET

START OF THE RIDGEWAY

NARROW PATH UP THROUGH TREES

RIVER KENNET

FOLLOW ROAD TO JUNCTION THEN TURN LEFT

THE SANCTUARY

A4

EAST KENNET

BUS STOP

THROUGH GATE OUT OF ONE FIELD AND STRAIGHT THROUGH GATE INTO THE NEXT

BUS STOPS

PATH THROUGH FIELD

STOP AT THE TOP OF WADEN HILL TO ENJOY THE VIEW

THROUGH GATE THEN FOLLOW RIVER

TURN RIGHT HERE IF YOU WANT TO VISIT THE LONG BARROW

WADEN HILL

SILBURY HILL

CAR PARK

FOLLOW BUSY A4 ROAD FROM CAR PARK TO TURN FOR WEST KENNET LONG BARROW

WEST KENNET LONG BARROW

¼ mile   500m   APPROX SCALE

FORK IN ROAD   30–45 MINS   WEST KENNET LONG BARROW

GATE 25–35 MINS ROAD 20–30 MINS WEST KENNET LONG BARROW

(cont'd from p81) The climb up is a bit tiring, but will get you in good shape for the Ridgeway.

After visiting the Long Barrow and admiring the views, you should retrace your steps to the path junction where you need to take a right turn, heading for **East Kennet** village. This is an idyllic place. Take a few minutes to look at the church and wander past the attractive village houses before you get to the fork in the road. At this point you should follow the other lane, almost doubling back on yourself. This lane turns into a path and you cross the River Kennet once more, heading up to **The Sanctuary** (see box opposite) by the side of the A4.

When you feel you have soaked up the atmosphere of this place you should cross the road to the official start of the Ridgeway and make your way up the

---

❏ **Silbury Hill**

Despite the enormity of this hill it's often neglected in favour of the stone circle up the road. But do make the effort to come here as it's only at this closer proximity that you can start to understand the almost super-human effort that must have been required to build this structure.

The history of the hill dates back to around 2600BC when construction started. The first phase created a stepped structure. The steps were then filled in with chalk and after that earth was shaped over the steps to create a smooth face. You can still see one of these steps near the top of the hill but it's only clear when viewed from the eastern side. The top of the mound was left flat, but not level, and is 39m high and 30m wide. The base is perfectly round with a diameter of 167m. Just to really impress you, the hill contains around a quarter of a million cubic metres of chalk.

Why was it built? No one really knows, but there have been some earnest efforts to find out. The first of these was in 1776 when a shaft was dug from the summit down to the base. Nothing was found apart from construction materials. In 1849 another approach was tried, this time digging a tunnel from the base to the centre. Again, nothing was found. Yet another investigation took place in the late 1960s but the new tunnel into the base, again, revealed no evidence to point to Silbury Hill's raison d'être.

The hill was previously open to the public but slippages of the top soil were detected and any more human trampling would have only accelerated this deterioration. In 2000 a large hole also opened up on the summit, owing to a collapse of the shaft dug in 1776. It was infilled with polystyrene blocks and then covered with chalk. Investigations by English Heritage around the base of Silbury Hill in 2007 discovered evidence of a Roman settlement and later in the same year a major task was undertaken to stabilise the hill. Tunnels which had previously been dug into the hillside were filled with hundreds of tonnes of chalk to prevent any more collapses. As this work was sealing up the tunnels for good, English Heritage also took the opportunity to undertake one final archaeological survey in a bid to finally understand why the hill was built. Although they ultimately didn't come any closer to finding an answer to the question, the stabilisation work on the hill was carried out successfully.

Naturally, various theories regarding Silbury Hill's purpose have been developed to fill the vacuum, among them that it was a solar observatory or was symbolic of a Mother Goddess, but none really explains why such a gargantuan effort was made to build something so seemingly purposeless.

❑ **The Sanctuary**
Opposite the official start of the Ridgeway is The Sanctuary. It's not one of the more
memorable relics in the Avebury area but is worth a visit nonetheless. The site consists of various concentric circles marked out with small concrete posts in the ground.
  This was the site of a circular wooden building, possibly a temple, dating back
as far as 2500BC. The smaller circle marks out the boundary of the original building
while the larger ones suggest that the structure was considerably and repeatedly
expanded over the course of the next thousand years. Eventually, the wooden buildings were replaced by two stone circles, noted by John Aubrey in 1648, and these
were connected to Avebury by a stone avenue (West Kennet Avenue), parts of which
you can still follow. The views from here over to Silbury Hill and West Kennet Long
Barrow are particularly good.

hill to the junction with **Green St**. Turn left onto this track and follow it down
to the Red Lion at Avebury. It's a handy place to finish for obvious reasons.

AVEBURY TO MARLBOROUGH WALK
[See Map A p82, Map C p86, Map D p87, Map E p88]

If you're spending time around the beginning of the Ridgeway, the chances are
you'll need to get from Avebury to Marlborough, or vice versa, at some point.
You could always take one of the regular buses but walking the route is far more
interesting.

  The route in fact follows the course of the Wessex Ridgeway (see pp184-5)
and is an easy 6 miles/10km across the Marlborough Downs with the only mildly strenuous section being at the Avebury end of the route. Although most of this
route is very exposed to the elements, the conditions underfoot are generally
excellent, consisting mainly of hard gravel tracks. From the Red Lion at Avebury
to Marlborough High St it'll take between 2 and 2³/₄ hours in either direction.

  From the Red Lion leave the village via **Green St**. The road soon fades into
a track that broadens into a series of roughly parallel deep ruts as it climbs up
to meet the Ridgeway. At this junction you walk straight across the Ridgeway
and through the gate into **Fyfield Down NNR** (Map C). To most people it's just
another attractive area for a stroll, but for geologists it's one of the most important sites in Britain. The sides and bottom of the valley in the reserve are littered
with sarsen stones – the very same type of stones that were used to build
Avebury and many of the more recent buildings in the vicinity. Some of these
sarsens are also home to rare mosses and lichens. There is something of a fan-
tasy-world feel to this place, as if you might pass by a wandering hobbit or see
an elf resting on a sarsen.

  You'll pass an underground **reservoir** to the left of the path which looks
rather anomalous in this landscape and as the well-made gravel track meanders
along with various paths and other tracks joining it, you'll notice plenty of evidence of the racehorse business (see box p96). Gallops parallel the track for
long stretches and if you're lucky you could see some thoroughbreds being

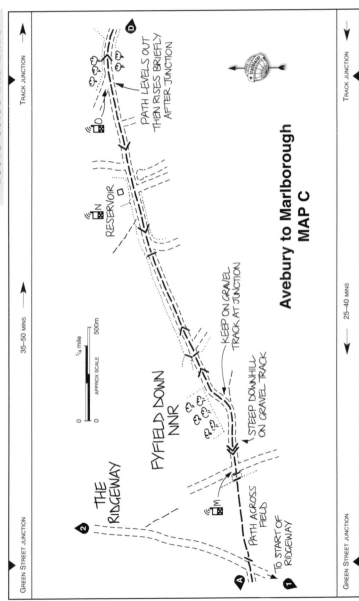

THE RIDGEWAY

FYFIELD DOWN NNR

RESERVOIR

PATH LEVELS OUT THEN RISES BRIEFLY AFTER JUNCTION

KEEP ON GRAVEL TRACK AT JUNCTION

STEEP DOWNHILL ON GRAVEL TRACK

PATH ACROSS FIELD

TO START OF RIDGEWAY

Avebury to Marlborough MAP C

GREEN STREET JUNCTION

35–50 MINS

TRACK JUNCTION

¼ mile

500m

0   APPROX SCALE

0

GREEN STREET JUNCTION

25–40 MINS

TRACK JUNCTION

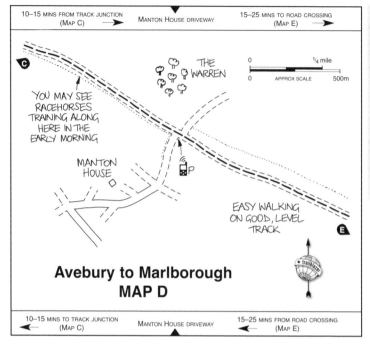

10-15 MINS FROM TRACK JUNCTION (MAP C) →   MANTON HOUSE DRIVEWAY   15-25 MINS TO ROAD CROSSING (MAP E) →

THE WARREN

YOU MAY SEE RACEHORSES TRAINING ALONG HERE IN THE EARLY MORNING

MANTON HOUSE

EASY WALKING ON GOOD, LEVEL TRACK

0   ¼ mile
0   APPROX SCALE   500m

Avebury to Marlborough MAP D

10-15 MINS TO TRACK JUNCTION ← (MAP C)   MANTON HOUSE DRIVEWAY   15-25 MINS FROM ROAD CROSSING ← (MAP E)

exercised. When walking on the edge of the grassy gallops instead of on the gravel track you'll notice just how soft and springy the ground is: this is one of the main reasons that this area is so favourable for training racehorses. You'll also pass the driveway for Manton House where there is a well-established stable and stud that has been operating since the 19th century.

At the end of the long, neat, straight track you come to a minor road that you must cross and you eventually end up walking on the edge of a golf course for a spell before crossing the road to two **cemeteries**. You should pass the new one but enter the old one via the rusty iron double gates. Someone has thoughtfully provided a roughly hewn wooden seat for resting on, in the middle of this peaceful place. Identical iron gates bound the other side of the cemetery and once through these you simply have to turn left and follow the track, then road, down into Marlborough town centre, passing by some immaculate cricket, rugby and hockey pitches.

The road joins the southern end of the High St with the library and tourist information point on your left (see map p71) and the **Sun Inn** on your right. There is a bench outside the library should you need it but it's perhaps a better idea to head to one of the many pubs lining the High St for a well-earned drink.

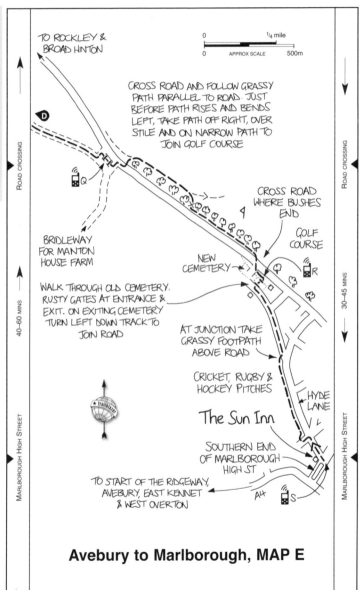

TO ROCKLEY &
BROAD HINTON

0   ¼ mile

0   APPROX SCALE   500m

CROSS ROAD AND FOLLOW GRASSY
PATH PARALLEL TO ROAD. JUST
BEFORE PATH RISES AND BENDS
LEFT, TAKE PATH OFF RIGHT, OVER
STILE AND ON NARROW PATH TO
JOIN GOLF COURSE

D

CROSS ROAD
WHERE BUSHES
END

GOLF
COURSE

BRIDLEWAY
FOR MANTON
HOUSE FARM

NEW
CEMETERY

R

WALK THROUGH OLD CEMETERY.
RUSTY GATES AT ENTRANCE &
EXIT. ON EXITING CEMETERY
TURN LEFT DOWN TRACK TO
JOIN ROAD

AT JUNCTION TAKE
GRASSY FOOTPATH
ABOVE ROAD

CRICKET, RUGBY &
HOCKEY PITCHES

HYDE
LANE

trailblazer

The Sun Inn

SOUTHERN END
OF MARLBOROUGH
HIGH ST

TO START OF THE RIDGEWAY,
AVEBURY, EAST KENNET
& WEST OVERTON

A4

S

ROAD CROSSING

ROAD CROSSING

40–60 MINS

30–45 MINS

MARLBOROUGH HIGH STREET

MARLBOROUGH HIGH STREET

Q

Avebury to Marlborough, MAP E

ROUTE GUIDE AND MAPS

The route guide

ALTERNATIVE STARTS TO THE RIDGEWAY [See map p79]

If you are staying in Avebury before you start the Ridgeway, there are three options for starting the walk from the village. It is generally agreed that starting by walking out from Avebury makes for a far more exciting beginning than simply being dropped off at the official start by the side of the A4 road.

Alternative start – Route A

This is the longest alternative start. It involves walking out of the village along West Kennet Avenue which runs parallel to the B4003. It's easy walking on the soft grass along here with the large sarsen stones flanking you on either side. After a hundred metres or so the road cuts into the avenue before leaving it intact again a hundred metres later.

The avenue finishes all too soon and you must exit the field through a gate and continue on the grass verge by the side of the road. Although this is a narrow road, some people drive too fast along here so take care.

Follow this road until you reach the T-junction and turn left onto the A4. Walk past the rather grand West Kennet House before crossing the road as it's easier to continue walking on the southern side of the road. You'll reach a right-hand turning for East Kennet with a pet hotel on the corner and should take this turning off the A4. There are always plenty of dogs here barking at each other. Just after the pet hotel there is a stile on your left leading into a field. Climb over this and walk up the field, parallel to the A4, to reach the top corner where you

---

❏ **Signposts on The Ridgeway**

The Ridgeway is one of the most comprehensively signposted long-distance trails in the country. At nearly every junction on the path there will be a dedicated and distinctive black 'Ridgeway' signpost, not only to keep you going in the right direction, but also to inform you of other options.

At a glance these waymarkers look to be made in the traditional manner from wood that has been treated with creosote, but in fact the material used is Plaswood. This is an environmentally friendly plastic material made from 30% consumer waste and 70% from other waste sources. It is strong, durable and impervious to water so it will not rot or splinter as wood does. This also means that it is maintenance free.

You will see many traditional wooden signs along the Ridgeway in various states of decay while the Plaswood signs will remain looking the same as the day they were set into the ground for years to come. Some of the Plaswood signs on the Ridgeway have been standing for more than ten years already.

Plaswood is now used for many other products, often as a substitute for wood in outdoor areas. Items such as benches, planters, walkways and street furniture are all being constructed from the material.

❏ **Change to the start of the Ridgeway**
Anyone who has walked the Ridgeway will agree that the official start is really rather lacking in atmosphere. This is surprising when one considers how packed with character the surrounding area is. With this in mind, there have been calls to change the starting point, though at the time of writing the situation hasn't changed much from when the first edition of this book was published. It is still very much on the wish list but these things tend to take a long time to be agreed and organised, not to mention the costs involved. However, a more salubrious starting point could be a serious possibility in the future.

Avebury is the obvious place for the relocation of the starting point. The path would then lead out of the village along Green St and join the Ridgeway just 1.8 miles (3km) into its current route. It's probable that many people do choose to walk this route anyway and as you really don't lose anything by not walking the first couple of miles of the trail it is a sensible choice. If you'd like to do this, follow alternative start routes B or C.

should climb over another stile and find yourself in The Sanctuary. From here you simply have to cross the A4 to arrive at the official start of the Ridgeway.

Alternative start – Routes B & C
Both these routes leave Avebury via Green St. The only part of Green St that could be vaguely described as a conventional 'street' peters out very quickly before becoming a sealed track.

Even on the busiest days in Avebury, you don't have to take many steps down Green St before leaving the crowds behind. You'll pass several houses on your right as Green St clears the village and then come to Manor Farm. This is the last building on the 'street' and is where the tarmac finishes. It can be muddy around here owing to the farm vehicles.

You will see Green St stretching into the distance up the hillside and it's at this point that you need to make the first decision of your walk. Either follow Green St up the hill (B), or take the signposted track that turns off right, immediately after Manor Farm (C).

If you choose to follow Green St straight up the hill (B) you'll find that the track broadens out and becomes grassy, making for easy walking despite the increasing gradient. Look behind on your way up here to see the view getting better all the time.

Green St joins the Ridgeway at the top of the climb and from here you have a choice of turning left or right. Turning left will take you onto the Ridgeway, heading towards Barbury Castle, whereas turning right will take you onto the Ridgeway and down to the official start. It's up to you, though there seems little point turning right, walking down to the beginning of the Ridgeway, then doing an about-turn and walking back up again. However, you might feel a bit of a cheat if you miss out this 1³/₄ miles/3km of the path, especially as it's the first part.

A compromise solution is to take the right turn after Manor Farm (C) as described earlier. Soon after joining this track it becomes grassy but deeply rutted and can be really muddy after rain. The path is level for the first half-mile after which it bends right and begins to climb the side of Overton Hill.

As you reach a **tumulus** (see box below) with a coppice on top, the path bends right more sharply than before and you'll see ahead where you will join the Ridgeway. When you do so you'll have the same choice as walkers on Alternative start route B.

Although Alternative start route C isn't as attractive as route B it finishes a lot closer to the start of the Ridgeway, giving less backtracking, should you prefer.

OVERTON HILL TO FOX HILL   [MAPS 1-10]

Overview

This first **16¹/₂-mile/26.3km** stage of the Ridgeway includes many interesting sights but most of them are before Ogbourne St George. By comparison, thereafter, it can seem a bit of a slog in parts, especially the last section from Liddington Hill to Fox Hill.

The full length of this stage will leave you tired after your first day but you'll have to push on to Bishopstone to find accommodation. Alternatively you could stay at Ogbourne St George which is only 9 miles/14.5km from the start of the Ridgeway. It would make an easy first day's walking and would also allow time to investigate the Fyfield Down National Nature Reserve and take a long break at Barbury Castle.

Route

There are several alternative starts to the Ridgeway (see pp89-91) that are all more interesting than the official one. It just depends how serious you are about following every step of the real path.

The official, but rather uninspiring, starting point is at the side of the Beckhampton to Marlborough road (the A4) and if you've taken Alternative start route A you will arrive here. However, you soon gain enough height on the broad track on Overton Hill to lose the sight and noise of this busy road. It's at this point that Alternative start route C joins the Ridgeway from the left.

In clear weather there are excellent views west to the obelisk monument on Cherhill Hill, 5 miles/8km away. It was built on an Iron Age hillfort in 1845/6

❏ **Tumuli**

Especially on the first half of the Ridgeway, and in particular on the first 15 miles of it, you will see many tumuli (see Map 1, p93) – burial mounds dating from around 4000 to 4500 years ago which now just look like raised grassy humps. In fact there are three right next to the start of the Ridgeway and you'll see a couple more just ten minutes up the path. Sometimes they are planted over with trees, so if you see an isolated bunch of trees in the middle of a field, this could suggest a tumulus underneath.

They are generally marked on Ordnance Survey maps, though not all marked tumuli are necessarily burial mounds. They could be just, as yet, unidentified lumps on the landscape.

in memory of Sir William Petty, the 17th-century economist. **Windmill Hill** (see box below), 2¹/₂ miles/4km to the west, is another easily spotted landmark. After the track levels out, you'll arrive at the Green St junction (Map 2).

If you have taken Alternative start route B from Avebury you will join the Ridgeway from the left, while to the right is a gate leading into **Fyfield Down NNR**. Up here it's exposed to the elements with few trees or bushes to shelter you and the walking is mainly level on a broad, grassy track with numerous byways and bridleways joining from both sides.

When you get to the junction (Map 3) where the Broad Hinton to Marlborough road crosses the Ridgeway you'll have the opportunity to see the **Hackpen White Horse** cut into the chalk of the hillside. You can't see it from the track as you are above it so you'll need to make a slight diversion. It is not an ancient White Horse – this one was cut into Hackpen Hill in 1838 – so don't feel the steep detour is obligatory, especially as you will be seeing the original white horse at White Horse Hill, further along the Ridgeway. This section of the Ridgeway path is also part of the **White Horse Trail**, a 90-mile circular route connecting eight white horses in Wiltshire. *(cont'd on p96)*

❏ **Windmill Hill**

This 20-acre site forms the largest of the 66 known Neolithic causewayed enclosures in Britain, with evidence of activity here dating from about 3700BC. A causewayed enclosure is a piece of land, usually oval in shape, bounded by one or more segmented banks or ditches. Windmill Hill has three such series of banks and ditches, with the outermost series being by far the most substantial. These sites represent the earliest examples of artificially enclosing an open area in Britain.

The findings of excavations by Rev H G O Kendall and Alexander Keiller, that took place here in the 1920s, not only established Neolithic causewayed enclosures as a distinct class, but also granted Windmill Hill its status as the most important one in Britain. The site even lent its name to 'Windmill Hill Ware', a distinctive type of pottery found at this and other similar sites in Britain.

From the 1920s onwards, the theory was that Neolithic people had lived in 'pit dwellings' – in the ditches of the enclosure – owing to the large quantity of animal bones and pottery found there. Keiller's findings from the 1920s were not properly written up at the time and it wasn't until 1965 that a summary of the excavations was published. This led to renewed excavations on the site and by the late 1960s the theory of 'pit dwellings' had totally lost favour. Although we now know that this was not a site of permanent settlement it is still unclear exactly what its purpose was. We can presume that ceremonies and feasts took place here, but the size of the enclosure would suggest a more substantial use. Several round burial mounds on Windmill Hill have also been excavated but these have been dated to the Bronze Age.

Despite the significance of Windmill Hill to archaeologists, a casual visit can prove disappointing. Apart from the views of the surrounding countryside there really isn't much to see on the hill itself as large sections of the banks and ditches have been ploughed into farmland. It's certainly far less visually dramatic than an Iron Age hill fort like Barbury Castle, only 5 miles (9km) along the Ridgeway from Avebury. If you want to visit Windmill Hill you should walk to the western end of Avebury High St and follow the signposts from there; it's about 2 miles (3km) from the village.

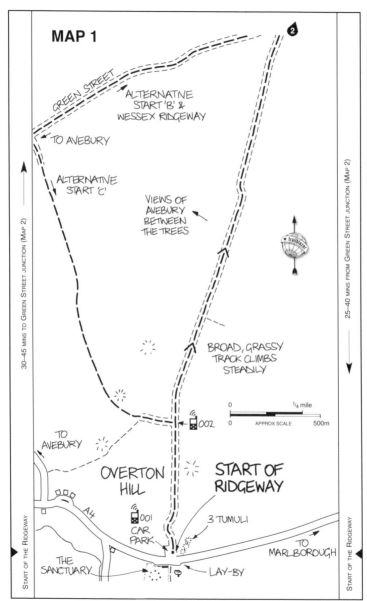

MAP 1

GREEN STREET

ALTERNATIVE START 'B' & WESSEX RIDGEWAY

TO AVEBURY

ALTERNATIVE START 'C'

VIEWS OF AVEBURY BETWEEN THE TREES

BROAD, GRASSY TRACK CLIMBS STEADILY

002

0   ¼ mile
0   APPROX SCALE   500m

TO AVEBURY

OVERTON HILL

START OF RIDGEWAY

001 CAR PARK

3 TUMULI

THE SANCTUARY

LAY-BY

TO MARLBOROUGH

30–45 MINS TO GREEN STREET JUNCTION (MAP 2)

25–40 MINS FROM GREEN STREET JUNCTION (MAP 2)

START OF THE RIDGEWAY

START OF THE RIDGEWAY

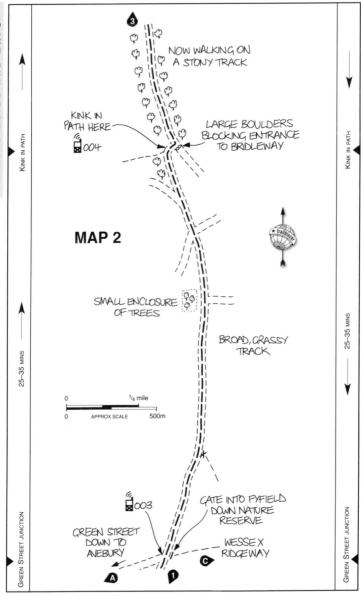

KINK IN PATH

NOW WALKING ON
A STONY TRACK

KINK IN
PATH HERE
📟004

LARGE BOULDERS
BLOCKING ENTRANCE
TO BRIDLEWAY

MAP 2

SMALL ENCLOSURE
OF TREES

BROAD, GRASSY
TRACK

KINK IN PATH

25-35 MINS

0   ¼ mile
0   APPROX SCALE   500m

25-35 MINS

GREEN STREET JUNCTION

📟003

GREEN STREET
DOWN TO
AVEBURY

GATE INTO FYFIELD
DOWN NATURE
RESERVE

WESSEX
RIDGEWAY

GREEN STREET JUNCTION

A   1   C

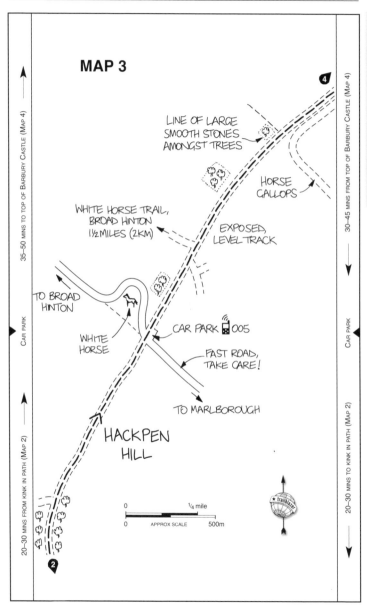

MAP 3

LINE OF LARGE
SMOOTH STONES
AMONGST TREES

HORSE
GALLOPS

WHITE HORSE TRAIL,
BROAD HINTON
1½ MILES (2KM)

EXPOSED,
LEVEL TRACK

TO BROAD
HINTON

WHITE
HORSE

CAR PARK 📱 005

FAST ROAD,
TAKE CARE!

TO MARLBOROUGH

HACKPEN
HILL

35–50 MINS TO TOP OF BARBURY CASTLE (MAP 4)

CAR PARK

20–30 MINS FROM KINK IN PATH (MAP 2)

30–45 MINS FROM TOP OF BARBURY CASTLE (MAP 4)

CAR PARK

20–30 MINS TO KINK IN PATH (MAP 2)

0   ¼ mile

0   APPROX SCALE   500m

trailblazer

2

4

(cont'd from p92) At the foot of **Barbury Castle** (Map 4) the 'Ridgeway Route For Vehicles' continues straight ahead across the road but walkers, cyclists and horses can follow the steep grassy slopes up onto the top of Barbury Castle itself. Apart from this one there are two more Iron Age forts on the Ridgeway (Liddington Castle and Uffington Castle), but this is the only one that the path cuts directly through. The 11-acre fort is ringed by double ramparts and deep ditches with entrances at both ends through which the Ridgeway passes. Some Iron Age finds from the castle are on display at Devizes Museum. Its defensive position is indisputable and this guaranteed its importance long after the Iron Age finished. In fact the name 'Barbury' is thought to come from the Old English name, 'Bera', after the Saxon chief who controlled the castle around AD550. Even as late as the Second World War it was being used as a potentially defensive position by allied troops.

The views from up here on a clear day are fantastic and it's a popular place at weekends with walkers, cyclists and horseriders. On some weekends it's also home to the White Horse Kite Fliers. You might wonder how all the people managed to get up here but when you get to the other side of the castle you'll understand. There you'll find a large car park, picnic tables, public toilets, a café and the road north to Wroughton, 3^1/$_2$ miles/6km away. *Castle Café* (☎ 01793 845346) is open Mon-Fri 10am to dusk, Sat & Sun 9am to dusk in the summer; weekends only in the winter. They serve tea (£1), coffee (£1.20), ice creams, snacks and meals: the cooked breakfast for £4.50 is well worth it, but there's also the mega-breakfast for £6.50 if you're really, really hungry. **Camping** is also available here for £10 per person including breakfast; they have toilets and are hoping to have showers by early 2009.

When the weather is good the walking on **Smeathe's Ridge** (Map 5) makes for some of the most enjoyable parts of this stage. The soft grass under foot makes walking easy and you can daydream as you walk. Although the official path doesn't go into Ogbourne St George you can follow the signposted footpath, about half a mile/1km, into this attractive village if you want to stop here.

❏ **Racehorses**
From virtually the start of the Ridgeway up until past East Ilsley you are likely to see racehorses. They won't be on the path itself, but will be training along the gallops that often run parallel to the path, sometimes with brushwood hurdles set up on them. As you may have noticed, the ground here is soft and springy and very open which makes it ideal for racehorse training. The early morning is the best time to see the small groups of horses being put through their paces with their trainers. When the Ridgeway is right next to the gallops you can feel the power of the horses as they thunder by.

When you are at Barbury Castle you can look down onto the Marlborough Downs and see the Barbury Castle racecourse, but it's the Lambourn Downs area, further east, that is really famous as a centre for racehorse training. There are around 50 racing yards around Lambourn which train up to 2000 horses at any one time.

If you visit East Ilsley (see p124) and the Crown & Horns pub there, you'll notice that the walls in the bar are covered with horse-racing memorabilia, connected to the landlord's involvement in the business.

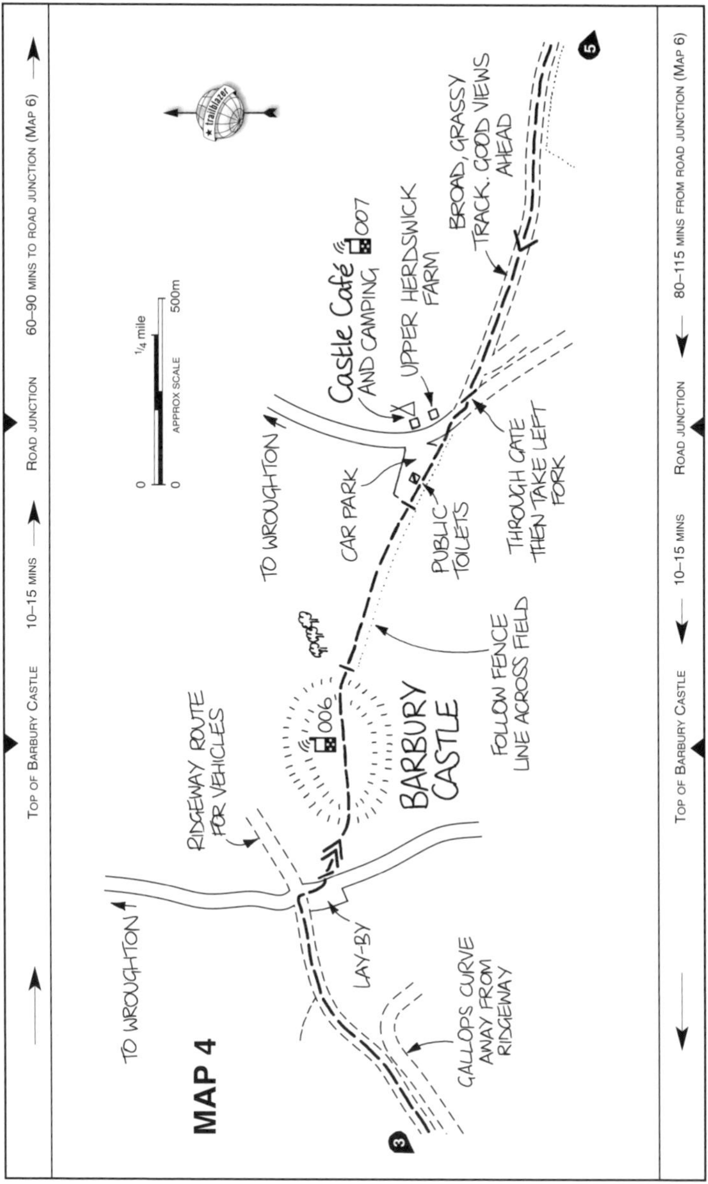
MAP 4
Top of Barbury Castle
10–15 mins
Road Junction
60–90 mins to Road Junction (Map 6)
80–115 mins from Road Junction (Map 6)
Road Junction
10–15 mins
Top of Barbury Castle
APPROX SCALE
0
1/4 mile
0
500m
trailblazer
3
5
TO WROUGHTON
GALLOPS CURVE AWAY FROM RIDGEWAY
LAY-BY
RIDGEWAY ROUTE FOR VEHICLES
006
BARBURY CASTLE
FOLLOW FENCE LINE ACROSS FIELD
TO WROUGHTON
CAR PARK
PUBLIC TOILETS
THROUGH GATE THEN TAKE LEFT FORK
Castle Café AND CAMPING
007
UPPER HERDSWICK FARM
BROAD, GRASSY TRACK. GOOD VIEWS AHEAD

ROUTE GUIDE AND MAPS

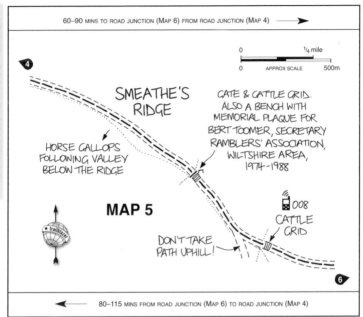

60–90 MINS TO ROAD JUNCTION (MAP 6) FROM ROAD JUNCTION (MAP 4) ⟶

0   ¼ mile

0   APPROX SCALE   500m

4

SMEATHE'S
RIDGE

GATE & CATTLE GRID.
ALSO A BENCH WITH
MEMORIAL PLAQUE FOR
BERT TOOMER, SECRETARY
RAMBLERS' ASSOCIATION,
WILTSHIRE AREA,
1974-1988

HORSE GALLOPS
FOLLOWING VALLEY
BELOW THE RIDGE

008
CATTLE
GRID

MAP 5

★ trailblazer

DON'T TAKE
PATH UPHILL!

6

⟵ 80–115 MINS FROM ROAD JUNCTION (MAP 6) TO ROAD JUNCTION (MAP 4)

OGBOURNE ST GEORGE
[See map p100]

The name of this village refers to the river Og (Map 6) and the name of its church, St George's. A mile or so south of here is the village of Ogbourne St Andrew, named in the same way. Ogbourne St George is a pretty-enough village but unless you are planning to stay the night, there really isn't much point making the detour. There are no shops but there are three decent places to stay, two good places to eat, and there's also a campsite nearby.

The **buses** calling here are Stagecoach's Nos 70 & 71, which operate between Swindon and Marlborough and stop in the village, and Wilts & Dorset Buses' No 95 between Pewsey and Swindon which stop on the A346 just outside the village; see pp42-5 for further details.

If you need a **taxi**, call one of the firms in Marlborough, see p70.

Where to stay, eat and drink

The Inn with the Well (☎ 01672 841445, 🖳 www.theinnwiththewell.co.uk; 2D/3T/1F, food Mon-Sat noon-2pm & 6.30-9pm, Sun noon-2pm) is a deservedly popular place with both locals and people travelling from the surrounding area. They serve a range of real ales including Wadworth 6X. Their bar menu includes various kinds of ploughman's for £5.75 and ham, egg and chips for £6.75. The varied restaurant menu has dishes such as balti chicken for £8.95 or venison casserole for £9.95. B&B accommodation here is in en suite double/twin rooms from £60, or £50.50-52.50 if you are on your own. The family room costs from £80.

A couple of minutes away is *The Sanctuary* (☎ 01672 841473, 🖳 www.the-sanctuary.biz; 1D or T/1F), a well-run, friendly B&B that's used to walkers. They serve large breakfasts to set you up for the

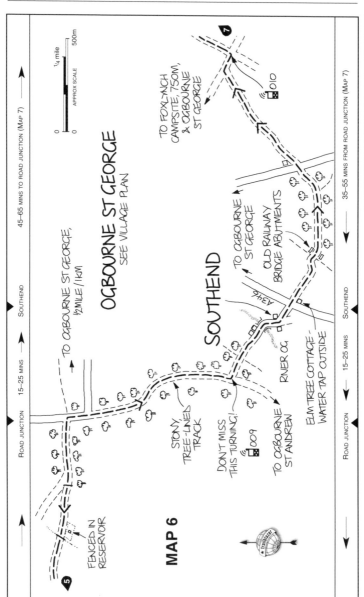

day. The double/twin is en suite and the family room has a private bathroom next door but each costs from £60; the single occupancy rate is from £45. They now have their own chickens so your breakfast eggs will be as fresh as possible.

Surprisingly for such a small village, there is a hotel: *Parklands Hotel* (☎ 01672 841555, 🖳 www.parklandshoteluk.co.uk; 6D/6D or T) has modern en suite rooms starting at £85 (single occupancy from £70). The restaurant here, *Bentley's* (Mon-Sat noon-2pm & 6.30-8.30pm, Sun noon-2pm & 6.30-8pm) changes its menu regularly. It may include tuna steak seared with ginger, honey and soy sauce: you can probably have a two-course lunch for about £14 and an evening meal for about £17. You need to book in advance for both lunch and dinner but they are used to walkers and don't have a strict dress code.

Campers should head for *Foxlynch* (☎ 01672 841307; 1T, D or F). It costs £5 per person to camp here including use of a toilet and shower. Breakfast (£5) is also available if requested in advance. They also offer **B&B** in a centrally heated bunkroom with an en suite bathroom. The bunkroom has a sofa bed and a bunk bed so up to four

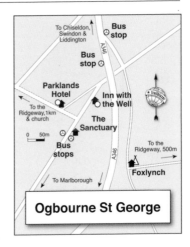

Ogbourne St George

can sleep here. It's £20 per person, including breakfast though it must be booked in advance. Although Foxlynch is not quite in the village, it's only about five minutes' walk away and, better than that, it's only 750m from the Ridgeway: for the most direct route, see Map 6.

The official path skirts around the south of the village on shady farm tracks. You get occasional glimpses of Ogbourne St George through the trees on your left and you soon arrive in the hamlet of **Southend** (Map 6). This must rate as one of the most picturesque collections of cottages anywhere and is so perfect it's almost twee. Apart from the few buildings at Barbury Castle, this is the most heavily built-up area you have passed through since setting off.

After the hamlet you start a steady climb up a stony track closed in by trees and bushes and come to pass between the hefty stone abutments of an old railway bridge which was once the route of the Midland and South Western Junction Railway. This section opened in the 1880s but has long since disappeared. It linked Swindon and Chiseldon, to the north, with Marlborough, to the south. It's now been developed into the Chiseldon & Marlborough Railway Path and is popular but muddy.

Much later on when you arrive at the crossroads with the **reservoir** (Map 7) on the left corner that looks like a fortified concrete bunker, there is the opportunity to visit the former village of **Snap**. A small farming community existed on this site for hundreds of years until the late 19th century when farming became less economically viable owing to cheap imports and spare land was bought up by wealthy local landowners for use as sheep-grazing. Most of the

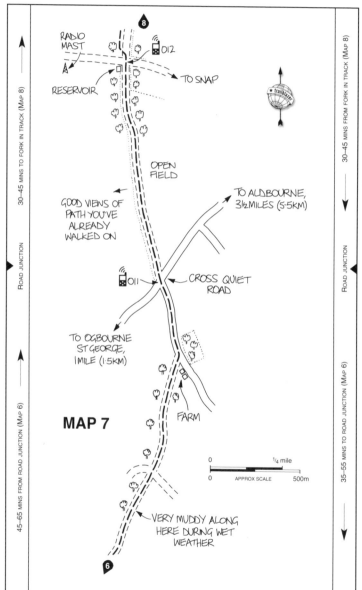

8

RADIO MAST

□ 012

TO SNAP

RESERVOIR

OPEN FIELD

GOOD VIEWS OF PATH YOU'VE ALREADY WALKED ON

TO ALDBOURNE, 3½ MILES (5.5KM)

011

CROSS QUIET ROAD

TO OGBOURNE ST GEORGE, 1 MILE (1.5KM)

MAP 7

FARM

0   ¼ mile
APPROX SCALE
0   500m

VERY MUDDY ALONG HERE DURING WET WEATHER

6

30–45 MINS TO FORK IN TRACK (MAP 8)

ROAD JUNCTION

45–65 MINS FROM ROAD JUNCTION (MAP 6)

30–45 MINS FROM FORK IN TRACK (MAP 8)

ROAD JUNCTION

35–55 MINS TO ROAD JUNCTION (MAP 6)

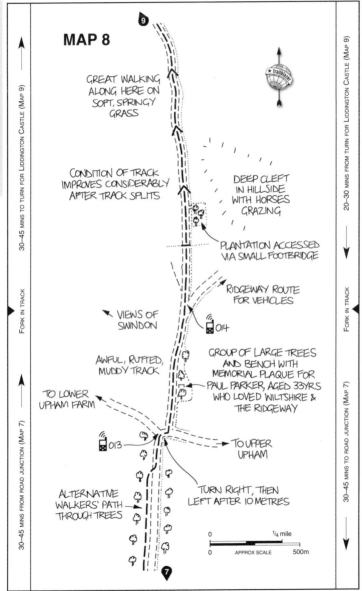

MAP 8

GREAT WALKING
ALONG HERE ON
SOFT, SPRINGY
GRASS

CONDITION OF TRACK
IMPROVES CONSIDERABLY
AFTER TRACK SPLITS

DEEP CLEFT
IN HILLSIDE
WITH HORSES
GRAZING

PLANTATION ACCESSED
VIA SMALL FOOTBRIDGE

RIDGEWAY ROUTE
FOR VEHICLES

VIEWS OF
SWINDON

014

AWFUL, RUTTED,
MUDDY TRACK

GROUP OF LARGE TREES
AND BENCH WITH
MEMORIAL PLAQUE FOR
PAUL PARKER, AGED 33YRS
WHO LOVED WILTSHIRE &
THE RIDGEWAY

TO LOWER
UPHAM FARM

013

TO UPPER
UPHAM

ALTERNATIVE
WALKERS' PATH
THROUGH TREES

TURN RIGHT, THEN
LEFT AFTER 10 METRES

0   1/4 mile
0   APPROX SCALE   500m

30–45 MINS TO TURN FOR LIDDINGTON CASTLE (MAP 9)

FORK IN TRACK

30–45 MINS FROM ROAD JUNCTION (MAP 7)

20–30 MINS FROM TURN FOR LIDDINGTON CASTLE (MAP 9)

FORK IN TRACK

30–45 MINS TO ROAD JUNCTION (MAP 7)

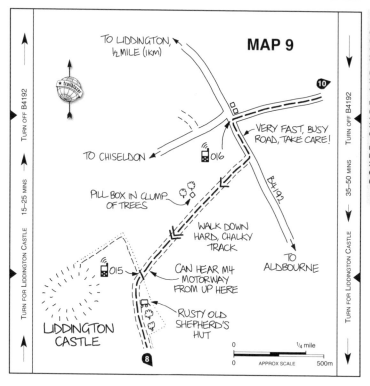

MAP 9

TO LIDDINGTON,
½ MILE (1KM)

★ trailblazer

10

VERY FAST, BUSY
ROAD, TAKE CARE!

TO CHISELDON

016

B4192

PILL BOX IN CLUMP
OF TREES

WALK DOWN
HARD, CHALKY
TRACK

TO
ALDBOURNE

015

CAN HEAR M4
MOTORWAY
FROM UP HERE

RUSTY OLD
SHEPHERD'S
HUT

LIDDINGTON
CASTLE

8

0   ¼ mile

0   APPROX SCALE   500m

TURN OFF B4192

15-25 MINS

TURN FOR LIDDINGTON CASTLE

TURN OFF B4192

35-50 MINS

TURN FOR LIDDINGTON CASTLE

population left the village to find work elsewhere and by the early 20th century the village was empty. To get there turn right and follow the track straight on for about half a mile/1km. Since being abandoned, the village has all but disappeared into the landscape, so unless you have plenty of time…

The 'Snap crossroads' is worth noting because just a short way down the track to the left is the **radio mast** that you'll probably have seen by now. If you haven't it will certainly be a prominent landmark every time you do look back, all the way to Liddington Castle.

When you eventually reach **Liddington Castle** (Map 9) you'll get views of the M4 over to the north-east and if you turn around you'll see the aforementioned radio mast, now on the horizon behind you.

The Ridgeway does not actually go through Liddington Castle so if you'd like to visit follow the signpost that directs you along the fence line rather than going directly to the castle; it's about 500m. The trig point on top of the castle displays a height of 277m and the hill is a popular launch site for paragliders.

After descending Liddington Hill and joining the fast B4192 you'll have the possibility of walking to Liddington; though it is only worth going if you want a drink or meal, or to get a bus. To get there simply continue down the B4192 for about half a mile/1km, crossing the M4 en route.

LIDDINGTON

The Village Inn (☎ 01793 790314; food Mon-Sat 11.30am-1.45pm & 6.30-8.45pm, Sun noon-2pm & 7-8.45pm) provides a friendly focus for the village and is usually busy. This creeper-clad inn was built in the late 19th century and was originally called The Bell. They serve Arkell's ales and their excellent food keeps the place full, particularly at weekends.

There are two **bus** stops in this village. Thamesdown's No 46 goes to Fox Hill, Marlborough and Swindon from the stop at Spinney Close. This is also the stop for RH Transport's X47 service to Fox Hill. You can also get a bus to Marlborough or Swindon (Thamesdown's No 48) from the

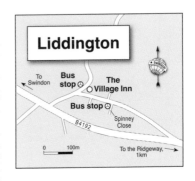

stop opposite the Village Inn; see pp42-5 for further details.

After enduring a stretch of road walking you must cross the bridge over the M4. You'll be surprised just how noisy and smelly it is, and although the fumes disappear quickly when you reach the other side, the noise will stay with you all the way to the Shepherds Rest pub at the end of this stage.

There is still about 700m of walking to go between the bridge and the pub in **Fox Hill** but it's all on a neat grassy verge along the edge of the grounds of *The Liddington* (☎ 01793 791000, 🖳 www.theliddington.co.uk; 198D) – a hotel and conference centre aimed mainly at the corporate sector. Their room rates are from £100 for a double (£85 if you're on your own) but special offers for online bookings are often available through their website. Their restaurant is open daily noon-1.30pm & 7-9pm and bar snacks are available 9-10pm. I wonder if any Ridgeway walkers have ever stayed there?

At the time of writing, the *Shepherds Rest* (🖳 www.shepherds-rest.co.uk), on the crossroads at Foxhill, was under new ownership and closed. In the past it was a welcome sight for walkers, especially those who had started the day at Avebury. The landlord was 'walker-friendly' and opened the bar daily from 11am-11pm. Food was served daily noon-9pm. Hopefully the new owners will carry on serving up the hearty meals and selection of real ales that the previous landlord did as this is the only pub directly on the western part of the Ridgeway.

Thamesdown's Nos 46 & 48 **buses** call here as does RH Transport's X47 service; see pp42-5 for further details.

FOX HILL TO COURT HILL [MAPS 10-16]

Overview

This second stage of the Ridgeway totals **11¹/₂ miles/18.4km** and on the whole the walking is easy along very broad grassy tracks. Although there are a few ascents, they're none too draining. There are some great views plus several interesting archaeological sites and natural phenomena worth investigating. This is also the most remote section of the Ridgeway and is completely exposed to the elements with little shelter available. If it rains there is little you can do but continue walking and get very wet.

Route

About 200m past the Shepherds Rest you leave the road that goes to the villages of Hinton Parva and Bishopstone and take the track on the right. A large **radio mast** will be in the field on your right protected by a gate with a dozen padlocks on it. The path levels out after a short climb and you can see the trig point on **Charlbury Hill** (Map 10) ahead and to the left of the path.

The ever-spreading town of Swindon is clearly visible to the west and you can also see villages down in the valley, parallel to the Ridgeway. These include Hinton Parva, Bishopstone, Idstone and Ashbury. Paths run down off the Ridgeway to these villages and many people from the surrounding area bring their dogs up here for exercise.

The first turning off left to Bishopstone is a bridleway down a very steep-sided cleft, followed just a few hundred metres later by a narrow surfaced road headed to the same place from the crossroads at **Ridgeway Farm** (Map 11). From this latter turning it's about half a mile/1km to the village.

BISHOPSTONE [see map p106]

Although this is a fairly large village, facilities for the walker are a little thin on the ground. There is no shop or post office, but there are a couple of good places to stay and eat should you decide to stop the night here. It's an attractive place for a wander, especially by the village pond and on the shady shortcut paths around the village, but like some of the other settlements on this stretch of the walk, it's only worth coming all the way down off the Ridgeway if you plan to stay or eat here.

Thamesdown's No 47 **bus** passes through on its way from Swindon to Ashbury and Lambourn. You can also take RH Transport's X47 service to Fox Hill or Ashbury; see pp42-5 for further details.

Where to stay and eat

The Royal Oak (☎ 01793 790481, 🖳 www .royaloakbishopstone.co.uk; 2D, T or F;

food Mon-Sat noon-2.30pm, Sun noon-3pm, daily 6.30-9.30pm), located in a grand building set on a quiet lane is one of the two pubs in the village. It's been here for about two hundred years and is well worth a look. They're open all day, serve Arkell's ales and have a popular restaurant that has a selection of organic food including steak. Both their rooms are en suite and they charge £60 for B&B for two sharing, £75 for three and if you're on your own you'll pay £40.

The interestingly named *True Heart Inn* (☎ 01793 790080, 🖳 www.trueheart .co.uk; food Mon-Sat noon-2.30pm & 6-9pm, Sun noon-2.30pm & 7-9pm) is the other pub in the village. It's a freehouse serving a range of real ales. If you're there for lunch you could try the ploughman's for £7.95, or if you've worked up a real appetite maybe a 16" baguette, also £7.95.

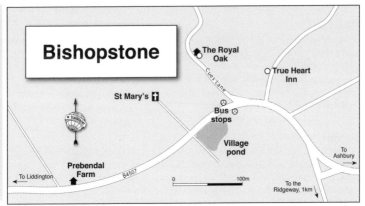

As for cooked meals, the extensive menu ranges from Somerset belly pork (£10.95), to fresh haddock and spinach (£9.95) to homemade squash and lentil strudel (£9.95) to create-your-own pizzas (from £5.45 for a 9" margherita).

Prebendal Farm (☎ 01793 790485, 🖳 www.prebendal.com; 3D/1T), a stately Victorian house set in beautiful gardens on a working farm, offers B&B from £70 per night and from £40 for single occupancy. Two of the doubles share a bathroom and the other rooms are en suite; wireless internet access is available.

Just after the junction at Ridgeway Farm, on the right, is a field of pigs. Most of them are saddleback and big with it, but you might spot the odd ginger-coloured beast, too. Unlike the sheep you sometimes pass, these animals will take little or no notice of you.

The track becomes lined with trees on both sides and the walking has been made easy along here owing to work over the last couple of years to upgrade the track surface with stone chippings and also the banning of motor vehicles.

At the next farm there is a track left, down Idstone Hill, to the hamlet of Idstone. From this junction to Bishopstone, via Idstone, it's a little over 1¼ miles/2km. There is also a **water tap** by the barn a few metres down the Idstone Hill turning. The sign says it is for trough water for animals, but if you are desperate… Otherwise wait until the next tap, 5½ miles/9km further on.

You're likely to hear the noise of the upcoming B4000 road crossing a good few minutes before you reach it. It comes up Ashbury Hill from Shrivenham and Ashbury, in the north, to cross the Ridgeway and continue south to the Lambourns. From this crossing (Map 12) it is about half a mile/1km down to the village of Ashbury.

ASHBURY   [see map p109]
This is another delightful village in the string of settlements running parallel to the Ridgeway. Unfortunately, like the other villages along here, there is no shop, but there is still a **post office**, though it has limited opening hours.

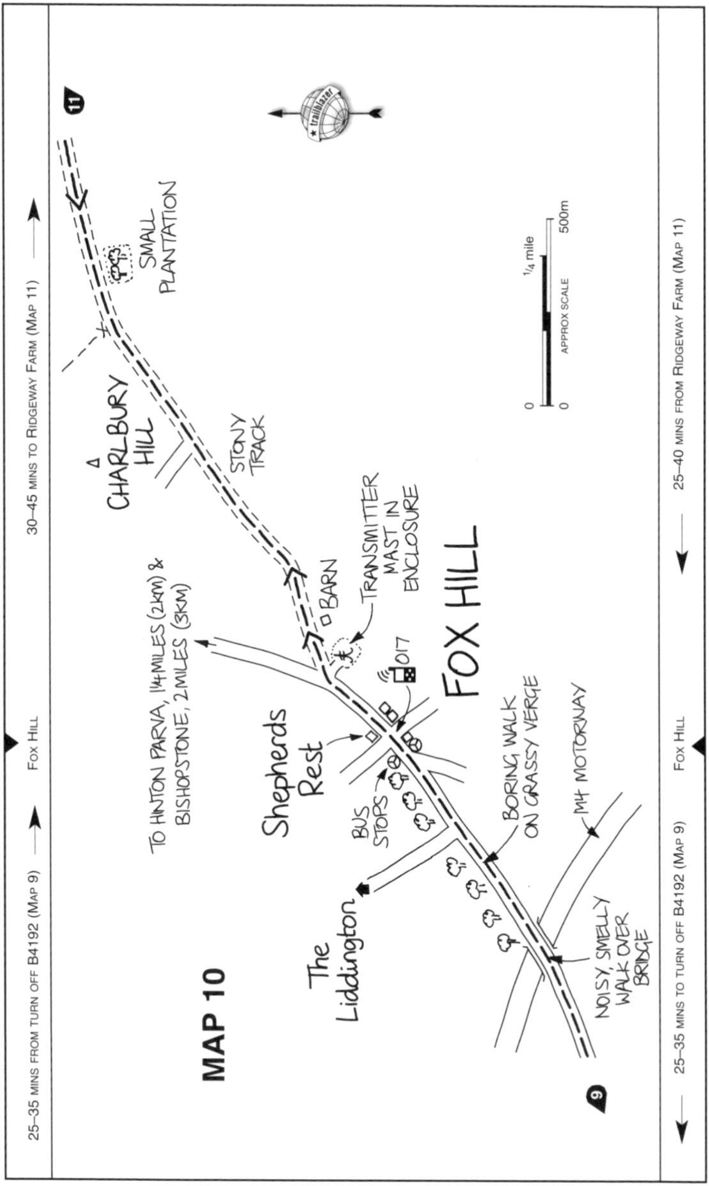

MAP 10

25-35 MINS FROM TURN OFF B4192 (MAP 9) ——→ ——→ FOX HILL

30-45 MINS TO RIDGEWAY FARM (MAP 11) ——→

CHARLBURY HILL

SMALL PLANTATION

STONY TRACK

BARN

TRANSMITTER MAST IN ENCLOSURE

FOX HILL

1017

TO HINTON PARVA, 1¼ MILES (2KM) & BISHOPSTONE, 2 MILES (3KM)

Shepherds Rest

The Liddington

BUS STOPS

BORING WALK ON GRASSY VERGE

M4 MOTORWAY

NOISY, SMELLY WALK OVER BRIDGE

trailblazer

¼ mile

0 ——— 500m

0 APPROX SCALE

25-40 MINS FROM RIDGEWAY FARM (MAP 11)

FOX HILL

25-35 MINS TO TURN OFF B4192 (MAP 9) ——→

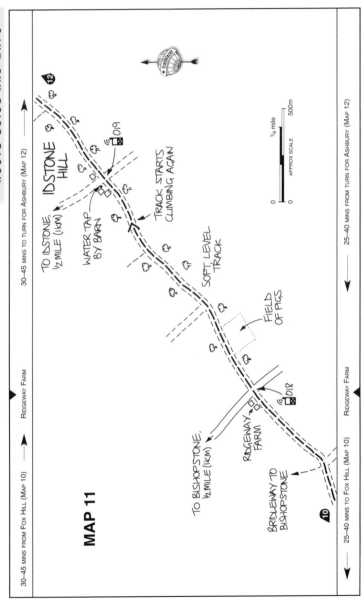

MAP 11

30–45 MINS FROM FOX HILL (MAP 10)

30–45 MINS TO TURN FOR ASHBURY (MAP 12)

RIDGEWAY FARM

TO IDSTONE, ½ MILE (1KM)

IDSTONE HILL

WATER TAP BY BARN

019

TRACK STARTS CLIMBING AGAIN

SOFT LEVEL TRACK

FIELD OF PIGS

018

TO BISHOPSTONE, ½ MILE (1KM)

RIDGEWAY FARM

BRIDLEWAY TO BISHOPSTONE

10

12

¼ mile

APPROX SCALE

0   500m

25–40 MINS TO FOX HILL (MAP 10)

RIDGEWAY FARM

25–40 MINS FROM TURN FOR ASHBURY (MAP 12)

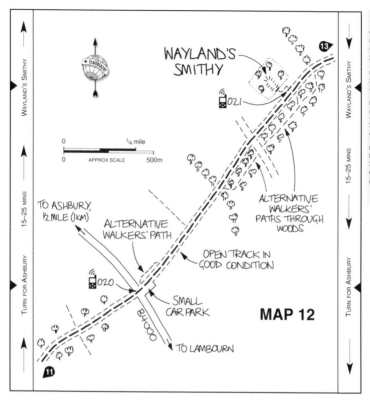

Thamesdown's Nos 47 **bus** service stops here as does RH Transport's X47 service; see pp42-5 for further details.

The only place to stay and eat here is at ***The Rose & Crown Hotel*** (☎ 01793 710222, 🖥 www.roseandcrownashbury.co .uk; 1S/3D/3T; food daily noon-2.15pm & 6.30-9.15pm). This large place occupies a commanding position in the centre of the village. The pub is open lunchtimes and evenings with Arkell's ales served. There is both a bar and a restaurant menu serving a wide range of main courses (£8.50-13.50) such as monkfish curry or venison sausage and mash. The single room is £40 a night and the (en suite) doubles and twins are £60, or £40 for single occupancy. This is a popular place for Ridgeway walkers to stay and they are always made to feel welcome.

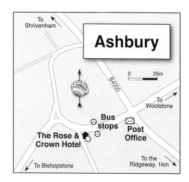

❏ Wayland's Smithy

This is a Neolithic long barrow. It was built in stages but was started around 2800BC as a burial place for members of the important ruling families in this area. The barrow itself is set in a small fenced wood and the entrance passageway that leads to the burial chamber is flanked by four huge sarsen stones. It's not possible to go into the underground chambers but nevertheless it's still an impressive construction when viewed just from the outside.

The name of this long barrow dates from a couple of thousand years after it was built and comes from 'Wayland', the Saxon god of smiths. Apparently he made the shoes for the Uffington White Horse and will even shoe your horse for you if you leave it here, overnight, with some payment – cash only.

Around fifteen minutes further along the closed-in track you will come to a short path on your left for Wayland's Smithy and by this time tall stands of trees will also be lining the track to your right. There is something a little eerie about this place, especially on a misty morning. **Wayland's Smithy** (see box above) isn't, and never really was, a smithy (a blacksmith's/forge).

The village of Woolstone can be reached by taking a left turn down the hill at the next crossroads (Map 13). It's about 1¼ miles/2km to the village.

WOOLSTONE

This is a very small, picturesque village at the foot of the steep Uffington Hill. There are many attractive buildings and the only place to stay and eat is one of the most enchanting buildings of all, *The White Horse* (☎ 01367 820726, 🖳 www.whitehorsewoolstone.co .uk; 3D/1T/1F sleeping up to 6, food Mon-Sat noon-2pm & 6.30-9pm, Sun noon-2pm). It is an attractive 16th-century coaching inn situated in the 'centre' of the village. The pub serves Arkell's ales and, worth noting, it's open all day, every day. They have both a bar and a restaurant menu with main courses costing between £8.50 and £16; the menu includes dishes such as steak and ale pie (£11) or a vegetable risotto also £11.

The comfortable en suite accommodation is in the more modern building next to

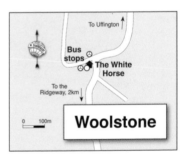

the pub and costs £75 for a double/twin, or £70 for single occupancy; the family room, which is really a suite, can accommodate up to six people and costs £130-140.

RH Transport's X47 **bus** service stops here; see pp42-5 for further details.

The climb up White Horse Hill to Uffington Castle (Map 13) is on a good track but it certainly gets steep towards the top; this is the toughest climb of this section but it doesn't last for long so count yourself lucky.

The National Trust area around this hill contains not only the aforementioned Uffington Castle and Uffington White Horse but also The Manger, a stunning coombe, lined with terraces, best viewed from the White Horse itself,

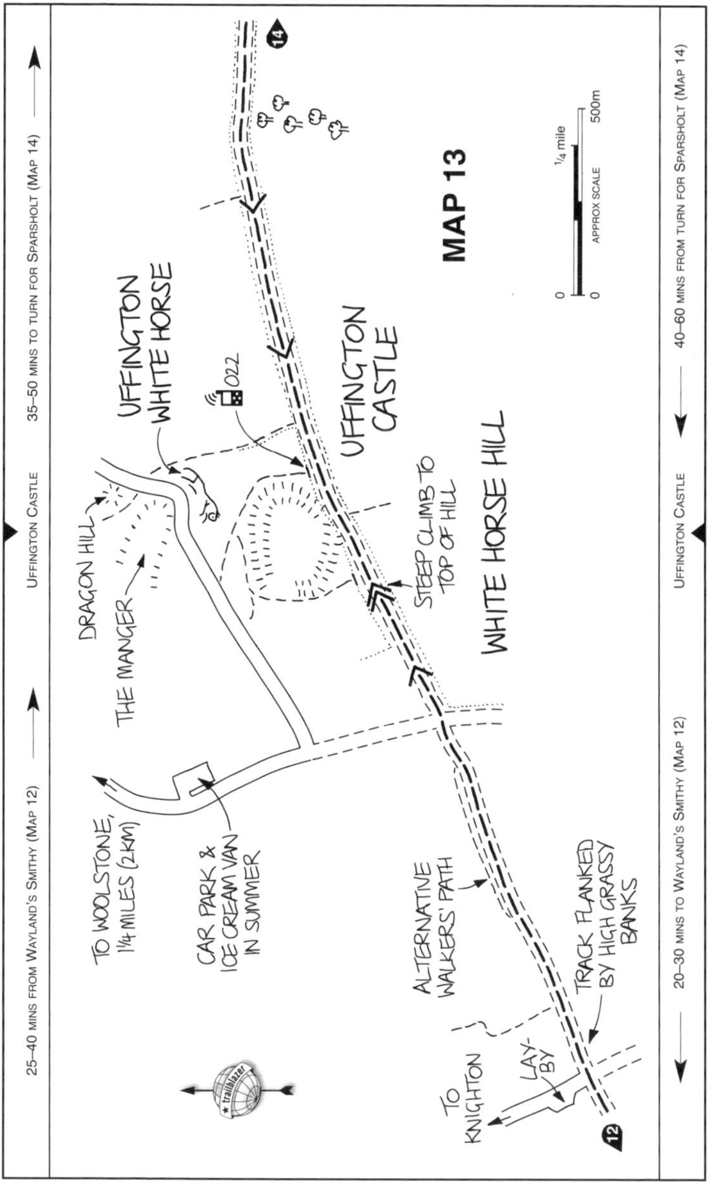

MAP 13

¼ mile

500m

0

APPROX SCALE

25–40 MINS FROM WAYLAND'S SMITHY (MAP 12)

UFFINGTON CASTLE

35–50 MINS TO TURN FOR SPARSHOLT (MAP 14)

20–30 MINS TO WAYLAND'S SMITHY (MAP 12)

UFFINGTON CASTLE

40–60 MINS FROM TURN FOR SPARSHOLT (MAP 14)

UFFINGTON WHITE HORSE

O22

UFFINGTON CASTLE

STEEP CLIMB TO TOP OF HILL

WHITE HORSE HILL

DRAGON HILL

THE MANGER

TO WOOLSTONE, 1¼ MILES (2KM)

CAR PARK & ICE CREAM VAN IN SUMMER

ALTERNATIVE WALKERS' PATH

TRACK FLANKED BY HIGH GRASSY BANKS

TO KNIGHTON

LAY-BY

14

12

and the perfectly formed, flat-topped Dragon Hill, just north of the White Horse, where St George battled with and slayed the dragon.

Uffington Castle is the third of the big Iron Age hill forts you will have passed – the previous two being Barbury Castle and Liddington Castle. The setting is certainly no less dramatic than Barbury's, though it's seven metres lower and only two-thirds its size. The double banks and ditches are still steep and well defined and the views from up here are magnificent.

❏ White horses

The **Uffington White Horse** (see Map 13) is the one that inspired them all. Scientists now think, after much debate, that it was first cut into the hillside around 800BC. It's over 100 metres long and superbly suggests the form of a horse rather than
simply defining its outline. It's still a
mystery how the creators of the horse
could cut it so well, given that the
whole horse is only properly viewable
from around a mile away in the valley.

Without a shadow of a doubt, Uffington White Horse is the best of the lot, but there are various other white horses scattered around the countryside near here. None of them is nearly as ancient and they don't even get close to the fluid beauty of the Uffington horse. By the time you reach this horse you'll have already passed another example at Hackpen Hill (Map 3) that was cut into the hillside in 1838.

The oldest and one of the most visible of all the modern horses is the **Westbury White Horse**. This was cut in 1778 but at some point in the 1950s it was concreted over. The concrete was then painted white. Owing to some unsightly deterioration and discolouration in the concrete, the horse was given another coating of concrete and paint in 1995. The logic was that concrete is easier to maintain. Using that logic maybe we should concrete over the Ridgeway, too? The **Cherhill White Horse** is on a hill of the same name that is south of the A4 near Cherhill village, 3¾ miles/6km west of Avebury. This horse is one of the older ones in the area having been cut into the hillside in 1780. It was fully restored in 2002 and is easily visible from the A4.

There are other **white horses**: between Milk Hill and Walkers Hill, close to the village of Alton Barnes, about 3¾ miles/6km due south of Avebury is a good speci-
men, cut in 1812 and cleaned up in 2002. There is a further example of a well cared for horse near Broad Town on a north-west-facing slope. This horse is about 5km north-west of the Hackpen Hill horse though it's unclear when it was cut – probably in the 1860s. On Pewsey Hill, just south of the village of Pewsey, about 4¼ miles/7km south of Marlborough, is a well-groomed 1937 white horse.

The youngest white horse in the area is on Roundway Hill in Devizes, about 7½ miles/12km south-west of Avebury. It was created for the millennium and is uncommon in that it faces to the right. There was a much older white horse close to here but it has long since disappeared.

There is now a recognised **White Horse Trail** that follows a roughly circular route and visits all the white horses in the area. The trail is around 90 miles/144km long and illustrated guides can be bought from tourist information centres in the area.

For further information visit 🖳 www.wiltshirewhitehorses.org.uk.

Opposite) The wide view from the Uffington White Horse, looking north.

❏ **Morris dancing**
If you hang around the pubs along the Ridgeway for long enough during the summer, you are likely to see some Morris dancing. Essentially the Morris teams are performing traditional country dances and will often be accompanied by musicians. Each group of Morris men has its own particular outfit: embroidered smocks, waistcoats, decorated hats, neckerchiefs and clusters of bells abound. Depending on the dance they might also be waving handkerchiefs or hitting sticks together, sometimes with great force.

It is thought that these dances, often named after the villages where they were originally performed (such as Adderbury, Bampton, Ducklington or Stanton Harcourt), have also been influenced by traditional European dances. It's fairly safe to say that they were performed as long as 500 years ago, though many traditions died out in the 18th and 19th centuries.

The beginning of the 20th century saw a concerted effort to record the dances and music before they disappeared forever and the last 30 years in particular have seen an increased interest in performing the traditions.

Morris groups based in the Ridgeway area include Ridgeway Step Clog, White Horse Morris Men, Liddington Hall and Icknield Way Morris Men, the latter being one of the more prolific. Many of the village pubs along the first half of the Ridgeway are popular venues for Morris dancers including the Rose & Crown at Ashbury, The Bell at Aldworth, the Royal Oak at Bishopstone, and The Greyhound at Letcombe Regis to name a few. For further information visit 💻 www.icknieldwaymorris men.org.uk.

The **Uffington White Horse** lies on the side of the hill to the north of the fort and although it really is spectacular this is certainly not the best place from which to view it. In fact it's very difficult to get a good view of the horse from the ground. Short of hiring a helicopter, the better views are from down in the valley: a steep descent and a very disappointing walk back up. If you don't think you can manage it, don't worry – even from down there the views are frustratingly incomplete. Perhaps remember to drive along the B4507 (the road running parallel to the Ridgeway along here) another time for views of the horse.

The **White Horse Hill area** really is one of the highlights of the Ridgeway trail so do take some time out to relax here and enjoy it. You've also got a fairly long stretch of plodding ahead, so you'll need the energy.

At the next crossroads (Map 14) a sealed road cuts across the Ridgeway. Turn left for Kingston Lisle (and RH Transport Service's **bus** No 67; see pp42-5 for further details) or right for Seven Barrows, a group of, well, yes, seven barrows.

After you descend Kingston Hill you will reach a crossroads that you should head straight across. It's also at this crossroads that you need to turn right to reach the B&B and camping at Down Barn Farm, about half a mile/1km away.

(**Opposite**) **Top**: Wayland's Smithy (see p110) is a Neolithic long barrow which became associated with Wayland, the Saxon god of smiths, about 2000 years after it was constructed. It is said that the shoes for the Uffington White Horse were made here. **Bottom**: On the path to Wayland's Smithy.

DOWN BARN FARM   [MAP 14]

For a unique experience you might like to stay at *Down Barn Farm* (☎ 01367 820272, mob ☎ 0779 983 3115, 🖳 pendomeffect @aol.com; 1D/2T). This place really is out on its own, set on a grassland farm that rears organic pigs and cattle. But don't worry about them, they won't intrude on the beautiful sense of peace and quiet that this isolated location promotes. The owner can prepare evening meals if given notice (£15-20 per person for three courses), which is just as well as the next nearest place to eat is a good couple of miles away.

Indoor accommodation costs £60-75 for a double/twin room or £40 if you're on your own. Outdoors there are several pitches for **campers** at £5 per person that are available all year, but it is exposed up here. Campers can use the toilet and a shower costs £3.

Alternatively, if you want to head to the Star Inn at Sparsholt, you could turn left here for the 1¹/₂-mile/2.5km walk to the village. Follow the track to the main road, turn right onto the road and follow it for 500m before turning left into the quiet village of Sparsholt.

SPARSHOLT   [off MAP 14]

The *Star Inn* (☎ 01235 751539, 🖳 www .starinn-sparsholt.co.uk; 2D/4T/2F, food Mon 6.30-9.30pm, Tue-Sat noon-2.30pm & 6.30-9.30pm, Sun noon-2.30pm, Sun evening residents only) is an inviting 17th-century country inn with en suite accommodation in a converted barn. During the week the bar is open 12.30-2.30pm & 6-11pm, but on Saturdays it's open noon-4.30pm & 6pm-midnight and Sunday noon-4.30pm & 6.30-11pm. They have plenty of filling dishes on their menu to satisfy the hungry walker with an emphasis on seasonal produce. A selection of sirloin, rump and ribeye steaks range from £8.95 to £11.95 and they have a very popular beer-battered fish & chips for £6.95. This well-kept accommodation starts at £70 for a double or twin, £50 for single occupancy and £80-90 for a family room.

There is no shop or post office in the village, but RH Transport's No 67 and X47 stop here; see pp42-5 for further details.

On your way up Hackpen Hill the valley drops away very steeply to the north giving you excellent views of the **Devil's Punchbowl** (Map 15). You can get closer to the punchbowl by taking the path that branches left from the track where there is a stile structure marking the path junction. Although this should be a path, it seems to run straight through a planted field with no visible trail.

You'll soon cross the road junction (Map 16) that has a left turn down to Letcombe Bassett and further on there is a track on the left that joins up with the road; using either of these turnings Letcombe Bassett is about half a mile (1km). You could also use these to walk to Wantage but it'd probably be better to wait for the next road junction for that. Shortly ahead there is a path on the left – yet another opportunity to head down to Letcombe Bassett.

It was just a little further on from here that, several years ago, I passed a nun on the track. She had walked from St Mary's Convent in Wantage, around three miles away. You might have some unlikely encounters on the Ridgeway – owls or deer, for instance, but I think that meeting a nun up here must now be added to the list. *(cont'd on p118)*

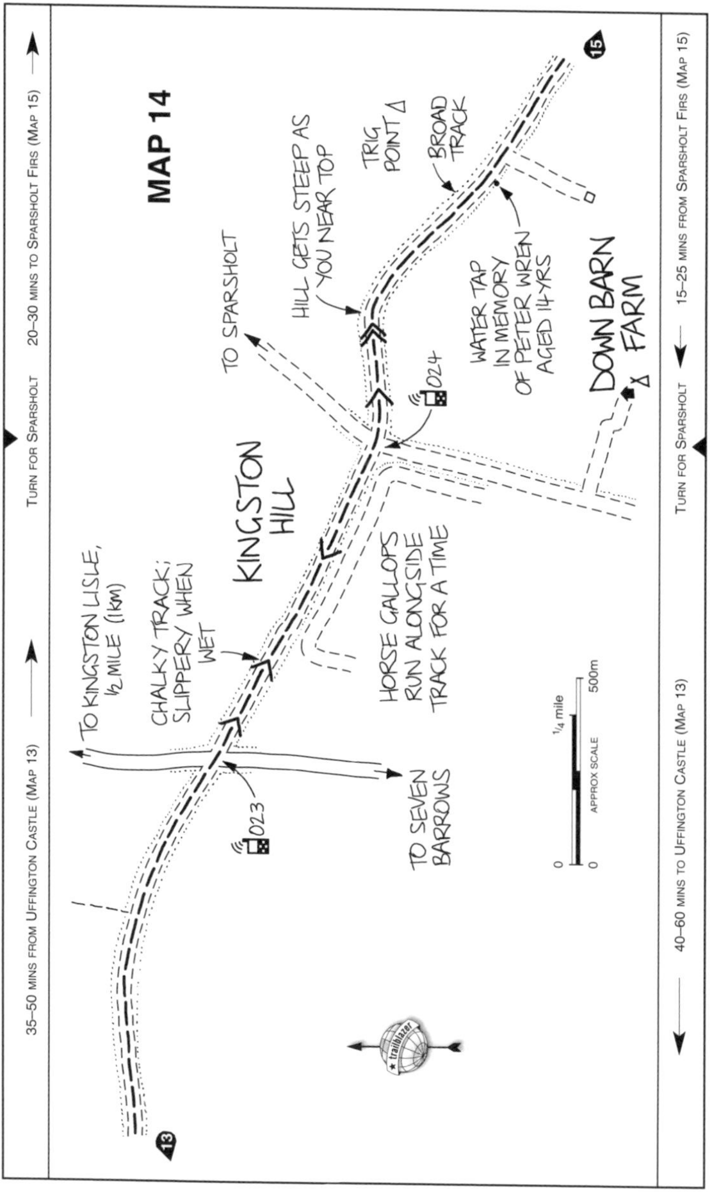
MAP 14
35–50 mins from Uffington Castle (Map 13)
Turn for Sparsholt
20–30 mins to Sparsholt Firs (Map 15)
40–60 mins to Uffington Castle (Map 13)
Turn for Sparsholt
15–25 mins from Sparsholt Firs (Map 15)
13
15
TO KINGSTON LISLE, ½ MILE (1KM)
CHALKY TRACK; SLIPPERY WHEN WET
023
TO SEVEN BARROWS
KINGSTON HILL
HORSE GALLOPS RUN ALONGSIDE TRACK FOR A TIME
TO SPARSHOLT
024
HILL GETS STEEP AS YOU NEAR TOP
TRIG POINT
BROAD TRACK
WATER TAP IN MEMORY OF PETER WREN AGED 14YRS
DOWN BARN FARM
APPROX SCALE
¼ mile
500m
0
0
trailblazer

ROUTE GUIDE AND MAPS

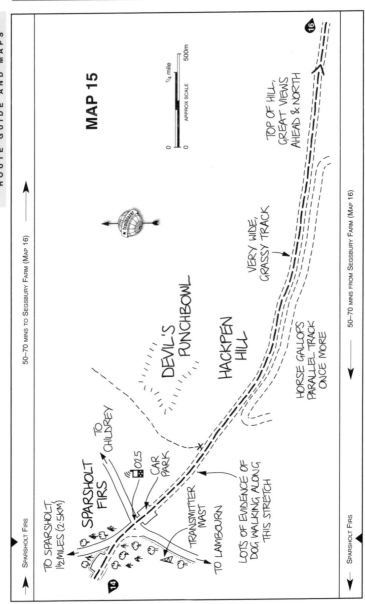

MAP 15

50–70 MINS TO SEGSBURY FARM (MAP 16)

SPARSHOLT FIRS

APPROX SCALE

0 ¼ mile
0 500m

TOP OF HILL,
GREAT VIEWS
AHEAD & NORTH

VERY WIDE,
GRASSY TRACK

DEVIL'S
PUNCHBOWL

HACKPEN
HILL

HORSE GALLOPS
PARALLEL TRACK
ONCE MORE

50–70 MINS FROM SEGSBURY FARM (MAP 16)

SPARSHOLT FIRS

TO SPARSHOLT
1½ MILES (2.5KM)

SPARSHOLT
FIRS

TO
CHILDREY

015

CAR
PARK

TRANSMITTER
MAST

TO LAMBOURN

LOTS OF EVIDENCE OF
DOG WALKING ALONG
THIS STRETCH

14

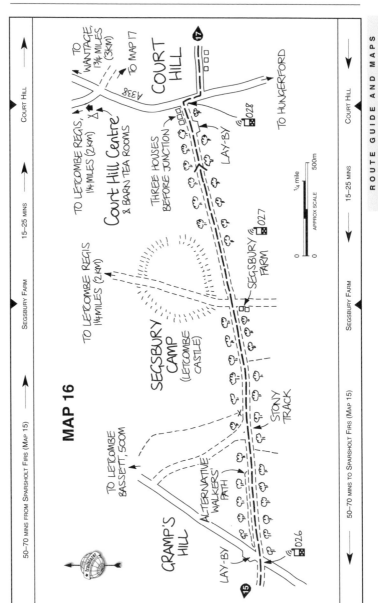

MAP 16

TO LETCOMBE BASSETT, 500M

CRAMP'S HILL

LAY-BY

D26

ALTERNATIVE WALKERS' PATH

STONY TRACK

SEGSBURY CAMP (LETCOMBE CASTLE)

TO LETCOMBE REGIS 1¼ MILES (2KM)

SEGSBURY FARM

027

TO LETCOMBE REGIS, 1¼ MILES (2KM)

Court Hill Centre & BARN TEA ROOMS

THREE HOUSES BEFORE JUNCTION

TO WANTAGE, 1¾ MILES (3KM)

TO MAP 17

A338

COURT HILL

17

LAY-BY

028

TO HUNGERFORD

¼ mile

APPROX SCALE

0   500m

50–70 MINS FROM SPARSHOLT FIRS (MAP 15)

SEGSBURY FARM

15–25 MINS

COURT HILL

50–70 MINS TO SPARSHOLT FIRS (MAP 15)

SEGSBURY FARM

15–25 MINS

COURT HILL

15

(cont'd from p114) On reaching **Segsbury Farm** (on your right), there is a 100-metre track (to the left) up to **Segsbury Camp**: this is also called Letcombe Castle. It's more than double the size of Barbury Castle but far less popular; you'll usually have the place to yourself. Like Barbury Castle, this was an Iron Age hill fort and evidence of roundhouses were found during excavations in the 1990s.

It's also this track that you should take if you want to visit Letcombe Regis. This isn't the only way to the village – you could follow the road past the Court Hill Centre – but it's the most convenient. You'll also have the bonus of passing through Segsbury Camp on your way. From the junction with the Ridgeway, it's about 1¼ miles/2km to the centre of the village.

LETCOMBE REGIS

This village, another in the chain of 'spring line' settlements below the Downs, dates back well over a thousand years although the 'Regis' part of the name was only added during the reign of Richard II (1377-99). However, the regal connections date from well before then as it was the property of King Stephen in the 12th century and there was a royal hunting lodge here in the 13th and 14th centuries.

The oldest remaining building in the village is the church, St Andrew's, parts of which date back to the 12th century though some of the houses don't look as if they are a great deal younger.

Letcombe Regis and its neighbour, Letcombe Bassett, are famous for the watercress beds that covered the land between them though 'Regis' is also home to four racing stables, which generate considerably more income.

There are no shops or services but nevertheless it would make a convenient and enjoyable overnight stop. The No 67 **bus**, operated by RH Transport, passes through on its route between Wantage and Faringdon and the X47 between Wantage and Swindon; see pp42-5 for further details.

Where to stay and eat

The Greyhound Inn (☎ 01235 771093; 2S/1D or T/1T/2F, food daily noon-2.30pm, Tue-Sat 6-9pm) is a Georgian-style, traditional country inn serving Greene King ales in a friendly atmosphere. The bar is open at

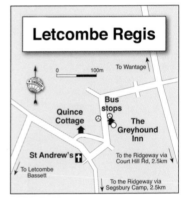

lunchtimes and evenings only Mon-Thu, but all day on Fri, Sat & Sun. The small but busy dining area provides sizable dishes from a menu focused on British food. You are advised to make a reservation if you want to eat here in the evening as this is a very popular place. The two single rooms and twin room share a bathroom but the other rooms have en suite facilities. They charge £30 per person including a full English breakfast.

Nearby is *Quince Cottage* (☎ 01235 763652, 🖳 bodens@supanet.com; 1T or F, private bathroom), a charming 18th-century thatched cottage that charges from £65 (£35 if you're on your own). Packed lunches (£3) are available if requested in advance. This is a friendly place and is deservedly popular with walkers: book well ahead!

Soon after here, at the foot of **Court Hill**, the Ridgeway crosses the main A338 road coming from Wantage in the north and Hungerford in the south. Turn left for Wantage – a town with plenty of shops, banks and other services two miles/3.5km away, and also for Court Hill Centre, about 500 metres along the road.

Court Hill Centre (☎ 01235 760253, 🖥 www.courthill.org.uk; 60 beds) was previously the *Ridgeway Youth Hostel*. It's virtually on the Ridgeway and has accommodation in a **bunkhouse**: there are family and dormitory rooms at £17 per night (£13 for under 18s). They also have two **tipis** (Mar-Sep only) each of which costs £70 per night and sleeps 5/6. You need to bring your own bedding if staying in a tipi, but you do have access to all the facilities. A limited number of **camping pitches** (£7.50 per night, £5.50 for under 18s) are also available. Breakfast, from £5, and an evening meal, from £8.50, are available as are packed lunches but all must be ordered in advance. There is a small food shop, open during hostel hours, and a self-catering kitchen. The hostel also has limited WiFi access for anyone with a computer.

If you're just passing by and not staying the night, you could always stop off at the *Barn Tea Rooms* (Thu-Mon 10.30am-5pm) where you'll find teas, coffees and cold drinks along with cakes, light lunches and ice-creams.

COURT HILL TO GORING   [MAPS 16-25]

Overview

This is an easy **14-mile/22.7km** section. From Court Hill up to the crossing of the A34 road, the path is level, broad, grassy and exposed, similar to what you've become used to from the previous stages. After the A34 there is more tree cover and the path starts to undulate, though it hardly ever gets steep. The Ridgeway then gradually descends into the small town of Streatley, on the west bank of the river Thames, before crossing into Goring on the opposite bank.

Route

Where the Ridgeway arrives at the A338 (Map 16) to Wantage you need to make a right turn and follow it for all of a minute before turning left, back onto the track. The track is sealed for a while now and you'll pass several houses on your right before reaching Whitehouse Farm (Map 17) on the left; the tarmac fades to soft grass or mud, depending on the weather conditions. When you arrive at the T-junction, you'll have another chance to visit Court Hill Centre by turning left.

After you have crossed the B4494 and rejoined the broad grassy track, you will come to a large **monument**, on your right. It consists of a marble column set on a large square base with steps on all sides. At the top of the column is a cross. It is in memory of Baron Wantage (1832-1901) who, amongst other things, expanded the nearby Lockinge estate.

A further mile down the track, but this time on the left, you will see a **reservoir** (Map 18). It's a low, square red-brick structure, surrounded by trees and fenced in. The walking along here is on the same broad grassy track you have been on for some time and it will be with you for a while yet. *(cont'd on p123)*

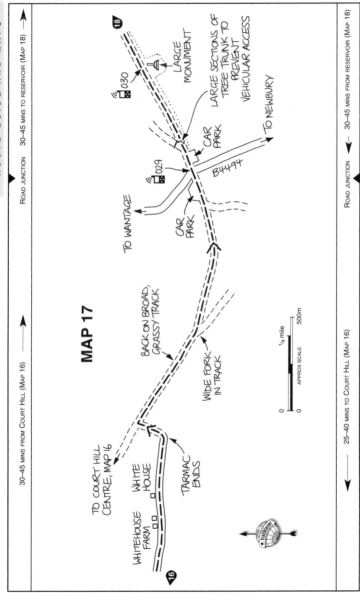

MAP 17

LARGE SECTIONS OF TREE TRUNK TO PREVENT VEHICULAR ACCESS

LARGE MONUMENT

030

TO NEWBURY

CAR PARK

B4494

029

TO WANTAGE

CAR PARK

BACK ON BROAD, GRASSY TRACK

WIDE FORK IN TRACK

¼ mile

500m

APPROX SCALE

TO COURT HILL CENTRE, MAP 16

WHITE HOUSE

WHITEHOUSE FARM

TARMAC ENDS

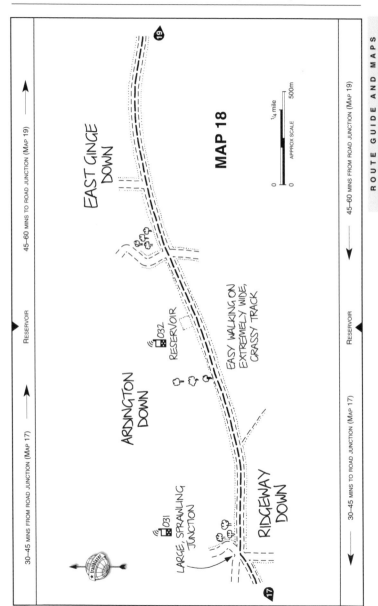

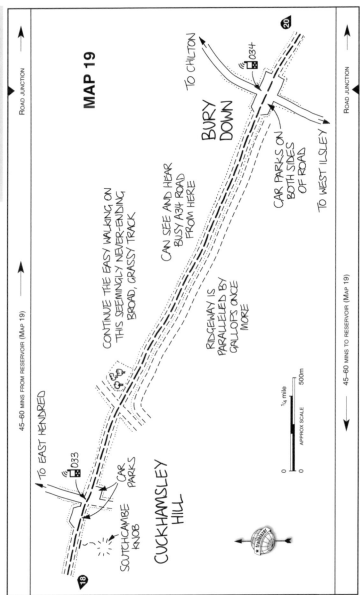

MAP 19

ROAD JUNCTION

45–60 MINS FROM RESERVOIR (MAP 19)

TO CHILTON

A34

BURY DOWN

CAR PARKS ON BOTH SIDES OF ROAD

TO WEST ILSLEY

20

CAN SEE AND HEAR BUSY A34 ROAD FROM HERE

CONTINUE THE EASY WALKING ON THIS SEEMINGLY NEVER-ENDING BROAD, GRASSY TRACK

RIDGEWAY IS PARALLELED BY GALLOPS ONCE MORE

TO EAST HENDRED

033

CAR PARKS

SOUTHCAMBE KNOB

CUCKHAMSLEY HILL

18

¼ mile

500m

APPROX SCALE

0

0

trailblazer

(cont'd from p119) Around 20 minutes after passing the reservoir you will come to a sealed road crossing (Map 19) the Ridgeway. This is the road to East Hendred, 2½ miles/4km to the north.

After this junction the Ridgeway is joined by gallops on the right that will stick with the track until the next road junction at the **Bury Down** car parks – the road here goes north to Chilton and south to West Ilsley, about one mile away. The Harwell International Business Centre is clearly visible just over a mile to the north from here. It's perhaps as far back as Swindon since something on this scale has been visible. You'll also start to hear the noise of the A34 along this stretch.

When you arrive at the A34 junction (Map 20) you can either use the tunnel underneath or try to cross it. There are paths catering to both these options but it makes sense to use the subway. The track down to it drops steeply and bends to the right then the left. Inside the tunnel, on the right side, are some murals depicting traditional historical scenes from the area and on both sides various amateur graffiti. The floor is littered with empty beer cans and other

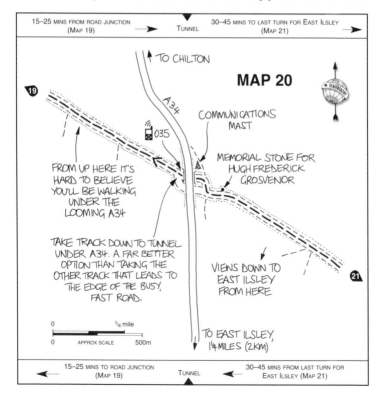

15–25 MINS FROM ROAD JUNCTION (MAP 19) → ▼ TUNNEL → 30–45 MINS TO LAST TURN FOR EAST ILSLEY (MAP 21) →

TO CHILTON

MAP 20

trailblazer

A34

COMMUNICATIONS MAST

035

MEMORIAL STONE FOR HUGH FREDERICK GROSVENOR

FROM UP HERE IT'S HARD TO BELIEVE YOU'LL BE WALKING UNDER THE LOOMING A34

TAKE TRACK DOWN TO TUNNEL UNDER A34. A FAR BETTER OPTION THAN TAKING THE OTHER TRACK THAT LEADS TO THE EDGE OF THE BUSY, FAST ROAD.

VIEWS DOWN TO EAST ILSLEY FROM HERE

0 ¼ mile
0 APPROX SCALE 500m

TO EAST ILSLEY, 1¼ MILES (2KM)

ROUTE GUIDE AND MAPS

waste so although people have obviously made an effort with the murals, it's not the kind of place that particularly invites you to linger for a closer look.

Just a few minutes after the tunnel, on the left of the track, almost enclosed by the shrubbery, is a **stone memorial** inscribed with the name of Hugh Frederick Grosvenor, a 2nd Lieutenant in the Lifeguards who was killed here in an armoured car accident on 9 April, 1947. He was aged just nineteen.

Look to the south occasionally and soon you'll get a glimpse of East Ilsley – a very welcome sight if you started at the Shepherds Rest pub earlier in the day. There is still the best part of two miles to go, however. These follow the same broad grassy track that has by now become very familiar.

There are four possible ways down into **East Ilsley** from the Ridgeway and they are all less than a mile apart. There's a **water tap** and trough on the path between the second and third turns. If you're visiting the village, the second way is the probably best choice – it's the most direct with easy walking. However, as the last two leave the Ridgeway that bit later, they give you slightly more of a head-start when you pick it up again. It doesn't really matter though – leaving by any of the tracks you'll have to walk about 1 mile/1.5km into the village.

EAST ILSLEY

The village of East Ilsley is famous as the venue for huge sheep markets from the 17th century onwards. At their peak, drovers would descend on the town filling it with up to 70,000 sheep.

The last market was in 1934 and since then the village has been a lot quieter. Today it's an attractive-enough place with three pubs, all of which provide food and accommodation, and this makes it a convenient place to break your journey along the Ridgeway. However, at the time of writing there was no shop or post office in the village.

Buses serve Newbury, Chievely and Compton on a circular route (Newbury Buses Nos 6 & 9, Mon-Sat); see pp42-5 for further details.

Where to stay and eat

The *Crown & Horns* (☎ 01635 281545; 6D/4T, food Mon-Sat noon-2.30pm & 6-9.30pm, Sun noon-2.30pm & 6-9pm) is a free-house with a cosy interior and a shady garden. It's always popular with walkers. The pub is open all day and has separate dining areas. The walls in the bar are covered with horse-racing memorabilia (see box p96) and in the colder months there is a welcoming open fire to sit beside. The

food here is recommended with main dishes such as paella or a pan-fried pork chop with a mushroom and tomato sauce costing from £8 to £13. To wash it down they serve Brakspear's and Fuller's ales and various guest beers. The accommodation is in well-kept en suite rooms and they charge £75, or £65 for single occupancy including breakfast.

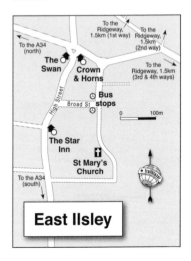

East Ilsley

Opposite is *The Swan* (☎ 01635 281238, 🖳 www.theswaneastilsley.co.uk; 5D en suite, food Mon-Sat noon-8.45pm, Sun noon-2.30pm), a 16th-century coaching inn in the centre of the village with a pleasant garden that is open all day. From lunchtime until 6pm they serve lunch and 'light-bites' and after 6pm more substantial fare is on offer. Steak, ale and mushroom pie, a Thai green curry or various pasta dishes are all on the menu with main courses ranging from £6.95 to £16.95. B&B here costs £70, or £65 if you are on your own.

Just a couple of minutes away, up the High St, is *The Star Inn*. At the time of writing, this former 15th-century inn was undergoing a complete renovation, though it should be open again by early 2009 adding another food and accommodation option for visitors to the village.

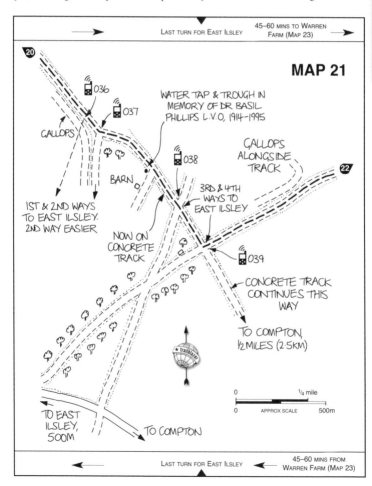

MAP 21

LAST TURN FOR EAST ILSLEY

45–60 MINS TO WARREN FARM (MAP 23)

20

036
037

GALLOPS

WATER TAP & TROUGH IN MEMORY OF DR BASIL PHILLIPS L.V.O, 1914–1995

038

GALLOPS ALONGSIDE TRACK

22

BARN

3RD & 4TH WAYS TO EAST ILSLEY

1ST & 2ND WAYS TO EAST ILSLEY. 2ND WAY EASIER

NOW ON CONCRETE TRACK

039

CONCRETE TRACK CONTINUES THIS WAY

TO COMPTON, ½ MILES (2·5KM)

0   ¼ mile
0   APPROX SCALE   500m

TO EAST ILSLEY, 500M

TO COMPTON

LAST TURN FOR EAST ILSLEY

45–60 MINS FROM WARREN FARM (MAP 23)

We start the Ridgeway again at the crossroads where the last of the four paths to East Ilsley turns off. If you want to go to Compton, 1½ miles/2.5km, it's best to leave the Ridgeway at this point.

COMPTON

The Saxon name given to this village means 'Coombe Town', or, 'town in the valley', but there is evidence of Bronze and Iron Age settlement in the area even before the Saxons were here. Plenty of Roman artefacts, coins in particular, have been found near Compton.

There is a **shop** (☎ 01635 578682; Mon, Tue, Thu & Fri 7am-5.30pm, Wed & Sat 7.30am-6pm, Sun 8-10.30am) in the village that stocks a surprisingly large range of groceries; it also contains the local **post office** (Mon-Fri 9.30am-5pm, Sat 9.30am-12.30pm).

The *Compton Swan* (☎ 01635 579400, 🖳 www.comptonswan.co.uk; 5D/1T, food Mon-Sat noon-10pm, Sun noon-3pm) is a large, white building on the main road through the village. In April 2006 this place was severely damaged by a fire. After major repairs and renovations it reopened in September 2008. It's a very popular place to eat and is often busy with a mixture of locals and visitors. If you are after a quick lunch they have 'doorstep' sandwiches for £5.25 and jacket potatoes for £5.75. Main courses such as pork cutlets with wild mushroom risotto and creamy tarragon sauce (£14.75) and ratatouille tartlet (£9.95) are on offer at lunchtimes and in the evenings. The stylishly furnished en suite accommodation is £85 for a large double/twin or £75 for a standard-sized room. Be sure to book ahead if you want to stay here.

From here you can take a **bus** (Newbury Buses' No 6 or 9, Mon-Sat) to Newbury, Chievely and East Ilsley; see pp42-5 for further details.

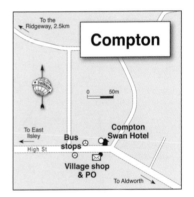

To the Ridgeway, 2.5km

Compton

0   50m

To East Ilsley

Bus stops

High St

Compton Swan Hotel

Village shop & PO

To Aldworth

Follow the broad grass track as it starts a slow descent, paralleled on the left by gallops. To a large extent, this is the last of the really exposed and lonely sections of the Ridgeway. The change isn't abrupt, but over the next few miles it will become obvious.

After passing the bridleway from Compton that joins the track from the right, you will cross a **concrete bridge** (Map 22). This takes you over the old, and dismantled, railway that was once the Didcot, Newbury and Southampton Junction Railway. It's been closed since 1962 and the strip where the track once lay is now covered by bushes and trees. The section that you cross lies between the old stations of Churn and Compton. This part of the line was opened in 1882 and owing to its course through remote countryside was given the nickname of the 'Desert Line'.

When you arrive at the slightly **staggered crossroads**, at which the left turning heads north to the wonderfully named Aston Tirrold while the right turning heads for the less enticing Greyladies, you should continue straight

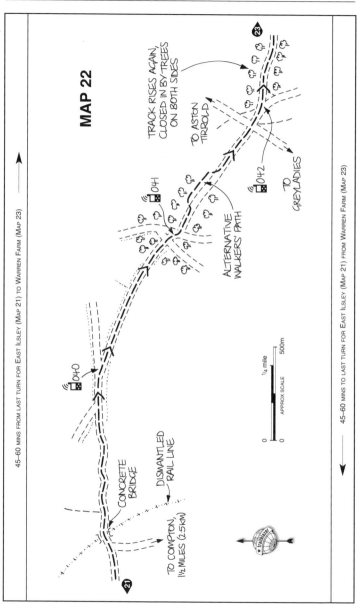

MAP 22

TRACK RISES AGAIN, CLOSED IN BY TREES ON BOTH SIDES

TO ASTON TIRROLD

TO GREYLADIES

042

040

040

ALTERNATIVE WALKERS' PATH

CONCRETE BRIDGE

DISMANTLED RAIL LINE

TO COMPTON, 1½ MILES (2.5KM)

¼ mile

APPROX SCALE

0   500m

0

Trailblazer

ahead for a short distance until the track forks. Make sure you are not day-dreaming when you reach here as you need to take the less obvious option, a turn to the left. It's an ascending flinty track, closed in by trees, which bends left after about 200m. It is signposted but if you're not paying attention the natural tendency is to carry straight on.

Just after you pass **Warren Farm** (Map 23), on your left, there is a path leading off right, down a 1¼ mile/2km track to Aldworth.

ALDWORTH

The main reason why you might like to detour to this quiet village is to visit *The Bell* (☎ 01635 578272; food Tue-Sat 11am-2.30pm & 6-9pm, Sun noon-2.30pm & 7-9pm). No doubt about it, this is a real country pub. The building dates back to the 15th century and the pub has been in the same family for over 200 years. Its high regard amongst real ale drinkers means that it's often very busy despite its quiet location. Take note that the pub is closed in the afternoons (3-6pm) and on Mondays, except Bank Holidays. Filled rolls (£2.60) and ploughmans (£5-6) are served to go with a choice of varied and interesting real ales and farmhouse cider. By the way, in case you need any more encouragement, it's been voted CAMRA (see box pp16-17) 'National Pub of the Year' twice, won the regional award various times and even won an award for being 'the most unspoilt pub in England'.

There is no shop, post office or public transport here but if needs be you can stay at the comfortable and quiet *Fieldview Cottage* (☎ 01635 578964, 🖥 www.fieldviewcottage.co.uk; 1S/1D/1T, all with private bathroom). The friendly couple who own this place charge £60-70 for the double/twin rooms and £35 for the single.

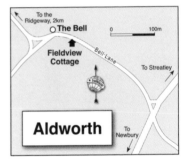

When you arrive at the sealed road by **Post Box Cottage** (Map 23) you have reached the beginning of a new type of Ridgeway. No more windswept wanderings up on grassy tracks 20 metres wide without a building in sight. For the next few miles at least, things are positively urban. You might welcome it after the previous stages, but it certainly lacks a lot of the wild feel. It's picturesque along this road, with each house having its own individuality; this helps to take your mind off the long walk on the tarmac.

The final sure symbol that you are about to leave all the tranquillity behind is the 30mph speed limit sign on the left of the road. This is, as far as I can remember, the first speed limit sign on the Ridgeway. From here on, there are houses on both sides of the road and just 100m further on you'll come to a T-junction where you join the A417 into the centre of Streatley.

(Opposite) Top: Walking through fields of crops just before the harvest, like this one near Nuffield, can prove hard going. **Bottom**: An unusual twin-railway viaduct with diagonally-laid brickwork (see p134) crosses the River Thames between South and North Stoke.

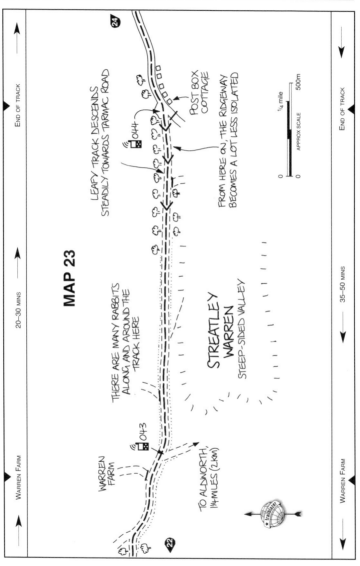

MAP 23

END OF TRACK

WARREN FARM

20–30 MINS

THERE ARE MANY RABBITS ALONG AND AROUND THE TRACK HERE

WARREN FARM

042 043

TO ALDWORTH, 1¼ MILES (2 km)

STREATLEY WARREN
STEEP-SIDED VALLEY

LEAFY TRACK DESCENDS STEADILY TOWARDS TARMAC ROAD

044

POST BOX COTTAGE

FROM HERE ON, THE RIDGEWAY BECOMES A LOT LESS ISOLATED

¼ mile

APPROX SCALE

0   500m

END OF TRACK

35–50 MINS

WARREN FARM

trailblazer

(Opposite) Top: You'll probably see more sheep than people on the Downs between Court Hill and East Ilsley. **Bottom**: The Boathouse pub in Wallingford (see p140) temporarily loses its waterside patio to the River Thames when it floods.

STREATLEY   [MAP 24]

This West Berkshire village is now very much smaller than its neighbour, Goring (see below), across the river in Oxfordshire, but historically it was the larger of the two. Both places were mentioned in the Domesday Book with Streatley being valued higher than its neighbour. Even up until the early 19th century it was larger owing to its location on the road to Reading.

For shops, restaurants and other services you should head across the bridge to Goring, just a couple of minutes' walk away. Two **bus** services, Thames Travel's No 132 (Goring to Pangbourne and Reading) and Heyfordian's Nos 134 & 135 (Wallingford to Goring), stop here; see pp42-5 for further details.

Where to stay, eat and drink

Streatley Youth Hostel (☎ 0845 371 9044, 🖥 www.yhastreatley.org.uk; 48 beds) is the main reason to stay here, rather than in Goring. The hostel is in a large white, Victorian house, just off the road. They provide cooked meals and packed lunches that you'll need to pre-order, and have a self-catering kitchen. It's £17.95 per night in a dormitory; family rooms range from £32 to £87.50 per night. Streatley will only save your booked bed until 6pm so it's worth phoning ahead to let them know if you're going to arrive later.

Other accommodation options include *The Bull* (☎ 01491 872392; 6D, food Mon-Sat noon-2pm & 6.30-9pm, Sun noon-2pm & 7-8.30pm), a 15th-century former coaching inn where the spacious bar, closed 3-6pm, has a relaxed atmosphere. The restaurant here serves a wide variety of food that gets consistently good reviews. The Bull Pie for £8.95 is recommended and they also have vegetarian options, such as butternut bake with spinach, cheese sauce, white beans and pesto crumble (£10.95). The accommodation is in a separate building, all rooms are en suite and cost £70, including breakfast, with no discount for single occupancy.

There is also a B&B at *3 Icknield Cottages* (☎ 01491 875152; 1S private bathroom); it has one single room for £30, which is very good value if you are walking on your own, and a good location too. Packed lunches are available on request.

Just before arriving in Goring is *The Swan* (Map 25; ☎ 01491 878800, 🖥 www .swanatstreatley.co.uk; 9S/36D or T, all en suite, food daily noon-2.30pm & 7-10pm), an up-market riverside pub/restaurant/hotel. This place is right on the bank of the Thames and boasts a spacious riverside terrace: an ideal spot for a break during a long day of walking. The bar menu (available 10am-10pm) includes a range of sandwiches from £5.95 and dishes such as roasted monkfish tail for £13.95. In the afternoon (daily 3-6pm) they serve a traditional cream tea (£7.50) or a full tea including sandwiches and cakes for £13.95. A three-course Sunday lunch is £22.95.

Accommodation here costs around £125 per night for two sharing and around £95 for a single room; this includes a full English breakfast.

Just a short walk across the double-span bridge from the village of Streatley is the town of Goring where you'll find pretty much everything you could need.

GORING   [MAP 25]

After the Great Western Railway came through here in 1840, the town started to grow larger than its neighbour, Streatley. This growth has continued up to the present day resulting in nearly all the shops, restaurants and services being located on this side of the river.

Services

There's a Lloyds TSB and a HSBC **bank** in the High St, but only HSBC has an ATM.

On the High St you'll also find a **chemist** (Mon-Fri 9am-5.30pm, Sat 9am-5pm), **newsagent** (Mon-Sat 6am-10pm, Sun 7am-10pm) which sells most groceries and also houses the **post office** (Mon-Fri

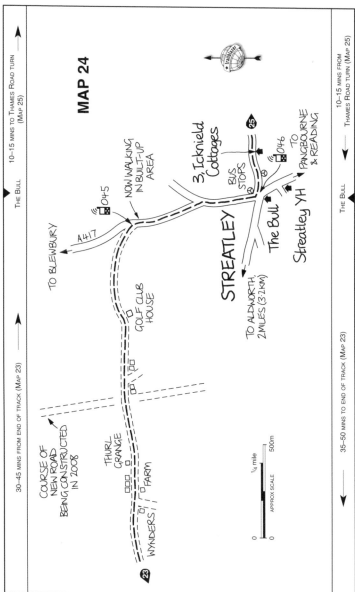

MAP 24

◄ TO BLEWBURY

A417

NOW WALKING IN BUILT-UP AREA

3 Icknield Cottages

045

046

BUS STOPS

STREATLEY

GOLF CLUB HOUSE

The Bull

Streatley YH

TO ALDWORTH, 2 MILES (3.2KM)

TO PANGBOURNE & READING

25

COURSE OF NEW ROAD BEING CONSTRUCTED IN 2008

THURL GRANGE

WYNDERS FARM

23

¼ mile

500m

0

0

APPROX SCALE

9am-5.30pm (closed 1-2pm), Sat 9am-12.30pm) and a **grocery** (Mon-Fri 9am-5pm, Sat 9am-4pm) which has an interesting selection of locally produced food. The **library** (Mon 9.30am-12.30pm, Tue 9.30am-12.30pm & 2-7pm, Thu & Fri 9.30am-12.30pm & 2-5pm, Sat 9.30am-1pm) has free **internet** access and **tourist information** (Mon-Sat 10am-noon) is available from the office on Station Rd.

There are **buses** from the railway station to Wallingford via South Stoke and North Stoke (Heyfordian's Nos 134 & 135) and also to Pangbourne and Reading on Thames Travel's No 132; see pp42-5 for further details. See box p39 for details of rail services to Goring & Streatley.

There is a **taxi** firm in the town called Golden Taxis (☎ 01491 871111) or you could try Pangbourne Taxis (☎ 01491 671979). Both of these services need to be booked in advance.

Where to stay

There are two recommended B&Bs: the first is *Melrose Cottage* (☎ 01491 873040, ✉ rosemary@howarth08.wanadoo.co.uk; 2T, shared bathroom), a 10-minute walk from the town centre. Twins here are £50 and single occupancy costs £30. Walk straight up Wallingford Rd, looking out for Milldown Rd on your right, but be careful not to confuse this with Milldown Avenue, also on your right. The B&B is pretty much at the far end of the road, again on your right.

The other B&B is *North View House* (☎ 01491 872184, ✉ isobel@goring-on-thames.freeserve.co.uk; 1D/1T, D or F/1T, shared bathroom), located right at the end of Farm Rd, just a few minutes' walk from the town centre. Prices here are £55, £30 for single occupancy and £70 for three in the larger room. The generous breakfasts will certainly set you up for a day of walking. They have a dog and two cats and welcome guests with dogs.

You can also stay at one of the inns in town such as *Miller of Mansfield* (☎ 01491 872829, ✉ www.millerofmansfield.com; 10D/1T). This lovely 18th-century building, situated right in the town centre, has a collection of striking, individually styled en

suite rooms ranging from £110-175 (single occupancy around £85).

The John Barleycorn (☎ 01491 872509, ✉ www.thejohnbarleycornpub.co.uk; 3D) is just two minutes' walk from the centre. The en suite accommodation in this place was refurbished in 2008. Very comfortable, modern doubles cost from £75, or £65 for single occupancy.

Where to eat and drink

If you're in one of the inns enjoying a drink anyway, you could try eating there. *Miller of Mansfield* (see left column; food daily noon-9.30pm) has a bar that is open all day and serves bar meals from £5.95 to £7.95, or platters to share for £11.95. Their interesting menu comprises dishes from all over Europe. They have a separate restaurant which has an equally varied menu including roast guinea fowl (£12.95) or Cornish scallops (£8.95). A three-course set menu (£19.95) is available at lunchtimes Mon-Sat and in the evenings Sun-Thu.

The John Barleycorn (see above; food Mon-Sat noon-2.30pm & 5-9pm, Sun noon-3pm), has a more traditional-style lunch menu with soup and bread (£4.25), and pork and apple casserole (£6.95). The evening menu includes gammon steak (£9.75) or toad-in-the-hole for £7.95.

One minute further along the road is the *Catherine Wheel* (☎ 01491 872379; food daily noon-2pm & 6.30-8.45pm). This welcoming place is probably the most traditional of the pubs in the town, serving Brakspear's ales and generous portions of home-cooked food including some vegan dishes. Booking for either lunch or an evening meal is recommended.

For lunch or snacks you could try the cheap and cheerful *Jan Marie* (☎ 01491 874264; Mon-Fri 7.30am-3pm, Sat 9am-3pm), a small café in the centre of town serving cakes, sandwiches and drinks.

There is also a standard Chinese restaurant/takeaway, *Chef King Restaurant* (☎ 01491 872485; daily noon-2pm & 5.30-11pm), in the arcade next to the café. The menu has all the standard dishes you'd expect, most for around £5-7. On the High St there is *Masooms* (☎ 01491 875078;

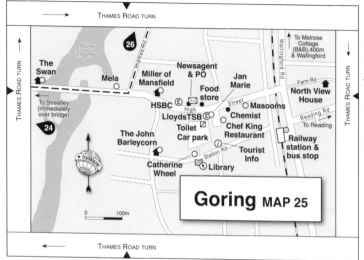

daily noon-2.30pm & 5.30-11pm), an Indian restaurant. The mouth-watering menu here is long and varied with most main courses costing between £7 and £12. The selection of fish curries is worth a look: the red mullet *biraan* is £13.95.

Just by the bridge is another Indian restaurant called *Mela* (☎ 01491 872243; daily Mon-Sat 5.30-11pm, to 10pm on Sun). They have a fairly basic menu, but the food is tasty and the prices for main courses range from £5.25 to £11.15.

GORING TO WATLINGTON   [MAPS 25-33]

Overview

This stretch of the Ridgeway totals **14¹⁄₂ miles/23.3km** and is very enjoyable, especially after the previous sections. From the twin towns of Streatley and Goring the path is easy and follows the Thames for around 5¹⁄₂ miles/9km, sometimes right on its bank, passing through the charming villages of South and North Stoke. Where the path turns east you can head into Wallingford or keep on the Ridgeway, heading along Grim's Ditch (see box p142) for several miles before emerging at Nuffield.

One of the most bizarre sections of the Ridgeway is here – a walk across a golf course – after which you head into woodlands and across open fields for the section to Watlington, passing through Ewelme Park Estate.

Route

Soon after you've crossed the bridge into Goring you need to take a left turn into Thames Rd. There are a couple of 'Ridgeway' signs here but it's still possible to miss this turning if you're not looking for it.

You will now be walking parallel to the Thames but won't be able to see it just yet. The Ridgeway follows a succession of roads and paths behind gardens as it gradually gets closer to and level with the Thames. Along here you'll pass a turning down to the *Leatherne Bottel* (Map 26; ☎ 01491 872667, 🖳 www .leathernebottel.co.uk; daily noon-2.30pm & Mon-Sat 7-9pm), a riverside inn and restaurant. It's a deservedly popular place serving high-quality food either on a terrace at the river bank or inside the restaurant itself. Prices for main courses start at just over £17.50 but they also have a two-/three-course set menu (£19.50/£24.50) at lunchtime. Booking is recommended.

Further along the path you veer away from the busy rail line and head diagonally across an open field, towards the village of South Stoke.

SOUTH STOKE   [MAP 26]

This is yet another attractive village on the route. The Ridgeway path follows 'The Street' through the village, lined with a real variety of old, new and renovated houses. You'll pass a primary school and a church, **St Andrew's**, but there are no shops.

The Goring to Wallingford **bus** (Heyfordian's Nos 134 & 135) stops on the main B4009 road just outside the village; see pp42-5 for further details.

The main place of interest to walkers will be the *Perch & Pike Inn* (☎ 01491 872415, 🖳 www.perchandpike.co.uk; 3D/ 1T all en suite, food daily noon-2.30pm & 6.30-9.30pm, except Sun eve), which is an excellent example of a rare phenomenon – a pub actually on the Ridgeway! For this reason it's a popular stop for many walkers and they are made more than welcome by the owners. The pub itself is a 17th-century coaching inn that has been tastefully refurbished and has open log fires in the colder months. They serve Brakspear ales, stock a select wine list and have both a bar and a restaurant menu. At the time of writing they were changing their menu; though the details were not decided they planned to include some South African dishes such as catemalay curry. Booking is recommended. The rooms are in a restored barn and cost £85-110 per night; there is no discount for single occupancy. One of them even has a Jacuzzi – just the thing after a long day's walk!

There is one other accommodation option in this village: *The Old Post Office* (☎ 01491 871872, 🖳 vanessa.guiver @btinternet.com; 1D, en suite shower) has a wonderful self-contained apartment in a converted oak barn. It costs £50/70 for one/two people including breakfast.

At the end of 'The Street' the Ridgeway branches left and Swan's Way turns right. Swan's Way is a 65-mile, long-distance bridlepath starting in Salcey Forest, on the border with Northamptonshire and finishing at Goring. The Ridgeway crosses it on numerous occasions up ahead.

After leaving South Stoke and following the Thames you'll come to the low, wide **viaduct** (Map 27) that carries the railway over the Thames. From a distance it looks like a standard four-arched viaduct with flattened elliptical arches, as opposed to the semi-circular ones more favoured at the time of its construction. It's only when you get fairly close, and even right under the viaduct, that you see it is really something special. It's not a single viaduct, but two viaducts, built alongside each other with a narrow gap between them. You'll also see that the viaducts are heavily skewed as they cross the Thames on an angle. *(cont'd on p138)*

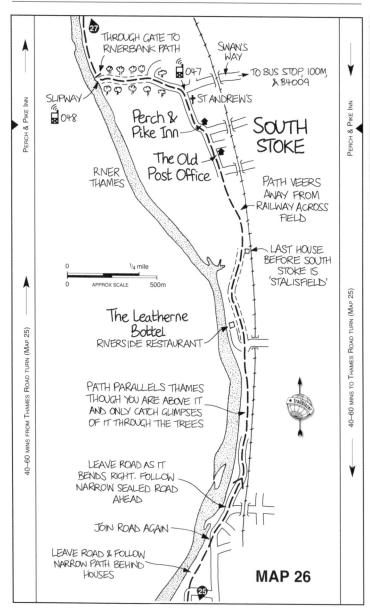

27

THROUGH GATE TO
RIVERBANK PATH

SWAN'S
WAY

047

→ TO BUS STOP, 100M,
& B4009

SLIPWAY

048

✝ ST ANDREW'S

Perch &
Pike Inn

SOUTH
STOKE

The Old
Post Office

RIVER
THAMES

PATH VEERS
AWAY FROM
RAILWAY ACROSS
FIELD

LAST HOUSE
BEFORE SOUTH
STOKE IS
'STALISFIELD'

0   ¼ mile
0   APPROX SCALE   500m

The Leatherne
Bottel
RIVERSIDE RESTAURANT

PATH PARALLELS THAMES
THOUGH YOU ARE ABOVE IT
AND ONLY CATCH GLIMPSES
OF IT THROUGH THE TREES

★ trailblazer

LEAVE ROAD AS IT
BENDS RIGHT. FOLLOW
NARROW SEALED ROAD
AHEAD

JOIN ROAD AGAIN

LEAVE ROAD & FOLLOW
NARROW PATH BEHIND
HOUSES

MAP 26

25

PERCH & PIKE INN

PERCH & PIKE INN

40–60 MINS FROM THAMES ROAD TURN (MAP 25)

40–60 MINS TO THAMES ROAD TURN (MAP 25)

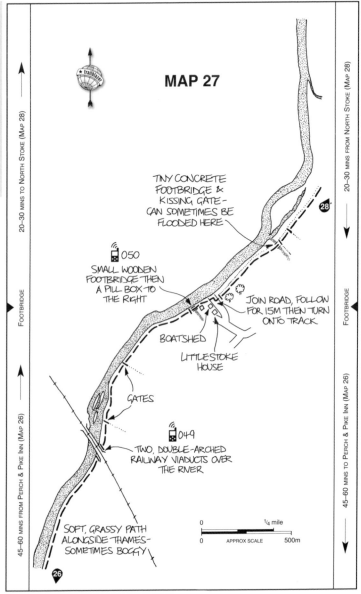

MAP 27

20-30 MINS TO NORTH STOKE (MAP 28)

20-30 MINS FROM NORTH STOKE (MAP 28)

FOOTBRIDGE

FOOTBRIDGE

45-60 MINS FROM PERCH & PIKE INN (MAP 26)

45-60 MINS TO PERCH & PIKE INN (MAP 26)

TINY CONCRETE FOOTBRIDGE & KISSING GATE - CAN SOMETIMES BE FLOODED HERE

28

050 SMALL WOODEN FOOTBRIDGE THEN A PILL BOX TO THE RIGHT

JOIN ROAD, FOLLOW FOR 15M THEN TURN ONTO TRACK

BOATSHED

LITTLESTOKE HOUSE

GATES

049 TWO, DOUBLE-ARCHED RAILWAY VIADUCTS OVER THE RIVER

0   1/4 mile

0   APPROX SCALE   500m

SOFT, GRASSY PATH ALONGSIDE THAMES - SOMETIMES BOGGY

26

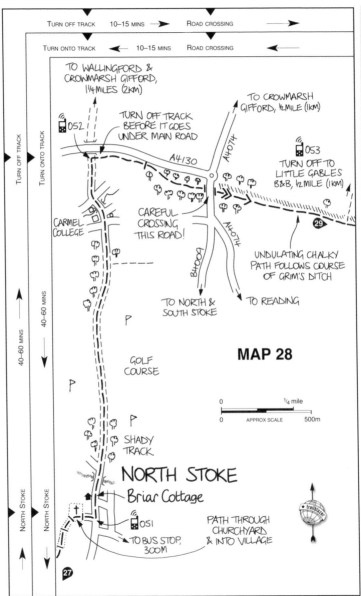

TURN OFF TRACK 10–15 MINS → ROAD CROSSING →

TURN ONTO TRACK ← 10–15 MINS ROAD CROSSING ←

TO WALLINGFORD & CROWMARSH GIFFORD, 1¼ MILES (2KM)

052

TURN OFF TRACK BEFORE IT GOES UNDER MAIN ROAD

A4130

TURN OFF TRACK

TURN ONTO TRACK

TO CROWMARSH GIFFORD, ½MILE (1KM)

A4074

053

TURN OFF TO LITTLE GABLES B&B, ½MILE (1KM)

29

CARMEL COLLEGE

CAREFUL CROSSING THIS ROAD!

B4009

A4074

UNDULATING CHALKY PATH FOLLOWS COURSE OF GRIM'S DITCH

40–60 MINS

40–60 MINS

TO NORTH & SOUTH STOKE

TO READING

P

GOLF COURSE

MAP 28

0 ¼ mile
0 APPROX SCALE 500m

P

P

P

SHADY TRACK

NORTH STOKE

NORTH STOKE

NORTH STOKE

Briar Cottage

051

TO BUS STOP, 300M

PATH THROUGH CHURCHYARD & INTO VILLAGE

trailblazer

27

(cont'd from p134) The red Berkshire brickwork is another interesting feature as the bricks are laid diagonally as opposed to horizontally. The visual effect of this, combined with the skewing of the viaduct, creates a sort of optical illusion as you stand under the arches following the lines of bricks with your eyes. The path keeps alongside the Thames until it reaches **North Stoke** village, after which it starts to turn away from the river.

NORTH STOKE   **[Map 28, p137]**

You arrive in this village via the grounds of the 14th-century **church**, the main building of which remains largely unaltered since its construction. Even some of the original stained glass remains in the windows. Once you've had a look at it there isn't much else to do here; the village is much smaller than South Stoke and there are no facilities for the walker.

However, *Briar Cottage* (☎ 01491 835833; 1D en suite) offers B&B for £60 (single occupancy £30). It's certainly a peaceful place to spend the night.

The Goring to Wallingford **bus** (Heyfordian's Nos 134 & 135) stops on the main B4009 road just outside the village, should you need to leave the Ridgeway; see pp42-5 for further details.

When you come up against the busy A4130 the Ridgeway branches off right, but if you want to visit the towns of Wallingford or Crowmarsh Gifford you should continue on the bridleway that crosses under the A4130. Along this path, to the centre of Wallingford, it is about 1¼ miles/2km; you can also use this path to get to the centre of Crowmarsh Gifford, about one mile/1.5km away, or walk about 500m further along the path and then walk to Crowmarsh Gifford on the A4074, though this is a less pleasant route.

WALLINGFORD   **[see map p141]**

This is the largest town you will have come across 'on' the Ridgeway so far which might merit it a visit, especially if you need to stock up, or just take some time out.

This historically important town was established by King Alfred in the 10th century and later a fortified castle was built here by William the Conqueror who arrived after the Battle of Hastings in 1066.

The fortifications were added to over the years until it became one of the most important castles in England and remained so for several centuries. It was, however, completely destroyed on the orders of Oliver Cromwell in 1652. You can still visit the Castle Gardens, the site of the castle, but there is virtually no evidence of the castle itself.

To reach Wallingford you'll have to walk across the **19-arch stone bridge** crossing the Thames. Believe it or not this was the main road crossing of the Thames

in this area until the A4130 bypass and new bridge were opened in 1993.

Although the railway was closed to passengers in 1959, it has since reopened as the **Cholsey and Wallingford Railway**, linking Wallingford, via the old GWR branch line to Cholsey, and the national rail network. Trains run on various weekends and bank holidays during the year and are sometimes pulled by a steam engine. For more information call ☎ 01491 835067 (24-hour recorded message), or go to the railway's website: 🖳 www.cholsey-walling ford-railway.com.

Services

There is a **tourist information centre** (TIC; ☎ 01491 826972, 🖳 ticwallingford @freenet.co.uk) in the Town Hall, built in 1670. The staff here are helpful and there is a huge amount of information for walkers in the form of free leaflets. It's open Mon-

Fri 10am-4pm (closed for lunch 12.30-1pm) and Sat 10am-2pm.

On the High St the **library** (☎ 01491 837395; Mon, Tue & Fri 9.30am-5.30pm, Thu 9.30am-7pm, Sat 9.30am-1pm) has free **internet access**. Almost next door is **Wallingford Museum** (☎ 01491 835065, 🖳 www.wallingfordmuseum.org.uk; Mar-Nov Tue-Fri 2-5pm, Sat 10.30am-5pm, Jun-Aug Sun 2-5pm) which traces the history of the town from its Saxon roots to the present day. Admission is £4 for adults and free for children if accompanied by an adult.

The **post office** (Mon-Sat 8.30am-5.30pm) is in K P Stationers on St Martin's St. On St Mary's St the Nationwide, Lloyds TSB and Barclays have **ATMs** as does the NatWest on the High St.

There is a **Lloyds Pharmacy** (Mon-Sat 9.30am-5.30pm) and a branch of **Boots** chemists (Mon-Sat 9am-5.30pm) on Market Place and a **laundrette** (daily 8am-7pm) on the High St, towards the river. If you need bicycle repairs try **Rides On Air** (☎ 01491 836289; Mon-Sat 9am-5.30pm) on St Mary's St. There is a large Waitrose **supermarket** (Mon-Sat 8am-8pm, Sun 10am-4pm) on the corner of St Martin's St and the High St and here you'll also find **public toilets**. There are more public toilets in the car park. There is also a monthly **farmers' market** (see box p15).

Wallingford has good **bus** links to the surrounding countryside. Destinations served include: Goring via North Stoke and South Stoke (Heyfordian's Nos 134 & 135); and the following services operated by Thames Travel: Goring, Pangbourne and Reading (No 132); Didcot Parkway Railway Station (No 130); Huntercombe (Nuffield) (No 139), Oxford (No 105); Watlington (No 125); Oxford and Reading (X39 & X40). Most services stop at Crowmarsh Gifford; see pp42-5 for further details. Buses stop either in front of the Baker's Oven, the Town Hall or on the western side of the Market Place so check you are at the correct stop.

If you need a **taxi** there is a taxi rank next to the Town Hall.

Where to stay

Pretty much in the centre of town is *Huntington House* (☎ 01491 839201, 🖳 www.huntington-house.co.uk; 1S/1D/1T), at 18 Wood St. This friendly place charges from £55 for a double/twin and from £35 for the single room. The single room has an en suite toilet and all the rooms share a bathroom, which also has a shower in it.

You could also try *The Dolphin* (☎ 01491 837377; 2T, private bathroom) which has accommodation above the pub: handy for a drink, but it's not the most peaceful place to stay. It's £60 (£45 if you're on your own) and although the price doesn't include breakfast, they serve food downstairs from 8am onwards (see p140).

The *George Hotel* (☎ 01491 836665, 🖳 www.george-hotel-wallingford.com; 9S/29D/1F, all en suite) is a large, upmarket place with a central location. The hotel is in a 16th-century building also incorporating a 'tavern' and a separate restaurant and bar called Wealh's (see p140). If you can afford the prices, you'll certainly be very comfortable: the rooms start from £110-130 for a double, £80-120 for a single, and £125-150 for the family room. Weekend rates include breakfast; during the week a continental breakfast is £10.50 and the full English breakfast is £12.50.

If all the accommodation in Wallingford is full, there is a campsite and B&B in Crowmarsh Gifford (see p142), within walking distance, across the bridge.

Where to eat and drink

There are plenty of places to eat in Wallingford and lots of variety, too. All the places listed below are in or around the town centre.

If you like Italian food you could try *The Pizza Café* (☎ 01491 826222; daily 10am-2.30pm, Mon-Thu 5.30-10.30pm, Fri & Sat 5.30-11pm), on St Mary's St, which has a large range of pizzas (£6-11) for such a small place, or the chain restaurant, *Pizza Express* (☎ 01491 833431; Sun-Thu noon-10.30pm, Fri & Sat noon-11.30pm), also on St Mary's St, dishing up much the same but for slightly higher prices and without the personal touch. *San Sicario* (☎ 01491 834078; Mon 6.30-10pm, Tue-Sat 11am-2pm & 6.30-10pm), on the corner of the High St, is another Italian restaurant serving pizzas, pasta, risotto and salads. It looks tiny from the outside but they have a large dining room seating up to 50 people upstairs.

There is also an Italian on the High St; *Avanti* (☎ 01491 835500, 🖳 www.avanti italian.com; Mon-Sat 12.15-2.30pm & 5.45-10.30pm) serves a range of pasta dishes from £7.50 to £9.35, plus all the usual pizzas and fresh seafood too.

If Spanish food is more your thing you could head for *La Vina* (☎ 0845 126 2954, 🖳 www.lavina.co.uk; Mon-Sat 10am-11pm, Sun 10am-10pm) where you'll find authentic Spanish tapas, salads and paella. The paellas are around £10.25 per person for a minimum of two people.

The best Indian restaurant in town is on the High St and called *Anokhi* (☎ 01491 838077; daily noon-2pm & 6-11.30pm, except Fri lunch). They have an extensive choice of chef's specialities (£6.95-12.95). Just past Anokhi is *Delhi Brasserie* (☎ 01491 826666, 🖳 www.delhibrasserie.co .uk; Mon-Sat noon-2pm & 5.30-11.30pm, Sun noon-11.30pm). Alternatively try *Wallingford Tandoori* (☎ 01491 836249, 🖳 www.wallingfordtandoori.com; Mon-Sat noon-2pm & 5.30-11.30pm, Sun noon-11.30pm) which has a standard menu and prices to match.

The only Thai restaurant in Wallingford is *Thai Corner* (☎ 01491 825050; Mon-Sat 5.30-11pm); it has an extensive menu with the *phed pad khing* (duck fried with ginger) at £8.50 well worth ordering.

Hong Kong House (☎ 01491 835453; Sun-Thu 5-11.30pm, Fri & Sat 11.30am-1.30pm & 5-11.45pm) and *Welcome Chinese Food* (☎ 01491 839112; Sun-Thu 4.30-11.30pm, Fri & Sat noon-1.15pm & 4.30-11.30pm) are both standard Chinese takeaways but you can eat in at the *Beijing Diner* (☎ 01491 835069; Mon-Thu 6-11pm, Fri-Sun noon-2.30pm & 6-11pm) at the southern end of St Mary's St. The menu

is fairly standard though they do have plenty of vegetarian options.

Fast food in Wallingford includes a *Smart's Fish & Chips* (Mon-Sat 11.30am-2pm & 4.30m-11pm, Sun 4-10pm) on the High St and *USA Chicken & Pizza* (daily noon-11pm), on St Martin's St.

There are plenty of pubs that serve food. If the weather is good you should visit the *Coach & Horses* (☎ 01491 825054; food daily noon-2pm) that faces out onto a large grassy area. The food here is good but only served at lunchtimes and includes large ploughman's and several vegetarian options. They serve a range of cask ales and have regular live music on Thursday evenings. *The Dolphin* (see p139; food daily 8am-2pm & 6-9pm), nearer the centre of town, has Greene King ales though only has a standard bar menu. From 8am to noon they serve 'full English' breakfasts for £5.50. *The Boathouse* (☎ 01491 834100; food Mon-Thu noon-9pm, Fri-Sun noon-7pm) has a large patio area for dining, right on the banks of the Thames. Although the menu is standard pub food it is done well. It can get quite noisy at weekends when they have live music in the evenings, but you can always sit outside if the weather is warm enough.

Wealh's, in the George Hotel (see p139), has a lovely outdoor eating area in the hotel courtyard; main courses here are £8-15 while lunchtime sandwiches cost from £4.95.

For lunch you might like to have a look in *Lamb Coffee Shop* (Mon-Fri 10am-4pm, Sat 10am-5pm), tucked away in Lamb Arcade. They have a tasty lunch menu including such choices as smoked haddock fishcake with salad and new potatoes (£5.25) and also do cream teas (£3.25) if you fancy a break in the afternoon.

Bloomers Sandwich Bar (☎ 01491 825465; Mon-Sat 8am-5pm) is a pleasant café that serves a wide range of filling baguettes, sandwiches and rolls from £2.95. The *Bakers Oven* (☎ 01491 836267; Mon-Sat 8am-5pm) has similar offerings (sandwiches £1.80-3).

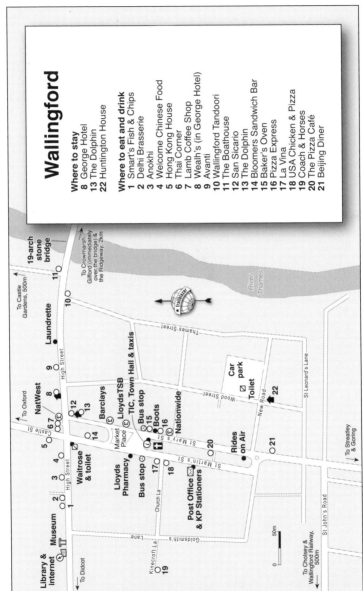

Wallingford

Where to stay
8 George Hotel
13 The Dolphin
22 Huntington House

Where to eat and drink
1 Smart's Fish & Chips
2 Delhi Brasserie
3 Anokhi
4 Welcome Chinese Food
5 Hong Kong House
6 Thai Corner
7 Lamb Coffee Shop
8 Wealh's (in George Hotel)
9 Avanti
10 Wallingford Tandoori
11 The Boathouse
12 San Sicario
13 The Dolphin
14 Bloomers Sandwich Bar
15 Baker's Oven
16 Pizza Express
17 La Vina
18 USA Chicken & Pizza
19 Coach & Horses
20 The Pizza Café
21 Beijing Diner

19-arch stone bridge

To Crowmarsh Gifford (immediately over the bridge) & the Ridgeway, 2km

To Castle Gardens, 500m

Laundrette

River Thames

To Oxford

NatWest

Barclays

LloydsTSB
TIC, Town Hall & taxis
Bus stop

Boots

Nationwide

Car park

Toilet

St Leonard's Lane

Wood Street

Thames Street

New Road

To Streatley & Goring

Castle St

High Street

Museum

Library & internet

To Didcot

Waitrose & toilet

Lloyds
Pharmacy
Bus stop

Market Place

Church La

St Mary's St

St Martin's St

Post Office & KP Stationers

Rides on Air

Kinecroft La

Goldsmith's Lane

St John's Road

To Cholsey & Wallingford Railway, 500m

trailblazer

0   50m

> ❏ **Grim's ditches**
> There are many Grim's ditches in England. The reason is that Grim is the Anglo-Saxon word for the devil and his name was often attributed to unnatural features in the landscape. This particular Grim's ditch (see Map 28, p137, but also Maps 29 & 30 (p144 & p145) was probably built during the Iron Age and is probably marking a boundary as it's not big enough to be a defensive earthwork. 'Probably' being the operative word, as even now little is known about this stretch.

CROWMARSH GIFFORD

This town has now become an extension of Wallingford. It's separated only by the bridge from its larger neighbour and to be honest, most shops and services are located on the other side of the bridge in Wallingford. There is, however, a campsite and B&B here and it's easy to walk into Wallingford should you need to.

The main claim to fame for this place is that **Jethro Tull** lived here. No, not them, but him, the inventor of the seed drill. You can still see his house on The Street where he lived from 1700 to 1710. It's only a couple of minutes' walk from the bridge, but not open to the public. It's the middle one of the three terraced Tudor houses.

The seed drill was essentially a device that enabled you to plant three rows of seeds at the same time. He also invented other machines in an effort to improve crop yields. At the time his ideas weren't implemented fully, but looking back he is now recognised as one of the most important figures in the modernisation of farming methods.

Services

There is a well-stocked **shop** (☎ 01491 837176; Mon-Sat 6.30am-7.30pm, Sun 8am-6pm) on The Street.

The number of **bus** services (operated by Thames Travel) here is almost as good as at Wallingford: Thames Travel's Nos 125, 132, 139, X39 and X40 services stop here; see pp42-5 for further details.

Where to stay

Just before you cross the bridge to Wallingford there is a campsite down a left-hand turning. **Riverside Park** (☎ 01491 835232, 🖳 www.soll-leisure.co.uk) is open from May to early September and is a very well-run **campsite**, with heated open-air swimming pools (daily 11am-6pm), on the banks of the Thames. There are 18 pitches (£13-16 per night) but it can get busy so you are advised to book ahead.

You could try the excellent B&B at **Little Gables** (☎ 01491 837834, 🖳 www .littlegables.co.uk; 3D or T), at 166 Crowmarsh Hill. Two of the rooms here are en suite and can also be made into a family room. Prices start from £50/60/75 for a single/double/family. There are a couple of places where you can eat within five minutes' walk but they will provide a sandwich tray (from £5 per person) and packed lunches (from £5). If booked in advance dogs and children are welcome. They will also transport your luggage to your next B&B (from £1.50 per mile).

Little Gables is in a cul-de-sac running parallel to the main road, a couple of hundred metres east of the large roundabout. Although you can walk here from Wallingford, the Ridgeway passes within about half a mile of this place (see Map 28, p137). To get there follow the Grim's ditch (see box above) and look for a path leading off through a field to your left. Take this path and when it joins the minor road continue on that, in the same direction. You will soon arrive at the cul-de-sac.

Where to eat and drink

There are basically two options but both are places that are part of nationwide chains so the menus are predictable: it just depends whether you prefer standard pub fare or Thai food.

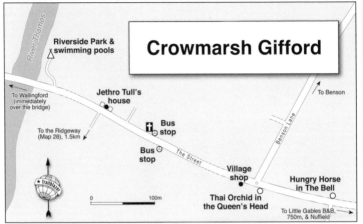

The Bell Inn (☎ 01491 835324; food Mon-Sat noon-10pm, Sun noon-9.30pm) on The Street, is a Greene King pub with a Hungry Horse restaurant and lots of facilities – the aim being that it will appeal to anyone that might walk through its doors. The menu is the same in all their branches: burgers with chips, steaks, or vegetable lasagne, but they pride themselves on the large servings and low prices. Most main courses are around £4.50-6.

The other place, ***Thai Orchid*** (☎ 01491 839857; food daily noon-2.30pm & 5.30-10.30pm), in the 13th-century Queen's Head pub, serves authentic Thai food. Since it's part of the group of *Thai Orchid* restaurants if you've been to one before you'll know what to expect. It's a good idea to go for one of their three-course set meals (between £19.95 and £24.95 per person) as they will choose the right dishes to complement each other.

From the junction at the A4130 the section of the Ridgeway more or less all the way to Nuffield comprises narrow, undulating paths following **Grim's ditch** (see box opposite). Sometimes the path is on top of the ditch and sometimes to one side. Most of the way is shaded by trees and you also pass through some attractive woodland. You are much more likely to meet other people, most of whom will be accompanied by a dog or two, on this stretch than the previous ones.

Several areas of woodland along this section (for example **Oaken Copse**, Map 29) are carpeted with bluebells in the late spring and make for a much-visited and very colourful sight.

Before you can finish this stage you must do something quite unexpected: walk across a golf course. It's called Huntercombe Golf Course and it's in the village of Nuffield. To cross the golf course you'll need to follow the strategically placed, numbered wooden posts. You don't skirt round the outside of the course discreetly; you actually have to cross several fairways. Just watch out for the bunkers! Once you've negotiated your way across you enter a small wooded area on a muddy path; this quickly turns into a gravelled track that leads you

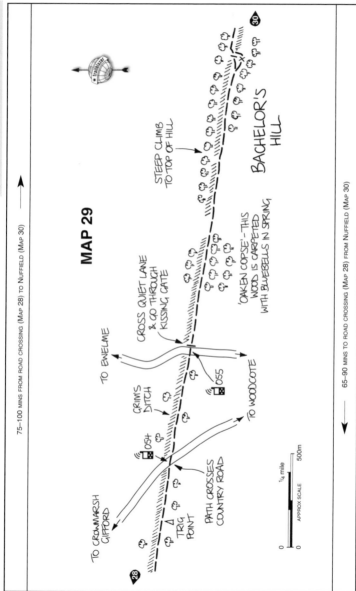

MAP 29

75–100 MINS FROM ROAD CROSSING (MAP 28) TO NUFFIELD (MAP 30)

65–90 MINS TO ROAD CROSSING (MAP 28) FROM NUFFIELD (MAP 30)

BACHELOR'S HILL

STEEP CLIMB TO TOP OF HILL

CROSS QUIET LANE & GO THROUGH KISSING GATE

'OAKEN COPSE' – THIS WOOD IS CARPETED WITH BLUEBELLS IN SPRING

TO EWELME

GRIM'S DITCH

055

TO WOODCOTE

054

TO CROWMARSH GIFFORD

TRIG POINT

PATH CROSSES COUNTRY ROAD

0   ¼ mile
0   500m
APPROX SCALE

28

30

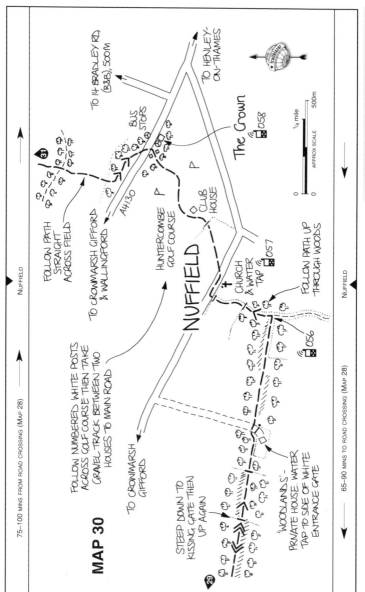

MAP 30

75-100 MINS FROM ROAD CROSSING (MAP 28) →

NUFFIELD

FOLLOW PATH STRAIGHT ACROSS FIELD

31

TO 14 BRADLEY RD (B&B), 500M

TO HENLEY-ON-THAMES

BUS STOPS

The Crown
058

FOLLOW NUMBERED WHITE POSTS ACROSS GOLF COURSE THEN TAKE GRAVEL TRACK BETWEEN TWO HOUSES TO MAIN ROAD

TO CROWMARSH GIFFORD & WALLINGFORD

A4130

HUNTERCOMBE GOLF COURSE

P

P

CLUB HOUSE

NUFFIELD

CHURCH & WATER TAP
057

FOLLOW PATH UP THROUGH WOODS

056

TO CROWMARSH GIFFORD

STEEP DOWN TO KISSING GATE THEN UP AGAIN

29

'WOODLANDS' - PRIVATE HOUSE. WATER TAP TO SIDE OF WHITE ENTRANCE GATE

NUFFIELD

¼ mile

APPROX SCALE

0   500m

65-90 MINS TO ROAD CROSSING (MAP 28) →

through a narrow gap between the two houses here, right past their front doors and down their drive. You may feel like a trespasser but this is the correct route. After curving round to the right, the path leads you almost straight to The Crown (see below), the only pub in the village.

NUFFIELD [Map 30, p145]

Nuffield is basically a small, quiet village with a church, a pub and a golf course: there is no post office or shop. The **Holy Trinity** church, built in 1189, is the final resting place of Viscount William Morris (1877-1963), founder of Morris Motors. He was the Henry Ford of England, starting a mass-production car factory to build the Morris Oxford car.

The Crown (☎ 01491 641335; food Mon noon-2pm, Tue-Sat noon-2pm & 6.30-9.30pm, Sun noon-3pm) serves Brakspear ales. It's closed on Sunday and Monday evenings except on Bank Holiday weekends. They have an extensive and varied lunch menu: a steak, mushroom and onion sandwich is £5.50 and a ploughman's £8. The dinner menu includes a delicious rustic lamb leg steak for £12 and there are also a few vegetarian options. It's a friendly place

and they are used to Ridgeway walkers dropping in for refreshment.

The only B&B is at *14 Bradley Road* (☎ 01491 641359, 🖳 dianamc@waitrose .com; 2D/1T), Huntercombe Place. Rooms here are £60 (single occupancy £30); one of the doubles is en suite and the other rooms share a bathroom. A packed lunch (£2-3) is available if requested in advance and there is a free transfer to Henley-on-Thames for meals when unavailable in the village. To get here walk past *The Crown* and take the first left turn. The B&B is at the far end of this road; it's about a ten-minute walk.

Thames Travel's No 139 **bus** (Wallingford to Henley via Crowmarsh Gifford) stops at The Crown (Huntercombe); see pp42-5 for further details.

From The Crown you need to cross the road and head down to where the Ridgeway path disappears into the trees. Once through them you have to walk on a path cutting straight through the middle of a field. In the summer, when the crops are at their highest, the bare trail cutting straight between them can look quite dramatic.

The first buildings you come to after starting from Nuffield are those of the picturesque **Ewelme Park Estate** (Map 31). This estate was formed around 450 years ago from several smaller estates and was an important royal deer park under Henry VIII, Elizabeth I, James I, and Charles I, before being broken up and sold. Nowadays the estate is better known for its pheasants rather than deer, though the finale for both animals is the same. A large cache of Roman coins was also found on the estate, among several other finds in the area. Local schools make trips to the estate to learn about its history and see the archery corridor used by Henry VIII. When you walk through you'll see the beautiful gatehouse and views of the main house itself which, despite its appearance, is not very old. You may also see some peacocks and will definitely hear several dogs barking, announcing your arrival in the area.

Not much further on is the 11th-century **St Botolph's church**. Considering the remote location it's a large place. The cemetery around the church is full and there is another diagonally across the crossroads. You may recognise the name of the church as it's famous for the carpet of snowdrops that grows around it in

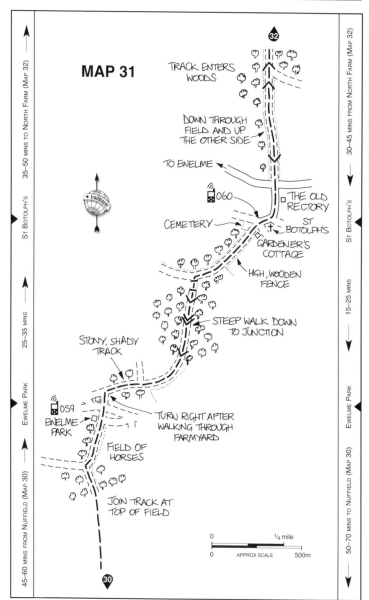

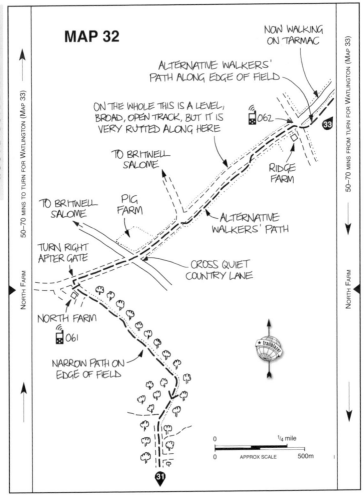

MAP 32

NOW WALKING ON TARMAC

ALTERNATIVE WALKERS' PATH ALONG EDGE OF FIELD

ON THE WHOLE THIS IS A LEVEL, BROAD, OPEN TRACK, BUT IT IS VERY RUTTED ALONG HERE

062

33

TO BRITWELL SALOME

RIDGE FARM

TO BRITWELL SALOME

PIG FARM

ALTERNATIVE WALKERS' PATH

TURN RIGHT AFTER GATE

CROSS QUIET COUNTRY LANE

NORTH FARM

061

NARROW PATH ON EDGE OF FIELD

31

0   1/4 mile
0   APPROX SCALE   500m

50-70 MINS TO TURN FOR WATLINGTON (MAP 33)

NORTH FARM

ROUTE GUIDE AND MAPS

50-70 MINS FROM TURN FOR WATLINGTON (MAP 33)

NORTH FARM

early February; so famous, in fact, that there have even been cases of snowdrop-bulb rustling in the churchyard.

A good couple of hours after leaving Nuffield you'll get to the two turnings for Watlington. If you're heading for the centre of town it matters little which you take, but if aiming for A. Woodgate Orchard Cottage B&B (see p150) you'll need the first turning and if aiming for the campsite (see p150) or Carriers Arms (see p150) you'll need the second. Either way it's about half a mile/1km into the town.

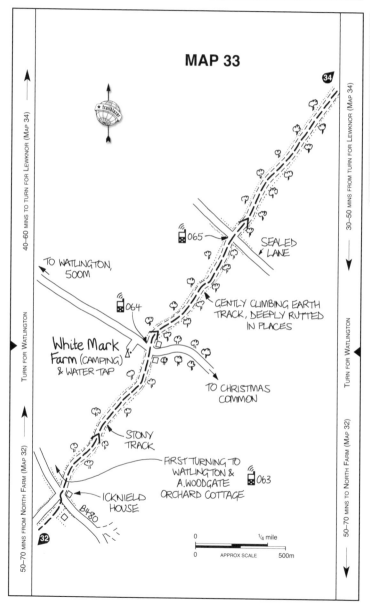

MAP 33

34

40–60 MINS TO TURN FOR LEWKNOR (MAP 34)

30–50 MINS FROM TURN FOR LEWKNOR (MAP 34)

📱 065

SEALED LANE

TO WATLINGTON, 500M

📱 064

GENTLY CLIMBING EARTH TRACK, DEEPLY RUTTED IN PLACES

TURN FOR WATLINGTON

White Mark Farm (CAMPING) & WATER TAP

TURN FOR WATLINGTON

TO CHRISTMAS COMMON

STONY TRACK

FIRST TURNING TO WATLINGTON & A. WOODGATE ORCHARD COTTAGE

📱 063

50–70 MINS FROM NORTH FARM (MAP 32)

ICKNIELD HOUSE

B480

32

50–70 MINS TO NORTH FARM (MAP 32)

0   ¼ mile

0   APPROX SCALE   500m

WATLINGTON

This is officially the smallest town in England. However, some people, the residents of Manningtree in Essex for instance, might like to take issue with this. For the record the royal charter giving town status to Watlington was issued in 1154.

If you are stopping here for the day most services and shops that you'll need are on one of two streets. The town is pleasant enough and has a few interesting old buildings to look at so it might be nice to relax here for an hour or two over lunch.

Services

There's a **post office** (Mon-Fri 9am-5.30pm, Sat 9am-12.30pm) and **Barclays Bank** (Mon-Fri 10am-3pm), on the High St, though the bank doesn't have an ATM; for that you'll have to go to the Co-op **supermarket** (Mon-Sat 7am-10pm, Sun 8am-9pm), on Couching St where an **ATM** is located just inside the door. Near the Co-op there is a **chemist** (Mon-Fri 9am-6pm, Sat 9am-1pm, closed for lunch 1-2pm) should you need it.

There is a **newsagent** (Mon-Fri 5.30am-5pm, Sat 5.30am-2pm, Sun 6.30am-noon, closed 1-2.15pm), on the High St, which sells snacks and drinks.

If you need to use the **internet**, you should head to the **library** (☎ 01491 612241; Mon 2-7pm, Tue 9.30am-12.30pm & 2-5pm, Thu 2-6pm, Fri 9.30am-12.30pm & 2-5.30pm, Sat 9.30am-1pm) on the High St where it's free of charge but they recommend booking in advance.

Buses from Watlington serve Stokenchurch, Reading Railway Station and Lewknor (Motts Travel's No M1), Wallingford via Crowmarsh Gifford (Thames Travel's No 125), Lewknor and Thame (Red Rose Travel's No 124); see pp42-5 for further details.

Where to stay

Close to the Ridgeway is a B&B at *A.Woodgate Orchard Cottage* (☎ 01491 612675, ✉ ronnieroper@onetel.com; 1D/2T). The prices start at £70, or £40-5 for single occupancy, with all rooms sharing a bathroom. The owner can provide packed lunches and luggage transport. Make sure to book well ahead if you want to stay here as it's very popular, especially with walkers. This place is just 400m from the Ridgeway; the easiest way to get here is to leave the path where it crosses the B480. Icknield House is on this junction. Head down the B480 towards Watlington and the B&B is on your right near the restriction signs.

Another good choice would be *The Fox & Hounds* (☎ 01491 613040, ✉ www.foxandhounds.net; 1S/7D/1F, all en suite). This is a delightful old pub near the centre of town serving Brakspear's ales and it's open all day. The accommodation here is in a tastefully converted coach barn next to the pub and each room is different. The single costs from £65 or £75 including breakfast.

Campers should head for *White Mark Farm* (☎ 01491 612295), just a few minutes' walk from the Ridgeway. There are lots of pitches on this friendly, well-run campsite and they charge £4.50 per person per night. There are toilet and shower facilities and campers can also use a microwave oven, kettle and fridge. It's no more than 10 minutes to walk to the centre of town from here. Officially they are closed from the end of October to the beginning of March but if you are walking between November and February and would like to camp here contact them.

Where to eat and drink

At lunchtimes you could try the *Bread Bin* (☎ 01491 613061; Mon-Fri 7.30am-4pm, Sat 9am-3pm) sandwich shop on the High St where you can eat in or takeaway.

On the way into Watlington, from the second turning off the Ridgeway, is the *Carriers Arms* (☎ 01491 613470; food Mon-Sat 10am-2.15pm, Sun 10am-4.30pm, Wed-Sun 7-9.15pm). Breakfast is served daily till 11.30am and on Sunday they serve a roast from 11.30am to 4.30pm. At other times you can get standard pub grub such as ham, egg and chips £5.50, or a plough-

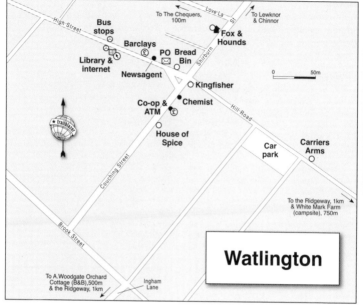

To The Chequers, 100m

To Lewknor & Chinnor

Love La

High Street

Bus stops

Fox & Hounds

Barclays

PO Bread Bin

Library & internet

Newsagent

Shirburn

Kingfisher

Co-op & ATM

Chemist

Hill Road

House of Spice

Car park

Carriers Arms

Couching Street

To the Ridgeway, 1km & White Mark Farm (campsite), 750m

Brook Street

Watlington

To A.Woodgate Orchard Cottage (B&B), 500m & the Ridgeway, 1km

Ingham Lane

0   50m

man's for £6. The place isn't particularly inviting, but is often busy at lunchtimes and is OK for a quick lunch. *The Fox & Hounds* (see opposite, food daily noon-2pm & 5-10pm, Sat & Sun noon-3pm & 5-10pm, Sun noon-3.30pm) would be a far more relaxing choice. Their bar menu includes baguettes and nachos, which cost £4-8 and their restaurant menu includes home-made pizza: a 12" pizza costs from £6.60, £3.50 for half a pizza.

The Chequers (☎ 01491 612874; food Tue-Fri noon-2pm & 7-9pm, Sat 7-9.30pm, Sun noon-2 or 3pm), a pub on Love Lane, is well known as one of the best places in town for food and has friendly staff. Their wide-ranging menu features English, Mediterranean and Thai dishes and main courses cost from £10 to £18.

There is also an Indian restaurant here, the *House of Spice* (☎ 01491 613552; daily noon-2.30pm & 6-11pm). The menu contains all the usual dishes with a chicken do-piaza and rice costing £7.90.

Alternatively *Kingfisher* (☎ 01491 613237; Mon-Sat 11am-2pm & 4-10pm) serves fish and chips and fried chicken.

WATLINGTON TO PRINCES RISBOROUGH

[MAPS 33-39]

Overview

Although this **11 mile/17.4km** section of the Ridgeway is pleasant enough, it's fairly uneventful. The walking is easy with few steep sections so you can really slow down, relax and enjoy the scenery. Perhaps take a diversion into Lewknor, Kingston Blount or Chinnor for a drink, or press on and finish early in Princes Risborough.

Route

Continuing on the Ridgeway from the road turn-offs for Watlington it's a long, straight 2¹/₂ miles/4km along shady tracks and through open fields, until you get to the turning for Lewknor. It's about half a mile/0.8km along this minor road to the village.

LEWKNOR   [MAP 34]

Lewknor is a small, picturesque village, much like many others around here. Easy access to the M40, and therefore London, has added to its value on the property market. It's a very quiet place as nearly all the traffic coming through is for the village itself.

Motts's M1 **bus** for Watlington and Reading stops at the Lewknor turning on the B4009 and Red Rose's No 124 (a limited service) stops at Ye Olde Leathern Bottel en route between Watlington and Thame. The Oxford Tube stops on the B4009, just off junction 6 of the M40 near Lewknor and runs every 15 mins between London and Oxford; see pp42-5 for further details.

At the crossroads in the village, and a good reason to come here, is *Ye Olde Leathern Bottel* (☎ 01844 351482; food Sun-Thu noon-2pm & 7-9.30pm, Fri & Sat noon-2pm & 6-9.30pm), a pub serving

Brakspear ales. It closes in the afternoons, so don't make the trek out here between 3 and 6pm. However, when it is open it can get very busy, especially at weekends, but they don't have a booking policy.

Another good reason to visit is for the excellent B&B at *Moorcourt Cottage* (☎ 01844 351419, 🖃 moorcourt2002@yahoo .co.uk; 1D private bathroom/1T en suite). Accommodation in this picture-perfect house is £65, or £40 if you're on your own. The friendly owners will even pick you up from where the Ridgeway joins the road to Lewknor, saving you a fairly tedious stretch of road walking at the end of the day. This is a popular place for walkers to stay so be sure to book well in advance. Packed lunches are available on request, and they will also transport your luggage to your next destination on the Way; a charge is made for both of these.

You'll hear the M40 motorway up ahead long before you see it. There are no two ways about it: this motorway completely dominates the countryside it passes through. The physically elevated status of the M40 at this point only acts to reinforce its dominance over the landscape. Luckily for walkers there is a large tunnel underneath it, albeit without murals, unlike the tunnel under the A34 back near East Ilsley.

Around 1¹/₂ miles/2.5km after you pass through the tunnel you'll come to a road crossing the path (Map 35). Turn left down this road to get to the village of Kingston Blount, about half a mile/1km away.

KINGSTON BLOUNT [see map p154]

This small village is probably worth a visit if you're planning to stay for the night. But on the other hand, if you are having an easy day of walking, you could stop at the pub for a long lunch.

In times gone by this place had a number of shops and pubs, a post office, a school and even a telephone exchange, but today just one pub survives. The local people

pronounce the 'Blount' part of the village name as 'blunt' – a reference to the Le Blunt family who were lords of this area for several hundred years.

Lakeside Town Farm (☎ 01844 352152, 🖃 www.townfarmcottage.co.uk; 2D/1T, all en suite) is a working farm with an old farmhouse that's full of character. The B&B is very-well run: the twin/double

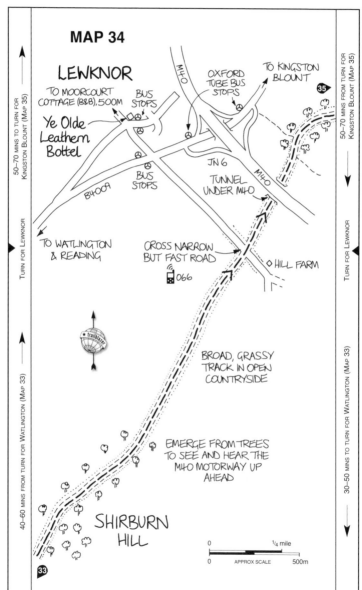

ROUTE GUIDE AND MAPS

MAP 34

LEWKNOR

TO MOORCOURT
COTTAGE (B&B), 500M

Ye Olde
Leathern
Bottel

BUS
STOPS

M40

OXFORD
TUBE BUS
STOPS

TO KINGSTON
BLOUNT

35

JN 6

BUS
STOPS

B4009

TUNNEL
UNDER M40

M40

TO WATLINGTON
& READING

CROSS NARROW
BUT FAST ROAD

066

HILL FARM

★ trailblazer

BROAD, GRASSY
TRACK IN OPEN
COUNTRYSIDE

EMERGE FROM TREES
TO SEE AND HEAR THE
M40 MOTORWAY UP
AHEAD

SHIRBURN
HILL

0   ¼ mile

0   APPROX SCALE   500m

33

50–70 MINS TO TURN FOR KINGSTON BLOUNT (MAP 35)

TURN FOR LEWKNOR

40–60 MINS FROM TURN FOR WATLINGTON (MAP 33)

50–70 MINS FROM TURN FOR KINGSTON BLOUNT (MAP 35)

TURN FOR LEWKNOR

30–50 MINS TO TURN FOR WATLINGTON (MAP 33)

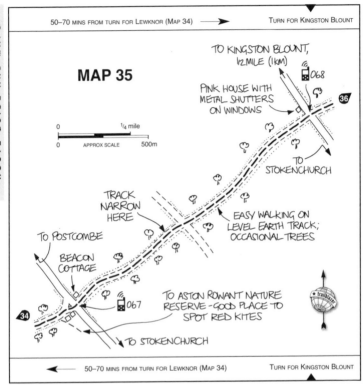

MAP 35

0   ¼ mile
0   APPROX SCALE   500m

TO KINGSTON BLOUNT, ½ MILE (1KM)   📱068

PINK HOUSE WITH METAL SHUTTERS ON WINDOWS

36

TO STOKENCHURCH

TRACK NARROW HERE

EASY WALKING ON LEVEL EARTH TRACK; OCCASIONAL TREES

TO POSTCOMBE

BEACON COTTAGE

TO ASTON ROWANT NATURE RESERVE - GOOD PLACE TO SPOT RED KITES

34   📱067

TO STOKENCHURCH

★ trailblazer

rooms are £85, or £60 if you're on your own. The beautiful gardens encompass lakes and have been featured on the BBC's Gardeners' World programme.

Alternatively, you could stay at ***The Cherry Tree pub*** (☎ 01844 352273, 🖳 www .thecherrytreepub.com; 4D, food Mon-Sat noon-2.30pm & 6.30-9.30pm, Sun noon-5pm); the modern double rooms in their converted barn cost £70, or £60 for single occupancy. The pub itself has a welcoming and contemporary feel and is a popular meeting place for locals. The bar is open all day Mon-Sat and noon-6pm on Sundays. It's well-worth eating here: a tasty dish such as crispy salmon fillet, wok fried noodles & spicy oriental sauce is £13.75.

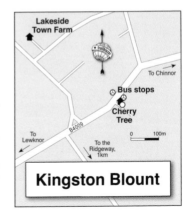

Lakeside Town Farm

★ trailblazer

To Chinnor

Bus stops

Cherry Tree

B4009

To Lewknor

To the Ridgeway, 1km

0   100m

Kingston Blount

Arriva's No 40 **bus** stops here en route between Thame, Chinnor and High Wycombe; see pp42-5 for further details. If you need a **taxi** you could call B&V Taxis (☎ 01844 342079); advance booking is recommended.

The cement works (Map 36) at Chinnor stand out for a mile, or two, and not long after you have spotted them the path becomes flanked by the huge pits that are the result of previous activity at the works. Although it's not easy to get a proper view of these, most have water at the bottom. On a sunny day the water is bright turquoise which contrasts with the brilliant white chalk-pit sides – a bizarre sight in the middle of this countryside.

When you reach the main road that crosses the Ridgeway, turn left and follow it into Chinnor, about a third of a mile/0.5km. Although Chinnor is a large village there isn't a great deal here, so if you don't want to go on the railway (see p156) or stay, and don't need to buy anything, you might want to keep walking.

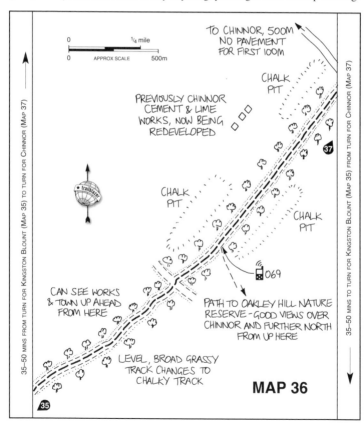

TO CHINNOR, 500M
NO PAVEMENT
FOR FIRST 100M

CHALK PIT

PREVIOUSLY CHINNOR CEMENT & LIME WORKS, NOW BEING REDEVELOPED

★ trailblazer

CHALK PIT

CHALK PIT

069

CAN SEE WORKS & TOWN UP AHEAD FROM HERE

PATH TO OAKLEY HILL NATURE RESERVE - GOOD VIEWS OVER CHINNOR AND FURTHER NORTH FROM UP HERE

LEVEL, BROAD GRASSY TRACK CHANGES TO CHALKY TRACK

MAP 36

35–50 MINS FROM TURN FOR KINGSTON BLOUNT (MAP 35) TO TURN FOR CHINNOR (MAP 37)

35–50 MINS TO TURN FOR KINGSTON BLOUNT (MAP 35) FROM TURN FOR CHINNOR (MAP 37)

0   ¼ mile
0   APPROX SCALE   500m

35

37

CHINNOR

This is the next town in the line of settlements along the Chilterns. In the 19th century this place was well known for producing lace and chair legs. The Chiltern beech forests were the source of wood for the legs.

In the early 20th century a cement factory was opened and this steadily expanded as new technology allowed for ever-increasing production levels. The population in the village grew as the works expanded but they were eventually closed in 1999. One thing that has survived is the **Chinnor & Princes Risborough Railway** that runs steam trains along a small section of line from here. By 1961 the line from Watlington to Chinnor had been closed completely, though the section from Chinnor to Princes Risborough remained in use by the cement factory. In the early '70s Chinnor station and platform were demolished and by the late '80s all traffic on the line from the cement works had ceased.

However, within five years the Chinnor & Princes Risborough Railway Association had rebuilt the platform and station and started running a public service. Since then they have extended the line twice and added a loop, enabling the engine to turn around. At the time of writing the round trip was seven miles (11km) though plans are afoot to extend the line to Princes Risborough. A steam or diesel engine runs most weekends, but check their talking timetable (☎ 01844 353535) or their website (🖳 www.cprra.co.uk) before making your way down there.

Services

On Church Rd there is a line of shops and this is more or less the centre of the village. This comprises a Spar **supermarket** (Sun-Thu 6.30am-9pm, Fri & Sat 6.30am-9.30pm), and a **bakery**.

The **post office** is just around the corner on the High St. The **library** (☎ 01844 351721; Mon & Wed 9.30am-12.30pm & 2-5.30pm, Thu 2-7pm, Fri 2-5.30pm, Sat 9.30am-1pm) offers free **internet** access.

There is an **ATM** outside the BP filling station on Oakley Rd and also a Co-op supermarket (Mon-Fri 6am-10pm, Sat & Sun 6am-9pm) and a **public toilet** here.

There are **bus** services from High Wycombe to Thame via Kingston Blount (Arriva's No 40) and to Princes Risborough (Carousel's No 320). Both services stop at the Red Lion and the Village Centre; see pp42-5 for further details.

If you want a **taxi** call Chinnor Cabs (☎ 01844 353637).

Where to stay

There is a B&B at *7 Station Road* (☎ 01844 351889; 1S/2T, share a bathroom) where a twin room is £50 for the first night and £45 per night for longer stays and the single is £35 or £30 for two nights or more. Packed lunches are available on request for £5 and they will also do luggage transfer, the charge depending on the distance.

Where to eat and drink

The Mayflower (☎ 01844 354034; Wed-Sun noon-2pm & 6-11pm, Tue 6-11pm), a Chinese restaurant, rustles up a delicious szechuan fried chicken for £6.45. If you'd prefer Indian, head to *Chinnor Indian* (☎ 01844 353038, 🖳 www.chinnorindiancuisine.co.uk; Mon-Sat noon-2.30pm & 6-11.30pm, Sun noon-3pm & 6-11.30pm) which is a couple of minutes' walk from the 'centre', but worth it if you like Indian food as this place is very good. The *kakra khani* (crab curry) would be a good choice at £5.50 for a starter and £9.50 for a main course.

Just across the road is the *Red Lion* (☎ 01844 353468; food daily noon-2pm & 7-9pm) serving pub grub including a steak night on Wednesdays for £6.95.

In the same part of the village is the rather grandly named *Kingston Fisheries* (☎ 01844 353874; Tue-Sat noon-1.45pm & 5-10pm). It's the only fish and chip shop in the village.

The *Village Centre* (☎ 01844 353733, 🖳 www.chinnorvillagecentre.co.uk; Mon-Fri 9.30am-5pm, Sat 9.30am-2.30pm) is a

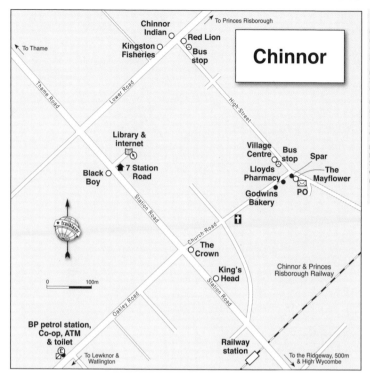

To Princes Risborough

Chinnor
Indian

Red Lion

To Thame

Kingston
Fisheries

Bus
stop

Chinnor

Thame Road

Lower Road

High Street

Library &
internet

Village
Centre

Bus
stop

Spar

Black
Boy

7 Station
Road

Lloyds
Pharmacy

The
Mayflower

Station Road

Godwins
Bakery

PO

trailblazer

0   100m

Church Road

The
Crown

King's
Head

Chinnor & Princes
Risborough Railway

Oakley Road

Station Road

BP petrol station,
Co-op, ATM
& toilet

Railway
station

To Lewknor &
Watlington

To the Ridgeway, 500m
& High Wycombe

meeting place for Chinnor residents but is mainly popular with the older generation. They serve tea and coffee (60p), sandwiches (£1.40-70), plus a decent all-day breakfast (£3.30).

Apart from the Red Lion, mentioned above, there are several other pubs in the village including: the *King's Head* (☎ 01844 351530; Mon-Thu 4-11pm, Fri 4pm-midnight, Sat noon-midnight, Sun noon-

11pm) that serves Greene King ales but no food; *The Crown* (☎ 01844 351244, food Mon-Wed noon-2.30pm & 6-8.30pm, Thu & Fri noon-2.30pm & 6-7.30pm, Sun noon-3pm), about a hundred metres further down Station Rd; and the *Black Boy* (☎ 01844 350426; food Mon-Sat noon-8.45pm, Sun noon-6pm). The Crown and the Black Boy are open all day.

Though the Ridgeway and Icknield Way have been sharing the same path since around Watlington, they eventually separate (Map 37) with the Icknield Way taking a straight course to Princes Risborough and the Ridgeway meandering along a much more roundabout route. Depending on how you are feeling at this point in the day, you might decide to take the Icknield Way as it meets up again with the Ridgeway before going into Princes Risborough. *(cont'd on p160)*

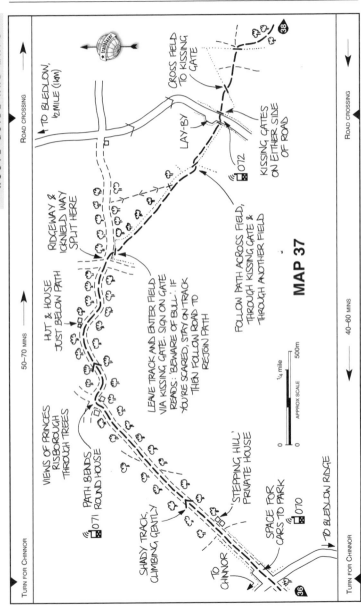

TURN FOR CHINNOR

50–70 MINS

ROAD CROSSING

TO BLEDLOW, ½ MILE (1KM)

CROSS FIELD TO KISSING GATE

LAY-BY

072

KISSING GATES ON EITHER SIDE OF ROAD

RIDGEWAY & ICKNIELD WAY SPLIT HERE

HUT & HOUSE JUST BELOW PATH

LEAVE TRACK AND ENTER FIELD VIA KISSING GATE. SIGN ON GATE READS: 'BEWARE OF BULL'. IF YOU'RE SCARED, STAY ON TRACK THEN FOLLOW ROAD TO REJOIN PATH

FOLLOW PATH ACROSS FIELD, THROUGH KISSING GATE & THROUGH ANOTHER FIELD

MAP 37

VIEWS OF PRINCES RISBOROUGH THROUGH TREES

071 PATH BENDS ROUND HOUSE

SHADY TRACK, CLIMBING GENTLY

'STEPPING HILL' PRIVATE HOUSE

SPACE FOR CARS TO PARK

070

TO CHINNOR

TO BLEDLOW RIDGE

36

APPROX SCALE
0 ¼ mile
0 500m

TURN FOR CHINNOR

40–60 MINS

ROAD CROSSING

38

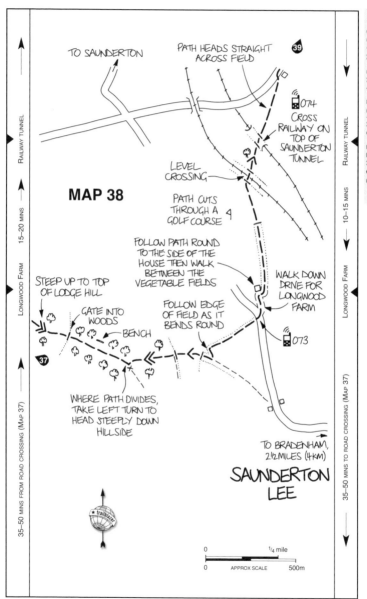

TO SAUNDERTON

PATH HEADS STRAIGHT ACROSS FIELD

39

074

CROSS RAILWAY ON TOP OF SAUNDERTON TUNNEL

RAILWAY TUNNEL

15-20 MINS

LEVEL CROSSING

MAP 38

PATH CUTS THROUGH A GOLF COURSE

RAILWAY TUNNEL

10-15 MINS

FOLLOW PATH ROUND TO THE SIDE OF THE HOUSE THEN WALK BETWEEN THE VEGETABLE FIELDS

WALK DOWN DRIVE FOR LONGWOOD FARM

LONGWOOD FARM

STEEP UP TO TOP OF LODGE HILL

GATE INTO WOODS

BENCH

FOLLOW EDGE OF FIELD AS IT BENDS ROUND

073

37

LONGWOOD FARM

WHERE PATH DIVIDES, TAKE LEFT TURN TO HEAD STEEPLY DOWN HILLSIDE

35-50 MINS FROM ROAD CROSSING (MAP 37)

TO BRADENHAM, 2½ MILES (4KM)

SAUNDERTON LEE

35-50 MINS TO ROAD CROSSING (MAP 37)

★ trailblaze

0   ¼ mile

0   APPROX SCALE   500m

(cont'd from p157) From where the two paths divide to where they rejoin, the Icknield Way is 1½ miles/2.5km and the Ridgeway is 2¾ miles/4.5km. Another factor that might sway your decision is that the Ridgeway heads off through a gate to which an unmissable yellow and black sign saying 'Beware of Bull' is fixed.

Some time after your encounter with the bull the Ridgeway cuts through a golf course (Map 38), the second so far, and crosses a railway track. It hardly needs to be mentioned to take great care here. A couple of minutes further on there is another railway crossing but this time you are walking on the roof of **Saunderton Tunnel**. From the path you get a great view of the extremely steep

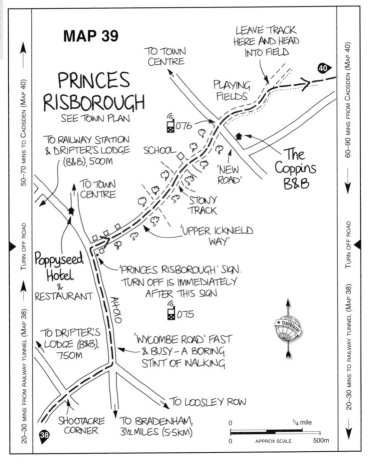

MAP 39

PRINCES RISBOROUGH
SEE TOWN PLAN

TO TOWN CENTRE

LEAVE TRACK HERE AND HEAD INTO FIELD

PLAYING FIELDS

40

076

TO RAILWAY STATION & DRIFTER'S LODGE (B&B), 500M

SCHOOL

'NEW ROAD'

The Coppins B&B

TO TOWN CENTRE

STONY TRACK

'UPPER ICKNIELD WAY'

Poppyseed Hotel & RESTAURANT

A4010

'PRINCES RISBOROUGH' SIGN. TURN OFF IS IMMEDIATELY AFTER THIS SIGN

075

TO DRIFTER'S LODGE (B&B), 750M

'WYCOMBE ROAD' FAST & BUSY - A BORING STINT OF WALKING

TO LOOSLEY ROW

SHOOTACRE CORNER

38

TO BRADENHAM, 3½ MILES (5·5KM)

0   ¼ mile

0   APPROX SCALE   500M

50-70 MINS TO CADSDEN (MAP 40)

TURN OFF ROAD

20-30 MINS FROM RAILWAY TUNNEL (MAP 38)

60-90 MINS FROM CADSDEN (MAP 40)

TURN OFF ROAD

20-30 MINS TO RAILWAY TUNNEL (MAP 38)

and deep cutting that leads to the tunnel. Turn left at Shootacre Corner (Map 39) if staying in Drifter's Lodge (see p162).

The final part of this section is the walk towards Princes Risborough along the busy A4010: it is as dull as most other walks along fast main roads. The Ridgeway only skirts the town so unless staying at Poppyseed Hotel (see p162), or needing the railway station, the best way to get to the centre is to turn off the A4010 after the Princes Risborough sign (following the Ridgeway path) and then left when New Road crosses the path: it's then about 500m to the centre of town.

PRINCES RISBOROUGH
[see map p162]

This is the biggest town you'll have visited so far on the journey. Despite this, the centre is still compact with most of the shops and services occupying the old High St and large supermarkets at either end. As the Ridgeway passes more or less through the town it makes a convenient overnight or lunch stop.

Like many of the towns around here, this one dates back a very long way, possibly to Roman times. The Saxons were certainly here and a couple of hundred years after they arrived there is a mention of this town in the Domesday Book as 'Riseburg'.

Edward, 'The Black Prince', had his palace here in the 14th century, hence the town's name, though the site of the palace is now unfortunately a car park, so not really worth investigating.

The arrival of the railway in 1862 caused the town to grow considerably and by the 1930s the previously separate towns of Princes Risborough and Monks Risborough had merged.

Services
There is a **post office** (Mon-Fri 9am-5.30pm, Sat 9am-12.30pm) on the High St along with NatWest, Barclays and Lloyds TSB banks, all with **ATMs**.

Near the roundabout at the bottom of the High St is the **Princes Risborough Information Centre** (☎ 01844 274795, 🖳 risborough_office@wycombe.gov.uk) that is open Mon-Fri 9am-5pm, Sat 10am-3pm; the staff can make accommodation bookings. Close by is the **library** (☎ 0845 230 3232; Tue 9.30am-7.30pm, Wed-Fri

9.30am-5pm, Sat 9.30am-1pm) where you can use the **internet** for 30 mins for £1.

Just off the High St is **Risborough Cycles** (☎ 01844 345949; Mon-Sat 9.30am-5pm), should you need any spares or repairs. You can find maps of the local area in the **bookshop** (Mon-Fri 9.15am-5.30pm, Sat 9.15am-5pm) on the High St. There is a **supermarket** at either end of the High St: **Tesco** (Mon-Sat 8am-10pm, Sun 10am-4pm) at the top and **M&S Simply Food** (Mon-Sat 8am-8pm, Sun 10am-4pm) at the bottom; both have **public toilets**. Next to M&S Simply Food there is a **newsagent** (Mon-Fri 6am-6pm, Sun 8am-1pm) and in the middle of the High St there is a **chemist** (Mon-Fri 9am-6pm, Sat 9am-5.30pm), a branch of Lloyds Pharmacy. There is a **farmers' market** once a month (see box p15).

If you need a **taxi** B&V Taxis (☎ 01844 342079) are very helpful and recommend advance bookings. The railway line here is still open, unlike in many of the surrounding towns and there are regular **trains** to London Marylebone and Birmingham, see box p39.

Arriva's No 300 **bus** from High Wycombe to Aylesbury passes through Princes Risborough; Carousel's No 320 goes to Chinnor; and the County Rider service to High Wycombe also calls at Saunderton. See pp42-5 for further details.

Where to stay
Conveniently located just 150m south of the Ridgeway is *The Coppins* (Map 39; ☎ 01844 344508, 🖳 www.thecoppins.co.uk; 1S/2D or T, shared shower room). It's

a quiet place with great views from the rear of the house towards Whiteleaf Cross. The rooms here are from £60 each or £35 if you are on your own. Packed lunches are available on request.

Another good place to stay, which is slightly out of town, is *Drifter's Lodge* (off Map 39; ☎ 01844 274773, 🖳 www.drifters lodge.co.uk; 1D/2T) at 60 Picts Lane. The bright and comfortable en suite rooms go from £59.50, or from £42 for single occupancy. Packed lunches are available on request.

Poppyseed Hotel (Map 39; ☎ 01844 345569; 3S/3D/3T) is also only a few minutes' walk from the Ridgeway, but further from the town centre. There's an Indian restaurant (see opposite) and pub downstairs and well-kept en suite rooms upstairs; singles/doubles go for £40/50 and breakfast costs £4.95. To get here follow the Ridgeway as it heads towards the town on the A4010. Where the Ridgeway turns off this main road, you need to simply keep on it for another 200m where the road forks either side of the Poppyseed.

Right in the centre of town you could try *The George & Dragon* (☎ 01844 343087, 🖳 www.georgeanddragonrisbor ough.co.uk; 4D). The accommodation at this place was being refurbished at the time of writing but the work was expected to be completed by February 2009. Contact them for further details.

Where to eat and drink

For a coffee and home-made cake, *Fired Up* (☎ 01844 275511; Tue-Fri 10am-5pm, Sat 10am-5.30pm) is at one end of the High St while *Crumbs Too* is located at the other.

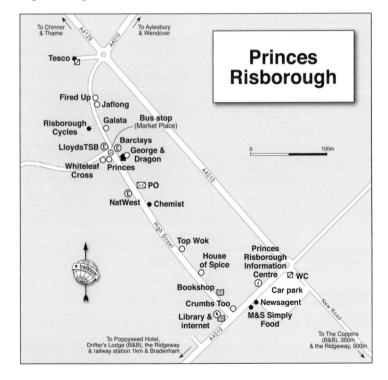

Princes Risborough

Alternatively, the *Top Wok* (☎ 01844 344333; Mon-Sat noon-2pm & 5.30-10.30pm, Sun noon-3pm & 5.30-10pm), on the High Street, is a canteen-style Chinese restaurant that also serves a range of pizzas for £5. For curry lovers the *House of Spice* (☎ 01844 345654; daily noon-2pm & 6-11pm), on the High St, is always busy but for a quieter Indian meal try *Jaflong* (☎ 01844 274443; daily 5.30-11.30pm) further up the road. The chef's special *lamb bemisall* here is well worth the £7.50.

The restaurant (daily 5.30-11pm) at the *Poppyseed Hotel* (see opposite) serves all the usual dishes on an Indian menu: mains cost £5.75 to £13.95.

For something different try *Galata* (☎ 01844 343134; Mon-Sat 10am-midnight, Sun noon-10pm), a Turkish restaurant towards the Tesco end of the High St. Main dishes range from £4.75 to £12.50 with the *hunkar begendi* (marinated lamb on a bed of creamed aubergine) costing £10.

The *George & Dragon* (see opposite; food Mon-Sat noon-2.30pm, Sun noon-4pm, Tue-Sat 7-9.30pm) has a French chef in the kitchen and the menu certainly reflects this Gallic influence. There are also some North African dishes on the menu. A set two-course lunch is £6.95 and includes beef and olive stew with mashed potatoes. The menu in the evening is á la carte but two courses should cost around £12.

On the corner of the High St, near Market Place, *Whiteleaf Cross* (☎ 01844 346834; food Mon-Thu 10am-2.30pm & 6-9pm, Fri 10am-2.30pm, Sat 10am-7pm, Sun noon-3pm & 6-9pm) is a friendly pub with a contemporary feel: it's popular with locals and serves standard but filling pub grub.

There is also a very busy fish and chip shop on the High St called *Princes* (☎ 01844 343751; Mon & Sat 11.30am-2pm & 4.30-9pm, Tue-Fri 11.30am-2pm & 4.30-10pm, Sun 4.30-9pm).

PRINCES RISBOROUGH TO WIGGINTON [MAPS 39-46]

Overview

This section is **12¹/₂ miles/20km** but be aware that there are many steep ups and downs to tire you out before the end is in sight. A great deal of the walking is through mature woodlands on good paths and there is plenty of variety. You'll pass by Chequers, the Prime Minister's country house, visit a Boer War monument on top of a hill with stunning views, and pass through the attractive and useful town of Wendover, amongst other things.

If you decide you want to walk right through to Ivinghoe Beacon in one day, be prepared for a tough time. On paper the 17¹/₂ miles/28km doesn't sound unreasonable, but the steep up and down sections will leave you weary well before you get your first sight of the Beacon. From there it's a strenuous last few miles to the end. Then there is the matter of walking from the Beacon to accommodation or to transport – a walk into Ivinghoe village is entirely possible but that would add another couple of miles. For this reason, starting the last day from somewhere reasonably close, such as Wigginton, can make a lot of sense. It'll also mean you'll have some energy left at the end of the day to celebrate finishing the Ridgeway.

Route

The section from Princes Risborough to Wendover is very popular with both day walkers and dog walkers. The Ridgeway and Icknield Way share the same path until they are out of Princes Risborough, then they split. The Icknield Way continues on the main path and rejoins the Ridgeway later.

At the top of the first steep climb you'll enter **Whiteleaf Nature Reserve** (Map 40). On the west side of the hill, facing Monks Risborough, there is a chalk cross on a triangular base cut into the hill – the **Whiteleaf Cross**. The history of this monument is hazy to say the least, but it was recorded as far back as the mid-1750s. It's probably been enlarged since then and now a concerted effort has been made to restore and maintain it. This nature reserve is also known for its variety of butterflies and wild flowers. Even if you're not looking specifically, you're bound to notice a chalkhill blue butterfly (see opp p64) or two and you'll probably also see the common blue. Flowers that grow well on this chalky soil have wonderful names, such as squinancy wort and viper's bugloss. The former is easy to spot having slender stems bearing pale-pink and white flowers. Viper's bugloss has a tall thick stem with purple funnel-shaped flowers.

After descending this hill, you come to **Cadsden** (Map 40), and more importantly a pub, *The Plough* (☎ 01844 343302, 🖥 www.ploughatcadsden .com; 5D or T en suite, food Mon-Sat noon-2pm & 6.30-9.30pm, Sun noon-2.30pm). Some may say this is Lower Cadsden but the pub sign says Cadsden. It's not hard to see why this well-maintained place is extremely popular for food and drink, particularly at weekends: it would be all too easy to get stuck here – especially as they now offer accommodation! They charge £60 for single occupancy and £90 for two sharing, including breakfast. Breakfast is eaten in a newly built orangery. Customers can also sit in their new miniature, heated barn. For dogs and walkers (!) there is a **water tap** in the pub's garden on the other side of the road.

Another steep climb will take you through woodlands and you'll eventually catch sight of Chequers (Map 41). The dwelling you might be able to see today dates from the 16th century though there has been a house on this site since the 12th century. Over time, Chequers has been modified by its various inhabitants, but a Mr Arthur Lee and his wife Ruth restored the house to its original Tudor glory in the early part of the 20th century. During the 1st World War Chequers was used as a hospital and convalescent home after which it was donated to the then prime minister, David Lloyd George, by the Lees. Since then it has been at the disposal of the current serving Prime Minister, though now it isn't used as much as it previously was. Its isolated position in the middle of the valley floor makes it impossible to miss, though at the time of writing not a great deal could be seen owing to the scaffold and tarpaulin covering extensive renovation works on the house.

Although the route cuts straight across the driveway, no other part of the grounds or the house is open to the public. Naturally, security around here is tight: you'll certainly see surveillance cameras and perhaps police on patrol.

After Chequers you rejoin the Icknield Way and there is another steep climb back onto high ground followed by some good walking through mature woodland which stays fairly level for some time. There are many paths through here and you'll need to look out for the black 'acorn marker' posts and the occasional Ridgeway signpost, to keep on the right path. *(cont'd on p168)*

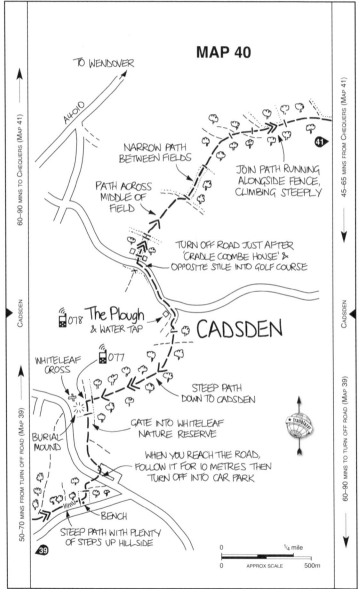

ROUTE GUIDE AND MAPS

MAP 40

TO WENDOVER

A4010

NARROW PATH
BETWEEN FIELDS

JOIN PATH RUNNING
ALONGSIDE FENCE,
CLIMBING STEEPLY

41

PATH ACROSS
MIDDLE OF
FIELD

TURN OFF ROAD JUST AFTER
'CRADLE COOMBE HOUSE' &
OPPOSITE STILE INTO GOLF COURSE

078 The Plough
& WATER TAP

CADSDEN

WHITELEAF
CROSS

077

STEEP PATH
DOWN TO CADSDEN

GATE INTO WHITELEAF
NATURE RESERVE

BURIAL
MOUND

WHEN YOU REACH THE ROAD,
FOLLOW IT FOR 10 METRES THEN
TURN OFF INTO CAR PARK

BENCH

STEEP PATH WITH PLENTY
OF STEPS UP HILL-SIDE

39

60-90 MINS TO CHEQUERS (MAP 41)

CADSDEN

50-70 MINS FROM TURN OFF ROAD (MAP 39)

45-65 MINS FROM CHEQUERS (MAP 41)

CADSDEN

60-90 MINS TO TURN OFF ROAD (MAP 39)

trailblazer

0   ¼ mile
0   APPROX SCALE   500m

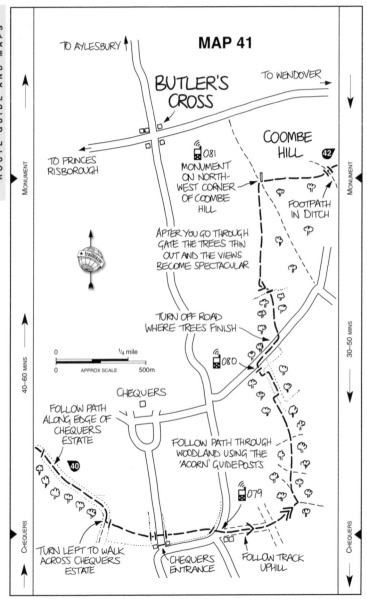

MAP 41

TO AYLESBURY

TO WENDOVER

BUTLER'S CROSS

COOMBE HILL

42

TO PRINCES RISBOROUGH

081
MONUMENT ON NORTH-WEST CORNER OF COOMBE HILL

FOOTPATH IN DITCH

AFTER YOU GO THROUGH GATE THE TREES THIN OUT AND THE VIEWS BECOME SPECTACULAR

TURN OFF ROAD WHERE TREES FINISH

080

CHEQUERS

FOLLOW PATH ALONG EDGE OF CHEQUERS ESTATE

40

FOLLOW PATH THROUGH WOODLAND USING THE 'ACORN' GUIDEPOSTS

079

TURN LEFT TO WALK ACROSS CHEQUERS ESTATE

CHEQUERS ENTRANCE

FOLLOW TRACK UPHILL

0   ¼ mile
0   APPROX SCALE   500m

MONUMENT

30–50 MINS

40–60 MINS

CHEQUERS

MONUMENT

CHEQUERS

ROUTE GUIDE AND MAPS

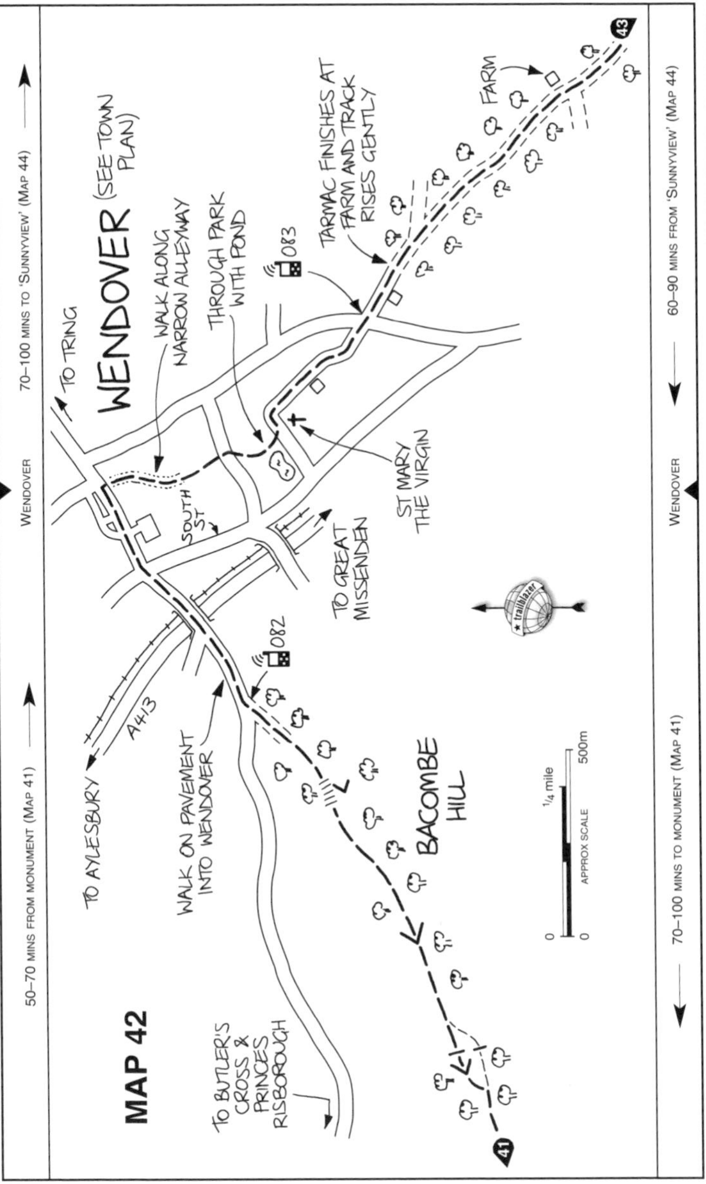

MAP 42

To BUTLER'S CROSS & PRINCES RISBOROUGH

WENDOVER (SEE TOWN PLAN)

WALK ALONG NARROW ALLEYWAY

THROUGH PARK WITH POND

TO TRING

SOUTH ST

TARMAC FINISHES AT FARM AND TRACK RISES GENTLY

FARM

083

ST MARY THE VIRGIN

TO GREAT MISSENDEN

TO AYLESBURY

A413

WALK ON PAVEMENT INTO WENDOVER

082

BACOMBE HILL

Trailblazer

¼ mile

APPROX SCALE

0   500m

50-70 MINS FROM MONUMENT (MAP 41)

70-100 MINS TO 'SUNNYVIEW' (MAP 44)

WENDOVER

60-90 MINS FROM 'SUNNYVIEW' (MAP 44)

WENDOVER

70-100 MINS TO MONUMENT (MAP 41)

41

43

(cont'd from p164) As the path opens out you'll have amazing views to the west before reaching the monument and trig point on the north-west corner of Coombe Hill. This is a popular place for day-trippers and after the lonely effort of the last couple of miles it's quite surprising to see so many people up here. The **monument** commemorates those men from Buckinghamshire who were killed in the Boer War. It was completed in 1904 but had to be partially rebuilt in 1939 after being damaged when struck by lightning.

From here you should be able to see Wendover, the next town on the Ridgeway, down below. It's all downhill to the town with the path joining the surfaced road to take you the last few hundred metres into the town itself.

WENDOVER

Even if the Ridgeway didn't go straight through the centre of Wendover it would still be a good idea to stop off here. It's an attractive town with a compact centre where all the shops and services are located.

This town was mentioned in the Domesday Book but probably dates from a good deal earlier than that. Its position on the road from London to Aylesbury has always ensured it plenty of passing trade and in days gone by it had a large number of inns to cater for weary travellers. There are still some very old pubs to stop off at for a few drinks.

Its proximity to London by train also means this is a popular place for city workers to commute from; as a result the town has an air of affluence.

Services

The **post office** (Mon-Fri 9am-5.30pm, Sat 9am-12.30pm) is on the High St along with a Lloyds TSB **bank** and ATM. Other useful services on this street include a branch of **Lloyds Pharmacy** (Mon-Fri 9am-6.30pm, Sat 9am-5.30pm) and a **newsagent** (Mon-Sat 6am-6pm, Sun 7am-3pm). Next to the newsagent is a Budgens **supermarket** (Mon-Sat 6.30am-10pm, Sun 9am-6pm). There is also a Barclays, with an **ATM**, on Aylesbury Rd.

If you're looking for outdoor clothing or equipment you'll probably find it at **Wendover Outdoors & Countrywear** (☎ 01296 624988; Tue-Fri 9.45am-5.30pm, Sat 9.45am-5pm, closed for lunch 1-2pm) on Back St. There's a monthly **farmers' market** (see box p15).

Wendover Tourist Information Centre (TIC; ☎ 01296 696759, 🖳 www .visitbuckinghamshire.org; Mon-Sat 10am-4pm) is in the clock tower at the bottom of the High St. The staff are very helpful and unless you're careful you come out laden with all manner of interesting leaflets about the area. There is also a **library** (☎ 0845 230 3232; Tue & Thu 9.30am-5pm, Wed & Sat 9.30am-1pm, Fri 9.30am-7pm), just off the High St, at the back of the car park, where you can access the **internet** for £1 for half an hour. You'll find **Wendover Book Shop** (☎ 01296 696204; Mon-Sat 9.30am-5pm) on the High St: it stocks a range of local interest books. There are **public toilets** in the car park.

Bus services from the town include Aylesbury (Arriva's No 54), Tring and Ivinghoe (Red Rose Travel's No 161); see pp42-5 for further details. There is a **taxi** firm at the railway station called Alexander's (☎ 01296 620888).

Wendover **train** station is on the Chiltern Line which runs from Aylesbury to London Marylebone; see box p39.

Where to stay

The most atmospheric place in which to stay is the ***Red Lion Hotel*** (☎ 01296 622266; 2S/16D/2T/2F). This is a 17th-century coaching inn that used to be the start/end point for coaches to London. The front of the hotel looks as if it has changed little since those days and the interior is just as authentic. This really is a place worth stopping off at even if you are not staying here – but if you are you can have a very

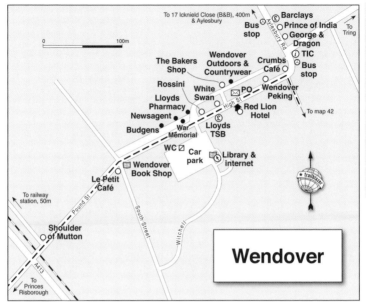

To 17 Icknield Close (B&B), 400m
& Aylesbury

Barclays
Bus stop
Prince of India
George & Dragon
To Tring
TIC
Bus stop
Wendover Outdoors & Countrywear
The Bakers Shop
Crumbs Café
Rossini
White Swan
PO
Wendover Peking
Lloyds Pharmacy
Red Lion Hotel
Newsagent
To map 42
Budgens
War Memorial
Lloyds TSB
WC
Car park
Library & internet
Wendover Book Shop
Le Petit Café
To railway station, 50m
Pound St
South Street
Witchel
Shoulder of Mutton
A413
To Princes Risborough

100m

Wendover

comfortable en suite room for £89.95 (the family rooms are £99.95).

If you'd prefer something a little cheaper, the B&B at *17 Icknield Close* (☎ 01296 583285, 🖳 grbr.samuels@ntlworld .com; 1S/2T, shared bathroom) might be just the thing. This friendly place is less than ten minutes' walk from the High St and charges £60 per room (£30 if you are on your own). To get there walk up Aylesbury Rd and turn into Wharf Rd which will be on your right. The turning for Icknield Close will then also be on your right.

Where to eat and drink
If you just want something quick you could try *The Bakers Shop* (☎ 01296 624642; Mon, Tue, Thu & Fri 7.30am-3.30pm, Wed 7.30am-3pm, Sat 7.30am-2pm), on Back St, or *Crumbs Café* (☎ 01296 622468; Mon-Sat 8am-5pm, Sun 9am-4pm) where you can get a sandwich and drink. There is also *Le Petit Café* (☎ 01296 624601; Tue-Fri 9.30am-4.30pm, Sat & Sun 9.30am-5.30pm) which serves much the same

things though with a touch more style. Sandwiches here cost £3.95-6.20.

On Pound St the *Shoulder of Mutton* (☎ 01296 623223; food Mon-Sat 11am-10pm, Sun noon-9pm) is a large, old Chef & Brewer pub serving a range of food from lamb rump to asparagus with crushed butternut squash.

The *Red Lion Hotel* (see opposite; restaurant Mon-Thu 9am-9.30pm, Fri & Sat 9am-10pm, Sun 10am-9.30pm) serves bar meals as well as a restaurant menu. The bar serves paninis and baked potatoes throughout the day and real ales that change on a regular basis. The restaurant menu changes every few months but main courses are around £10-13.

On the High St you'll find the Mediterranean-styled *Rossini* (☎ 01296 622257, 🖳 www.rossinirestaurant.co.uk; daily noon-2pm & 7-9.30pm). It's an upmarket place where a set two-course dinner is around £22 (£25.95 for three courses) and lunchtime specials include tuna nicoise or mushroom ravioli for £9.95.

Just down from the post office is the only Chinese restaurant in town, *Wendover Peking Restaurant* (☎ 01296 623991; Mon-Thu noon-1.45pm & 6-10.30pm, Fri & Sat noon-1.45pm & 6-11pm, Sun 6-10.30pm). They serve crispy chilli beef for £5.80. Inside the *George & Dragon* (☎ 01296 586152; food Wed-Sun noon-2.30pm, Tue-Sat 6-10pm, Sun 6-9pm) is a Thai restaurant and takeaway. With around 60 items on the menu, you are spoilt for choice but the *gai ped mamuang* (chicken stir fried with cashew nuts) is £6.50 and recommended. The *Prince of India* (☎ 01296 622761; daily noon-2.30pm & 6-11.30pm), almost next door to the George & Dragon, serves tasty Indian food: the *korai chicken* at £7.95 is good.

The *White Swan* (☎ 01296 622271, Sun-Thu noon-11pm, Fri & Sat noon-midnight) looks small from the outside but has several bar areas inside and is open all day. They do not serve food but appear to make up for that by selling plenty of drink.

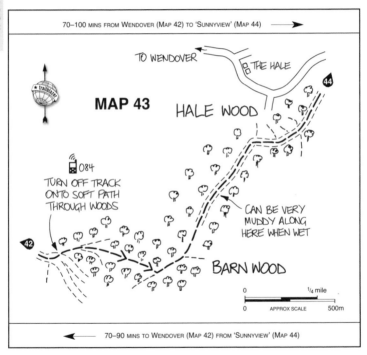

70-100 MINS FROM WENDOVER (MAP 42) TO 'SUNNYVIEW' (MAP 44)

TO WENDOVER

THE HALE

MAP 43

HALE WOOD

44

084

TURN OFF TRACK ONTO SOFT PATH THROUGH WOODS

CAN BE VERY MUDDY ALONG HERE WHEN WET

42

BARN WOOD

0   ¼ mile
0   APPROX SCALE   500m

70-90 MINS TO WENDOVER (MAP 42) FROM 'SUNNYVIEW' (MAP 44)

The path out of Wendover follows a pleasant route between houses and parks before emerging at a T-junction in front of the church of **St Mary the Virgin** (Map 42). This church was built in the 14th century and was used briefly as a camp by some of Oliver Cromwell's New Model Army troops during the English Civil War. Today it's still well used but for more sedate purposes such as afternoon tea and bellringing practice.

There's another long climb up into woodland that thankfully levels out for some time along the ridge through the Forestry Commission's **Hale Wood** (Map 43). This is a lovely walk along good paths surrounded by mature woodlands including many conifer trees. Although there are good views back to Wendover from here, the forest blocks them for most of the time.

You'll rejoin the Icknield Way after the woods. For many miles now the Ridgeway and Icknield Way have often been following the same route and at times the Icknield Way can provide you with a shortcut if you are in a hurry. For instance, both paths leave Wendover at roughly the same place, but by the time they meet up again Ridgeway walkers have gone 2³/₄ miles/4.5km whereas Icknield Way walkers have only gone 1³/₄ miles/3km. However, if you're going to walk the Ridgeway, you might as well do it properly.

Having said that, up ahead there is a part of the Ridgeway that it might be best not to do properly and I doubt many people do. You'll come to a **T-junction** (Map 44) in woodland and need to turn right. The official signpost for this is at the bottom of a steep ditch. So, you can descend into the ditch and follow

ROUTE GUIDE AND MAPS

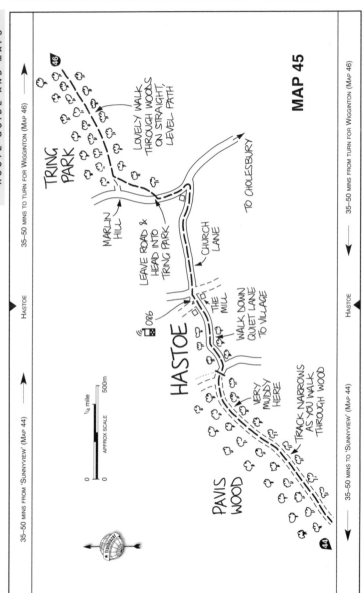

35–50 MINS FROM 'SUNNYVIEW' (MAP 44)   HASTOE   35–50 MINS TO TURN FOR WIGGINTON (MAP 46)

MAP 45

35–50 MINS FROM TURN FOR WIGGINTON (MAP 46)   HASTOE   35–50 MINS TO 'SUNNYVIEW' (MAP 44)

TRING PARK

LOVELY WALK THROUGH WOODS ON STRAIGHT, LEVEL PATH

MARLIN HILL

LEAVE ROAD & HEAD INTO TRING PARK

CHURCH LANE

TO CHOLESBURY

086

HASTOE

THE MILL

WALK DOWN QUIET LANE TO VILLAGE

VERY MUDDY HERE

TRACK NARROWS AS YOU WALK THROUGH WOOD

PAVIS WOOD

¼ mile
500m
APPROX SCALE

it up the hill, or simply continue walking on the woodland path parallel to the ditch. Having walked in the ditch I wouldn't recommend it unless you like muddy boots and hordes of flies for company.

After passing through the collection of houses and farms collectively known as **Hastoe** (Map 45), you'll enter **Tring Park**, leased to the Woodland Trust (see p58). This park used to be much bigger but in 1974 the A41 was cut straight through the centre of it in an east–west direction. The manor house is now located in the top half, while the Ridgeway passes through the bottom half. It's a really enjoyable section of the walk along decent paths with plenty of wildlife to look out for, including fallow deer.

The next village you come to is Wigginton (Map 46). The Ridgeway passes a few hundred metres from the 'centre' and it's a good place to stay the night if you want a relaxed last day of walking up to Ivinghoe Beacon.

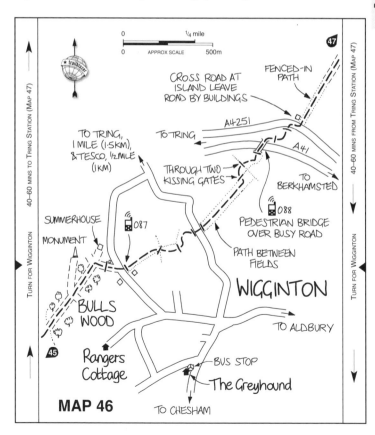

0 — ¼ mile
0 — APPROX SCALE — 500m

47

40–60 MINS FROM TRING STATION (MAP 47)

40–60 MINS TO TRING STATION (MAP 47)

TURN FOR WIGGINTON

TURN FOR WIGGINTON

CROSS ROAD AT ISLAND LEAVE ROAD BY BUILDINGS

FENCED-IN PATH

A4251

TO TRING

A41

TO TRING, 1 MILE (1·5KM), & TESCO, ½ MILE (1KM)

THROUGH TWO KISSING GATES

TO BERKHAMSTED

088

SUMMERHOUSE

087

PEDESTRIAN BRIDGE OVER BUSY ROAD

MONUMENT

PATH BETWEEN FIELDS

WIGGINTON

BULLS WOOD

TO ALDBURY

45

Rangers Cottage

BUS STOP

The Greyhound

MAP 46

TO CHESHAM

WIGGINTON [MAP 46, p173]

This small village has been here for centuries. It's a sleepy place with little to do, but has two good accommodation options and a decent pub in which you can wind down after a long day on the Ridgeway. It's probably best known for the exclusive Champneys Health Spa just out of the village on the Chesham Road.

There are no shops, nor is there a post office. A **taxi** can be ordered through Diamond Cars (☎ 01442 890303) which is just as well because Red Rose Travel's No 387 **bus** between Tring and Aldbury is the only service calling here; see pp42-5.

The Greyhound (☎ 01442 824631, ☐ www.the-greyhound.co.uk; 2D/1F, food Mon-Sat noon-2.30pm & 6-9.30pm, Sun noon-3pm) is the only pub in the village and hence popular with the locals. This friendly place is open all day and has a changing selection of real ales. Their menu includes scampi and chips or hand-carved ham with two fried eggs and chips for £7.95 and a 10oz Aberdeen Angus steak for £13.50. It's a deservedly popular place with walkers too, so book well ahead for the en suite accommodation. Rates are £60 for a double or £45 for one person. The family room is £75.

The other place to stay is *Rangers Cottage* (☎ 01442 890155, ☐ www.rangers cottage.com; 2D/1T) which is set in a beautiful and quiet location. All the rooms are en suite and have separate access from the main house. Single occupancy costs £65 and a room for two sharing is £75 plus £5 per room on a Friday or Saturday night. This is a very relaxing place to stay.

If you are heading for Tring you'll also need to leave the Ridgeway where the path crosses the road at Wigginton. It's about 1 mile/1.5km to the centre of Tring from here. The advantage that staying in Tring has over Wigginton is that there are far more facilities, but on the other hand it's not on the Ridgeway so you'll have to take into account the time and effort of walking there and back. If you are just after a bed and some food you are better off staying in Wigginton.

TRING

This is a large town near the end of the Ridgeway and it would be a good place at which to stop before you tackle the last stretch of walking up to Ivinghoe Beacon, but maybe it would be better to come here after you have finished the Ridgeway as, apart from all the shops and services you might need, there are good public transport links to get you back home. There aren't, however, many places to stay in Tring, so you might prefer to make your visit brief.

Like many of the towns in this chain of settlements along the edge of the Chilterns, there is evidence of Saxon settlement in Tring and it's also mentioned in the Domesday Book.

The town has always been on a natural pathway and when the Grand Junction Canal was cut through here in the late 18th century commerce in the town really started to expand. In the early 19th century a large silk mill was established in Tring and this gave employment to many of the town's women and children.

In 1835 a railway was built along the course of the canal which runs to the east of Tring. Although this meant that the railway station was not built in the town it still further improved Tring's accessibility, especially to London.

You might well expect a museum in this town to include some of this history, but in fact its subject is something altogether different. The **Natural History Museum at Tring** (☎ 020 7942 6171, ☐ www.nhm .ac.uk/tring; entry free) is just a few minutes' walk from the High St. It's at the corner of Akeman St and Park St and is open Mon-Sat 10am-5pm and Sun 2-5pm. It comprises about 4000 stuffed animals from Walter Rothschild's personal collection. You'll be able to see anything from a coelacanth to a great auk to a platypus. It really is worth a visit!

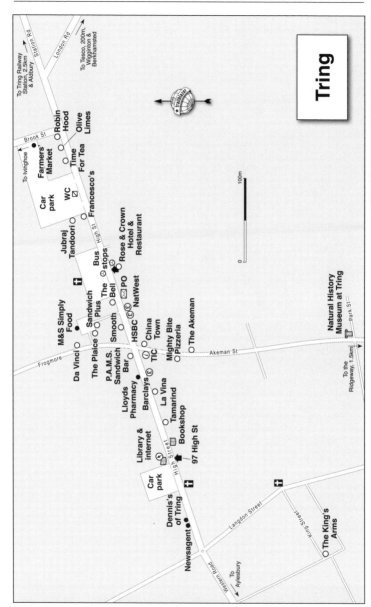

Tring

Services

The **post office** (☎ 01442 823211; Mon-Fri 9am-5.30pm, Sat 9am-12.30pm) can be found on the High St next to the NatWest and HSBC **banks**, both with ATMs. There's also a Barclays with an ATM further along the same street.

If you need more local info, **Tring Information Centre** (TIC; ☎ 01442 823347, 🖳 www.tring.gov.uk/info/info cent.htm) is conveniently located right in the middle of the High St but the entrance is on Akeman St. It has plenty of literature and advice, but its opening times (Mon-Fri 9.30am-3pm and Sat 10am-1pm) are limited. The **library** (Mon 10am-7pm, Tue, Thu, Fri 9am-7pm, Wed 9am-5pm, Sat 9am-4pm), also on the High St, has **internet** access at £1.50 for half an hour. A **bookshop** (Mon-Fri 9am-5.30pm, Sat 9am-5pm) with a small selection of maps covering the local area is near Barclays Bank and there are several newsagents on this street, too.

Dennis's of Tring (Mon-Fri 9am-5.15pm, Sat 9am-5pm), past the library, should be able to help with some walking-related supplies. There is an M&S Simply Food **supermarket** (Mon-Fri 8am-8pm, Sat 8am-7pm, Sun 10am-4pm) in a precinct just off the High St and a large branch of Tesco on London Rd. The **farmers' market** (see box p15) is held in the Market Place.

A branch of **Lloyds Pharmacy** (Mon-Fri 9am-6pm, Sat 9am-5.30pm) can be found on the High St.

Tring is a stop on Silverlink's frequent **rail** service from London Euston to Northampton, see box p39. There are a reasonable number of **bus services** from Tring to nearby villages such as Ivinghoe, Wigginton and places further away such as Aylesbury and Luton. The important thing is to make sure you go to the correct stop: Red Rose Travel's No 387 stops at both the Rose & Crown and the train station; Arriva's Nos 61 and 500 only stop at the Rose & Crown and their No 30 stops at the station; Red Rose Travel's No 161 stops only at the Rose & Crown; see pp42-5 for further details.

If you need a **taxi** you should phone John Executive Cars (☎ 01442 828828), based at Tring Station (Map 47).

Where to stay

You can't beat the location of the *Rose & Crown Hotel & Restaurant* (☎ 01442 824071, 🖳 www.roseandcrown-tring .co.uk; 4S/18D/2T/3F) and it's hard to miss it, too. This huge, mock-Tudor building stands out a mile on the High St. Its origins do date back to Tudor times, but in the early 20th century the building on this site was demolished and the current hotel constructed. The 27 en suite rooms are anything but mock-Tudor with all mod-cons and a price of £80/90 for singles/doubles or twins during the week and £70/80 at weekends; a family room costs £125 during the week and £110 at the weekend. If you fancy splashing out on a hotel to celebrate completing the Ridgeway, maybe this should be it?

In a great location, right in the town centre is *97 High Street* (☎ 01442 823678; 1D private bathroom) which charges £60, or £40 if you're on your own. Breakfast (with organic food) can either be a full English or continental. Packed lunches are available if requested in advance; a separate charge is made.

Where to eat and drink

There is no shortage of possibilities and the variety is good, too. This would make a good place to have a relaxing meal and a few drinks to finish off your Ridgeway trip.

If you fancy a lunchtime sandwich you could head for *P.A.M.S. Sandwich Bar* (☎ 01442 824262; Mon-Fri 9am-3pm, Sat 9am-2pm), on the High St. They do all the usual sandwiches, baguettes and rolls here and charge from £2 to £4. In the precinct near the supermarket, *Sandwich Plus* (☎ 01442 826489; Mon-Fri 8.30am-3pm) does much the same thing.

(Opposite) Top: St Mary the Virgin church in the centre of Ivinghoe village (see p182).
Bottom: The trig point atop Ivinghoe Beacon (see p181) marks the end of the Ridgeway.

For a light lunch there is the tiny *Time For Tea* (Mon-Fri 8.30am-5pm, Sat 9am-5pm, Sun 10am-3pm) where a serving of good old beans on toast with cheese is only £3.95. They also have veg chilli and salad for £5.25. If you want it cheap and cheerful the even smaller, *Smooth* (Mon-Sat 8am-4.30pm), on the High St, has takeway shakes, smoothies, paninis and baguettes.

The *Rose & Crown Hotel & Restaurant* (food Mon-Sat 12.30-2pm & 6.30-9pm, Sun noon-4pm & 6.30-9pm), mentioned opposite, is probably the most expensive place in town though the restaurant is popular: main courses range from £15 to £25.

There are several Indian restaurants and among them is the recommended *Jubraj Tandoori* (☎ 01442 890386; daily 12.30-2pm & 6-11.45pm), just off the High St. The *nababi hash* (flame-grilled duck in spices) is well worth £9.95. Other Indian restaurants include *Tamarind* (☎ 01442 827788; Mon-Thu 6-11.30pm, Fri & Sat 6pm-midnight, Sun 6-11.30pm) where one of the chef's specials is *tilapia bhaja* (£7.50). You could also head to *Olive Limes* (☎ 01442 828444; daily noon-2.30pm, Sun-Thu 5.30-11pm, Fri & Sat 6-11.20pm) which has a more contemporary feel to it. The *chicken achari* (£7.95) is delicious.

The Italian restaurant and café *Francesco's* (☎ 01442 827258; Mon-Sat 10am-3pm & 6-11pm, Sun noon-11pm) is a really popular place, especially in the day time when the café gets very busy. Authentic pizzas here are priced from £7.50. There's another Italian restaurant on Frogmore St called *Da Vinci* (☎ 01442 891300; Mon-Thu noon-3pm & 6-10pm, Fri & Sat noon-3pm & 6-10.30pm, Sun noon-9pm), which has all the usual pizzas and pasta dishes and also a selection of fish: the *pesctrice zenese* (monkfish with cherry tomatoes and thyme) for £13.95 is recommended.

If you'd prefer a Spanish flavour to your meal, *La Vina* (☎ 01442 824509, 🖥 www.lavina.co.uk; Mon-Sat noon-10.30pm, Sun noon-10pm), right on the High St, has a vast array of mouthwatering tapas ranging from £3.45 to £5.95 per dish. At the time of writing they opened at 10am and served coffee and pastries but this may not continue.

Several standard takeaways are dotted around Tring. They include: *China Town* (☎ 01442 824831; Wed & Thu noon-1.45pm & 5-11.30pm, Tue & Sun 5-11.30pm, Fri & Sat noon-1.45pm & 5pm-midnight) which serves exactly what you'd expect; *Mighty Bite Pizzeria* (☎ 01442 828556; Sun-Thu 5-11pm, Fri & Sat noon-11pm) serving pizzas, burgers and jacket spuds and *The Plaice* (☎ 01442 828248; Mon-Fri noon-2.30pm & 4-9.30pm, Sat noon-2.30pm & 4-9pm), a fish and chip shop.

There are plenty of pubs around town, most of them serving food. The most upmarket of them is *The Akeman* (☎ 01442 826027, 🖥 www.theakeman.co.uk; Mon-Sat 9am-midnight, Sun 9am-11pm) a café/pub/restaurant serving Mediterranean-style food. They serve an English-style breakfast (9am-noon; £6.25) and later on there's a wide choice of Spanish, Italian and Greek dishes ranging from £6.50 to £14.95.

The Bell Inn (☎ 01442 828357; food daily 12.30-2.30pm), on the High St, is full of young drinkers and can get quite lively in the evenings. They have paninis, jacket spuds, baguettes and some main meals for £2.70-5. The *Robin Hood* (☎ 01442 824912; food Mon-Sat noon-2.15pm & 6-9.15pm, Sun noon-2.15pm) is far more sedate and really rather quiet. Probably the most interesting choice is just a short walk away from the western end of the High Street; *The King's Arms* (☎ 01442 823318; food Mon-Sat noon-2.15pm, Mon-Thu & Sat 7-9.30pm, Fri 7-9pm, Sun noon-3pm & 7-9pm) on King St. This is a friendly place on a suburban street with various real ales and a relaxed atmosphere. All these pubs are open all day.

(Opposite) Top: There are superb views from Coombe Hill (see p168) and the monument that commemorates men from Buckinghamshire who died in the Boer War. **Bottom**: The Shoulder of Mutton pub, a welcoming sight on the road into Wendover (see p169).

WIGGINTON TO IVINGHOE BEACON [MAPS 46-48]

Overview
This final **5 mile/7.9km** section of the Ridgeway may not seem much of a challenge but as most of this stage is uphill, with a steep climb to the finish itself,
it'll probably be enough. From the finish you'll also have to walk at least to the
nearest road, or probably to the nearest village, Ivinghoe. This will add around
1¹/₂ miles/2.5km to your walk and you don't want to be too tired to celebrate
with a drink or two in one of the local pubs at the end.

Route
From Wigginton you'll soon come to the **pedestrian bridge** (Map 46) crossing
the crowded A41 that runs from Bicester down to the M25. Next up it's the fast
A4251 that you must cross without the aid of a bridge, so take care.

Soon after these two road crossings, the Ridgeway crosses the **Grand
Union Canal** (Map 47; see box below).

After crossing two roads and a canal, next up is a rail line. You pass by
Tring Station, now a minor stop for trains on the West Coast Main Line to/from
London Euston. The large building next to the station used to be a hotel but has
closed. There is a taxi company (see p176) in the station car park, but if you're
not catching a train here there is little reason to stop. You follow the road for a
few more minutes and when you leave it, you can consider yourself to be beginning the last stage of the Ridgeway. If you want to visit Aldbury, don't turn off
here, but continue on the road for another half a mile/1km.

ALDBURY [see map p180]
Aldbury is a picture-perfect English village,
complete with duck pond, church and pub. It
would be a good alternative to Wigginton if
the accommodation there is full. This idyllic
village has been captured on film many
times: *The Avengers*, *The Dirty Dozen*,
Inspector Morse, and, more recently, *Bridget
Jones's Diary: The Edge of Reason*.

You'll be surprised when you look
inside the **village shop** (Mon, Tue, Thu, Fri
6am-5.30pm, Wed & Sat 6am-7.30pm, Sun
7.30am-4pm). Not only is it very well
stocked and much larger than it looks from
the outside, but there is a **post office** in here
as well as an **ATM**.

Buses leave the village for Tring
(Arriva's No 30, Centrebus No 327 and
Red Rose Travel's No 387) and other desti-
nations; see pp42-5 for further details.

Where to stay and eat
Opposite the duck pond is *The Greyhound*
(☎ 01442 851228, 🖳 www.greyhoundald
bury.co.uk; 6D/1D or F, all en suite; food
Mon-Sat noon-9.30pm, Sun noon-8pm), a

❏ **The Grand Union Canal**
This runs from the River Thames in Brentford, up through the Chilterns via many
locks, then on to Birmingham where it finishes 137 miles/220km later. Initially this
was the Grand Junction Canal, which opened in 1805 and ran only from Brentford,
Middlesex, to Braunston, Northamptonshire, to link with the Oxford Canal. In 1929
it was linked to various other branches running up to Birmingham via Warwick and
was renamed the Grand Union Canal. Nowadays the main traffic on the canal is
barges rented by tourists. The towpath, from the Thames at Brentford to Birmingham,
is now also recognised as an official walking path.

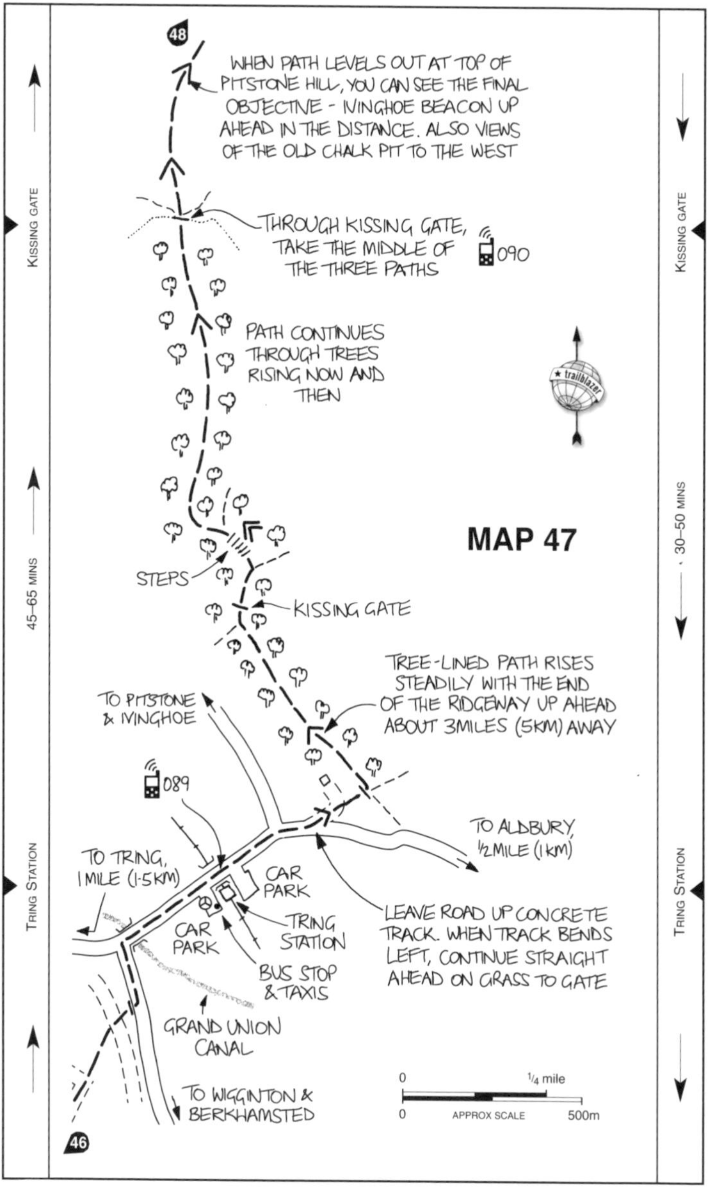

48

WHEN PATH LEVELS OUT AT TOP OF PITSTONE HILL, YOU CAN SEE THE FINAL OBJECTIVE – IVINGHOE BEACON UP AHEAD IN THE DISTANCE. ALSO VIEWS OF THE OLD CHALK PIT TO THE WEST

THROUGH KISSING GATE, TAKE THE MIDDLE OF THE THREE PATHS

📱090

PATH CONTINUES THROUGH TREES RISING NOW AND THEN

MAP 47

STEPS

KISSING GATE

TREE-LINED PATH RISES STEADILY WITH THE END OF THE RIDGEWAY UP AHEAD ABOUT 3 MILES (5KM) AWAY

TO PITSTONE & IVINGHOE

📱089

TO ALDBURY, ½ MILE (1KM)

TO TRING, 1 MILE (1·5KM)

CAR PARK

TRING STATION

CAR PARK

BUS STOP & TAXIS

GRAND UNION CANAL

LEAVE ROAD UP CONCRETE TRACK. WHEN TRACK BENDS LEFT, CONTINUE STRAIGHT AHEAD ON GRASS TO GATE

TO WIGGINTON & BERKHAMSTED

46

KISSING GATE

KISSING GATE

45–65 MINS

30–50 MINS

TRING STATION

TRING STATION

0   ¼ mile

0   APPROX SCALE   500m

much filmed and photographed place. Food is served all day and there is a varied menu: you could try the ginger-coated deep-fried chicken strips with a sweet chilli dip (£6.75) for lunch while the evening menu includes pan-fried sea bass (£14.50) and ribeye steak with chips (£16). B&B costs £75, £65 if you're on your own and £90 for three in a room.

A good option for food is *The Valiant Trooper* (☎ 01442 851203, 🖥 www.valiant trooper.co.uk; food daily noon-9pm). This pub is less than five minutes' walk from the centre of the village. Being a freehouse, they have a changing selection of real ales to accompany their food choices. The menu itself changes a couple of times a year but includes daily specials as well as standard pub fare. A little further along the road from the Valiant Trooper is a B&B at *16 Stoneycroft* (☎ 01442 851294; 1S/1D/1T); the double/twin rooms cost £50 and the single is £25. All share a bathroom.

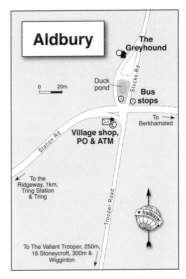

The path climbs through woodland, sometimes level, but more often than not climbing (Map 47). By now there will only be a few miles left and you might think it's all going to be over soon. Then you'll get your first glimpse of Ivinghoe Beacon, up ahead in the far distance. The word, 'far' is appropriate but at least the end is now always in sight. You can admire the increasingly stunning views from up here and plod on.

You can also see, down to your left a large, old chalk pit, now filled with water; this is a popular place for relaxing and swimming during the summer. The water takes on a turquoise colour, adding something almost tropical to the atmosphere of the place. If you are plodding your way up to the Beacon on a hot day, just the sight of it can make you want to run down there and dive right in.

When you reach the road and car park (Map 48) the Icknield Way puts in an appearance once more and stays with you all the way to the end of the Ridgeway. Gradually the Beacon gets closer until you are left with just one last climb to the end. This will just about finish you off if you started the day at Princes Risborough.

There is a Ridgeway information board and trig point at the end of the walk to go with the panoramic views. There are often other people up here but not many that have been on the Ridgeway for the last 87 miles, for sure. Take plenty of time to relax, enjoy the views and reflect on the previous stages. When you are ready to leave the Beacon you have several choices. If you are lucky, someone might be waiting to pick you up from the car park you passed on your way up here. If not, you'll need to walk down to Ivinghoe village. The best way to do this is to follow one of the many paths down the hillside to the main road. Be careful as it's very steep and there are plenty of hidden holes in the ground.

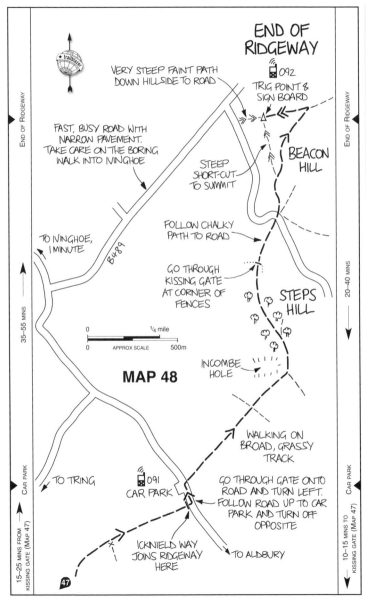

END OF RIDGEWAY

092
TRIG POINT & SIGN BOARD

VERY STEEP FAINT PATH DOWN HILLSIDE TO ROAD

FAST, BUSY ROAD WITH NARROW PAVEMENT. TAKE CARE ON THE BORING WALK INTO IVINGHOE

BEACON HILL

STEEP SHORT-CUT TO SUMMIT

TO IVINGHOE, 1 MINUTE

B489

FOLLOW CHALKY PATH TO ROAD

GO THROUGH KISSING GATE AT CORNER OF FENCES

STEPS HILL

0   ¼ mile
0   500m
APPROX SCALE

MAP 48

INCOMBE HOLE

TO TRING

091
CAR PARK

WALKING ON BROAD, GRASSY TRACK

GO THROUGH GATE ONTO ROAD AND TURN LEFT. FOLLOW ROAD UP TO CAR PARK AND TURN OFF OPPOSITE

ICKNIELD WAY JOINS RIDGEWAY HERE

TO ALDBURY

47

ROUTE GUIDE AND MAPS

End of Ridgeway

End of Ridgeway

20–40 MINS

35–55 MINS

15–25 MINS FROM KISSING GATE (MAP 47)

CAR PARK

CAR PARK

10–15 MINS TO KISSING GATE (MAP 47)

Most paths finish near to the B489 from where it's a boring walk into Ivinghoe. This road is not particularly wide but still people drive very fast along it so be careful. If you get on with it the 1¼ mile/2km walk from the top of Ivinghoe Beacon to Ivinghoe village shouldn't take more than about half an hour.

IVINGHOE

Given its name you'd be right in presuming that this village is the closest to the end of the Ridgeway at Ivinghoe Beacon. This means that most Ridgeway walkers will pass through, or stay here, at some point.

Services

The village **post office** (☎ 01296 668358; Mon, Tue, Thu & Fri 9am-1pm & 2-5.30pm, Wed 9am-1pm, Sat 9am-12.30pm) is located behind the **Village Centre**; just follow the signs round to the side of the building. The village centre sells soft drinks and biscuits, but nothing more substantial to eat. The **library** (☎ 0845 230 3232; Tue & Thu 2-5pm, Fri 2-7pm, Sat 10am-1pm) offers **internet access** at £1 for 30 minutes.

The nearest shop for groceries is **Mason's Stores** (☎ 01296 660052; Mon-Fri 6.30am-8pm, Sat 7am-8pm, Sun 7.30am-5pm) on Marsworth Rd in Pitstone village about ten minutes' walk away. It's also an **off-licence** and **newsagent**.

A number of **buses** (Arriva's Nos 61 and Red Rose Travel's Nos 161) stop here en route to destinations such as Aylesbury, Tring, Dunstable, Luton, Leighton Buzzard and Wendover but some of the services are limited; see pp42-5 for further details.

Where to stay

Despite a good deal of local opposition, Ivinghoe Youth Hostel closed in 2007.

However, accommodation can be found at the welcoming ***Bull Lake B&B*** (☎ 01296 668834, 🖳 www.bull-lake.co.uk; 2T, shared bathroom) where it's £30 per person. It's a popular place with a lot of regular bookings so advance reservations are essential. To walk here follow Station Rd out of the village centre for a few minutes. The farm is on your right.

There is also ***The Brownlow*** (☎ 01296 668787, 🖳 www.thebrownlow.com; 4D/1T, all en suite) about a mile out of the village where the road crosses the Grand

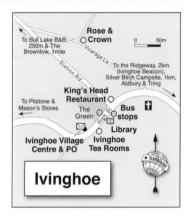

Union canal. Light, spacious rooms are available from £75 to £85 (£45-55 if you're on your own). To reach here, head out of the village on Station Rd.

If you want to camp, head for the ***Silver Birch Campsite*** (☎ 01296 668348; open Apr-Oct) which has ten pitches at £3.50 per person. It's a fairly basic campsite but has all the essentials. It's on the B488 road, about half a mile out of the village.

Where to eat and drink

Down Vicarage Lane is the cosy ***Rose & Crown*** (☎ 01296 668472; pub Mon-Sat noon-3pm & 6-11pm, Sun noon-3pm & 7-10.30pm, food Mon-Sat noon-2pm & 6-9.30pm, Sun noon-2pm) which serves real ales and meals. They have a specials board which includes various fish dishes, plus the usual pub grub such as gammon and eggs. Mains cost from £7.50 to £13.95.

In the centre of the village, ***Ivinghoe Tea Rooms*** (☎ 01296 660650; Thu-Sun 9am-4.30pm) have a lovely garden in which to relax with a post-walk cream tea (£4.60), or if you're after something more filling they do a range of soups, jacket potatoes, sandwiches and pies.

The 17th-century **King's Head Restaurant** (☎ 01296 668388, 💻 www.kingsheadivinghoe.co.uk; Mon-Sat noon-2.15pm & 6.45-9.30pm, Sun noon-2.15pm), right in the centre of the village, is known for its high-quality cuisine. It's not really the place for muddy walkers and with the average three-course meal costing £36.50-50, plus drinks, you'll probably not find many of them in there anyway. However, they do a three-course lunch menu Monday to Saturday for £17.95 which might be worth considering for a celebratory lunch.

In **Pitstone** village, next to Mason's Stores, there is a Chinese restaurant and takeaway called **May Fu Peking Restaurant** (☎ 01296 661969; Wed-Sat noon-2pm & 5.30-11pm, Sun noon-2pm & 6.30-10.30pm, Tue 5.30-11pm). You won't be stuck for choice at this well-liked place where main dishes cost between £5 and £8.

APPENDIX A: MAP KEYS

Town plan key

🏠	Where to stay	ⓘ	Tourist Information	☉	Bus stop
○	Where to eat	📖	Library/bookstore	☑	Public toilet
Δ	Campsite	Ⓢ	Internet	—▭—	Rail line & station
⊠	Post office	🏛	Museum/gallery		Park
Ⓔ	Bank/ATM	🛉	Church/cathedral	•	Other

Trail map key

Walking track		Stile		Building	
Subsidiary track		Gate		Accommodation	
4WD track		Bridge		Campsite	
Road		Fence		Church	
Steps		River		Public toilet	
Slope		Trees/wood		Bus stop	
Steep slope		Map continuation		GPS waypoint	

APPENDIX B: THE GREATER RIDGEWAY

LYME REGIS TO HUNSTANTON

After you've completed the Ridgeway you might like to consider a stroll along parts of the Greater Ridgeway that link Lyme Regis, in Dorset, with Hunstanton, in Norfolk. The Ridgeway covered in this book comprises just the middle section.

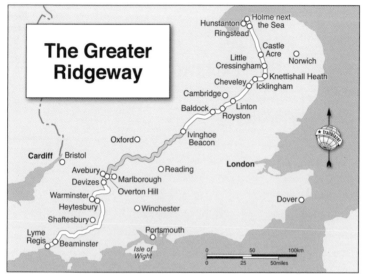

Starting from the popular seaside town of Lyme Regis, you can follow the Wessex Ridgeway 136 miles (219km) up to its finishing point at Marlborough in Wiltshire, crossing the Ridgeway near Avebury. From Lyme Regis the path goes through Beaminster before meandering through open country and numerous small villages and passing within a few miles of Shaftesbury. You then skirt round the edge of Salisbury Plain taking in the towns of Heytesbury and Warminster. From here you head towards the Westbury White Horse and on to Devizes before arriving in Avebury and finally Marlborough.

From there the Ridgeway in this book takes you up to Ivinghoe Beacon from where you can follow the Icknield Way on to Knettishall Heath in Suffolk, 103 miles (165km) away. The long history of this trail equals that of the Ridgeway and is made evident by the wealth of archaeological remains found along here. The route continues on the high chalky ground visiting numerous towns along the way including Baldock, Royston and Linton. From here the Icknield Way continues to Cheveley and Icklingham before finishing at Knettishall Heath Country Park.

Picking up where the Icknield Way finishes, the Peddars Way from Knettishall Heath to Hunstanton, clocks in at 46 miles (74km) and provides easy walking to the end of the Greater Ridgeway. This largely straight inland route follows a Roman road in open countryside with few villages en route. You will pass through Little Cressingham, Castle Acre and Ringstead before reaching the coast at Holme next the Sea. From here you walk along the coast to reach Hunstanton, and the end of the Greater Ridgeway.

Further information
The Wessex Ridgeway, Anthony Burton, Aurum, 1999; *Ancient Trackways of Wessex*, HW Timperley & Edith Brill, Nonsuch, 2005; *The Icknield Way Path: A Walkers' Guide*, Chris James, Icknield Way Association, 2006; *Walking the Peddars Way and Norfolk Coastal Path with Weavers Way: A Guide and Accommodation list*, Ian Mitchell, Ramblers Association Norfolk Area, 2005; *Peddars Way and Norfolk Coastal Path*, Bruce Robinson, National Trail Guides, 2002

APPENDIX C: GPS WAYPOINTS

Each GPS waypoint below was taken on the route at the reference number marked on the map as below.

MAP	REF	GPS WAYPOINT	DESCRIPTION
Map A	A	N51° 25.712' W01° 51.236'	Red Lion, Avebury
Map B	B	N51° 25.246' W01° 50.749'	Gate to Waden Hill
Map B	C	N51° 25.041' W01° 51.188'	Join River Kennet
Map B	D	N51° 25.130' W01° 51.336'	Left turn
Map B	E	N51° 24.967' W01° 51.705'	Silbury Hill car park
Map B	F	N51° 24.851' W01° 51.110'	Leave A4 road
Map B	G	N51° 24.732' W01° 51.045'	Turn to the Long Barrow
Map B	H	N51° 24.516' W01° 51.017'	West Kennet Long Barrow
Map B	I	N51° 24.496' W01° 50.096'	Join road into East Kennet
Map B	J	N51° 24.711' W01° 49.834'	Start of the Ridgeway
Map B	K	N51° 25.065' W01° 49.816'	Turn to Avebury
Map A	L	N51° 26.191' W01° 51.236'	Junction with Green Street
Map C	M	N51° 26.234' W01° 48.851'	Cross track
Map C	N	N51° 26.517' W01° 47.638'	Reservoir
Map C	O	N51° 26.597' W01° 47.109'	Junction in path
Map D	P	N51° 26.384' W01° 46.326'	Driveway to Manton House
Map E	Q	N51° 25.957' W01° 44.954'	Road crossing
Map E	R	N51° 25.565' W01° 44.213'	Gate into cemetery
Map E	S	N51° 25.113' W01° 44.031'	Marlborough High Street
Map 1	001	N51° 24.711' W01° 49.834'	Start of the Ridgeway
Map 1	002	N51° 25.065' W01° 49.816'	Turn to Avebury
Map 2	003	N51° 26.191' W01° 51.236'	Junction with Green Street
Map 2	004	N51° 27.312' W01° 49.245'	Kink in path
Map 3	005	N51° 28.294' W01° 48.913'	Hackpen Hill car park
Map 4	006	N51° 29.115' W01° 47.178'	Barbury Castle
Map 4	007	N51° 28.979' W01° 46.483'	Castle Café
Map 5	008	N51° 28.325' W01° 44.461'	Cattle grid
Map 6	009	N51° 27.752' W01° 43.303'	Turn to Southend
Map 6	010	N51° 27.746' W01° 41.822'	Crossroads

MAP	REF	GPS WAYPOINT		DESCRIPTION
Map 7	011	N51° 28.618'	W01° 41.520'	Road crossing
Map 7	012	N51° 29.224'	W01° 41.694'	Crossroads at reservoir
Map 8	013	N51° 29.688'	W01° 41.640'	Lower/Upper Upham junction
Map 8	014	N51° 30.036'	W01° 41.521'	Fork in path
Map 9	015	N51° 30.994'	W01° 41.695'	Gate near Liddington Castle
Map 9	016	N51° 31.429'	W01° 41.267'	Turn to Fox Hill
Map 10	017	N51° 31.803'	W01° 40.100'	Shepherds Rest, Fox Hill
Map 11	018	N51° 32.559'	W01° 38.213'	Road junction to Bishopstone
Map 11	019	N51° 33.010'	W01° 37.270'	Turn to Idstone
Map 12	020	N51° 33.432'	W01° 36.427'	B4000 road crossing
Map 12	021	N51° 33.969'	W01° 35.700'	Entrance to Wayland's Smithy
Map 13	022	N51° 34.459'	W01° 34.013'	Second gate, Uffington Castle
Map 14	023	N51° 34.452'	W01° 32.134'	Turn to Kingston Lisle
Map 14	024	N51° 34.217'	W01° 31.436'	Turn Sparsholt/Down Barn Fm
Map 15	025	N51° 33.826'	W01° 30.343'	Sparsholt Firs car park
Map 16	026	N51° 33.241'	W01° 28.012'	Turn to Letcombe Bassett
Map 16	027	N51° 33.317'	W01° 26.871'	Segsbury Farm
Map 16	028	N51° 33.437'	W01° 25.960'	A338 road crossing
Map 17	029	N51° 33.266'	W01° 23.906'	B4494 road crossing
Map 17	030	N51° 33.411'	W01° 23.408'	Large monument
Map 18	031	N51° 33.513'	W01° 23.086'	Large, sprawling junction
Map 18	032	N51° 33.648'	W01° 22.047'	Reservoir
Map 19	033	N51° 33.737'	W01° 20.428'	Turn to East Hendred
Map 19	034	N51° 33.194'	W01° 18.598'	Bury Down car park
Map 20	035	N51° 32.880'	W01° 17.679'	Tunnel under A34
Map 21	036	N51° 32.373'	W01° 16.590'	First turn to East Ilsley
Map 21	037	N51° 32.362'	W01° 16.544'	Second turn to East Ilsley
Map 21	038	N51° 32.125'	W01° 16.175'	Third turn to East Ilsley
Map 21	039	N51° 32.016'	W01° 16.059'	Fourth turn to East Ilsley
Map 22	040	N51° 32.262'	W01° 14.490'	Fork in path
Map 22	041	N51° 32.021'	W01° 13.844'	Crossroads
Map 22	042	N51° 31.786'	W01° 13.331'	Fork in path
Map 23	043	N51° 31.647'	W01° 12.551'	Turn to Aldworth
Map 23	044	N51° 31.639'	W01° 11.068'	Post Box Cottage
Map 24	045	N51° 31.726'	W01° 09.064'	Path joins A417 road
Map 24	046	N51° 31.363'	W01° 08.923'	Streatley crossroads
Map 26	047	N51° 32.929'	W01° 08.335'	Turn towards River Thames
Map 26	048	N51° 32.951'	W01° 08.701'	Slipway on bank of Thames
Map 27	049	N51° 33.454'	W01° 08.544'	Railway viaduct
Map 27	050	N51° 33.862'	W01° 08.072'	Small wooden footbridge
Map 28	051	N51° 34.306'	W01° 07.271'	North Stoke
Map 28	052	N51° 35.304'	W01° 07.232'	Turn before A4130 road
Map 28	053	N51° 35.121'	W01° 05.983'	Turn to Little Gables B&B
Map 29	054	N51° 35.069'	W01° 05.487'	Road to Crowmarsh Gifford
Map 29	055	N51° 35.012'	W01° 05.012'	Road to Ewelme & Woodcote
Map 30	056	N51° 34.716'	W01° 02.419'	T-junction in path
Map 30	057	N51° 34.862'	W01° 02.281'	Church & water tap, Nuffield
Map 30	058	N51° 35.048'	W01° 01.607'	The Crown, Nuffield
Map 31	059	N51° 35.833'	W01° 01.732'	Ewelme Park
Map 31	060	N51° 36.393'	W01° 00.979'	St Botolph's

MAP	REF	GPS WAYPOINT	DESCRIPTION
Map 32	061	N51° 37.392' W01° 01.316'	North Farm
Map 32	062	N51° 37.831' W01° 00.254'	Ridge Farm house
Map 33	063	N51° 38.022' W00° 59.954'	First turn to Watlington
Map 33	064	N51° 38.413' W00° 59.528'	Turn to White Mark Farm
Map 33	065	N51° 38.714' W00° 59.110'	Road crossing
Map 34	066	N51° 39.968' W00° 57.546'	Road to Lewknor
Map 35	067	N51° 40.404' W00° 56.903'	A40 road crossing
Map 35	068	N51° 40.908' W00° 55.741'	Road to Kingston Blount
Map 36	069	N51° 41.309' W00° 54.704'	Turn to Oakley Hill NR
Map 37	070	N51° 41.749' W00° 54.073'	Road to Chinnor
Map 37	071	N51° 42.264' W00° 53.218'	Path bends round house
Map 37	072	N51° 41.864' W00° 51.978'	Road to Bledlow
Map 38	073	N51° 41.741' W00° 50.531'	Longwood Farm drive
Map 38	074	N51° 42.205' W00° 50.498'	Saunderton railway tunnel
Map 39	075	N51° 42.930' W00° 50.118'	Leave A4010 road
Map 39	076	N51° 43.251' W00° 49.502'	Road crossing
Map 40	077	N51° 43.737' W00° 48.641'	Turn in path direction
Map 40	078	N51° 43.982' W00° 48.287'	The Plough, Cadsden
Map 41	079	N51° 44.221' W00° 46.578'	Leave road for track
Map 41	080	N51° 44.707' W00° 46.326'	Path joins road
Map 41	081	N51° 45.184' W00° 46.291'	Monument on Coombe Hill
Map 42	082	N51° 45.545' W00° 44.999'	Join road into Wendover
Map 42	083	N51° 45.366' W00° 44.098'	Crossroads
Map 43	084	N51° 44.949' W00° 43.456'	Path leaves track
Map 44	085	N51° 45.825' W00° 41.816'	Road crossing at Sunnyview
Map 45	086	N51° 46.532' W00° 40.269'	The Mill, Hastoe
Map 46	087	N51° 47.138' W00° 38.777'	Road crossing
Map 46	088	N51° 47.460' W00° 38.133'	Bridge over A41 road
Map 47	089	N51° 48.042' W00° 37.400'	Tring railway station
Map 47	090	N51° 48.956' W00° 37.379'	Take middle path
Map 48	091	N51° 49.496' W00° 36.931'	Car park
Map 48	092	N51° 50.531' W00° 36.502'	End of the Ridgeway

INDEX

Page references in **bold** type refer to maps

TRAILBLAZER GUIDES – TITLE LIST

Adventure Cycle-Touring Handbook	1st edn out now
Adventure Motorcycling Handbook	5th edn out now
Australia by Rail	5th edn out now
Azerbaijan with excursions to Georgia	3rd edn out now
China Rail Handbook	1st edn late 2009
Coast to Coast (British Walking Guide)	3rd edn out now
Cornwall Coast Path (British Walking Guide)	2nd edn out now
Corsica Trekking – GR20	1st edn out now
Cotswold Way (British Walking Guide)	1st edn out now
Dolomites Trekking – AV1 & AV2	2nd edn out now
Inca Trail, Cusco & Machu Picchu	3rd edn out now
Indian Rail Handbook	1st edn mid 2009
Hadrian's Wall Path (British Walking Guide)	2nd edn out now
Himalaya by Bike – a route and planning guide	1st edn out now
Japan by Rail	2nd edn out now
Kilimanjaro – the trekking guide (includes Mt Meru)	2nd edn out now
Mediterranean Handbook	1st edn out now
Morocco Overland – 55 routes (Atlas to the Sahara)	1st edn mid 2009
Nepal Mountaineering Guide	1st edn late 2009
New Zealand – The Great Walks	2nd edn mid 2009
North Downs Way (British Walking Guide)	1st edn out now
Norway's Arctic Highway	1st edn out now
Offa's Dyke Path (British Walking Guide)	2nd edn out now
Overlanders' Handbook – worldwide driving guide	1st edn late 2009
Pembrokeshire Coast Path (British Walking Guide)	2nd edn out now
Pennine Way (British Walking Guide)	2nd edn out now
The Ridgeway (British Walking Guide)	2nd edn out now
Siberian BAM Guide – rail, rivers & road	2nd edn out now
The Silk Roads – a route and planning guide	2nd edn out now
Sahara Overland – a route and planning guide	2nd edn out now
Scottish Highlands – The Hillwalking Guide	1st edn out now
South Downs Way (British Walking Guide)	3rd edn Mar 2009
Tibet Overland – mountain biking & jeep touring	1st edn out now
Tour du Mont Blanc	1st edn out now
Trans-Canada Rail Guide	4th edn out now
Trans-Siberian Handbook	7th edn out now
Trekking in the Annapurna Region	4th edn out now
Trekking in the Everest Region	5th edn out now
Trekking in Ladakh	3rd edn out now
Trekking in the Moroccan Atlas	2nd edn Aug 2009
Trekking in the Pyrenees	1st edn out now
The Walker's Haute Route – Mont Blanc to Matterhorn	1st edn out now
West Highland Way (British Walking Guide)	3rd edn out now

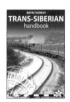

www.trailblazer-guides.com

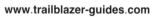

TRAILBLAZER'S LONG-DISTANCE PATH (LDP) WALKING GUIDES

We've applied to destinations which are closer to home Trailblazer's proven formula for publishing definitive route guides for adventurous travellers. Britain's network of long-distance trails enables the walker to explore some of the finest landscapes in the country's best walking areas and they are an obvious starting point for this series. These are guides that are user-friendly, practical, informative and environmentally sensitive.

● **Unique mapping features**
In many walking guidebooks the reader has to read a route description then try to relate it to the map. Our guides are much easier to use because walking directions, tricky junctions, places to stay and eat, points of interest and walking times are all written onto the maps themselves in the places to which they apply. With their uncluttered clarity, these are not general-purpose maps but fully edited maps drawn by walkers for walkers.

● **Largest-scale walking maps**
At a scale of just under 1:20,000 (8cm or 3¹/₈ inches to one mile) the maps in these guides are bigger than even the most detailed British walking maps currently available in the shops.

● **Not just a trail guide – includes where to stay, where to eat and public transport** Our guidebooks are a complete guide, not just a trail guide. They include: what to see, where to stay (pubs, hotels, B&Bs, campsites, bunkhouses, hostels), where to eat. There is detailed public transport information for all access points to each trail so there are itineraries for all walkers, both for hiking the route in its entirety and for day walks.

West Highland Way *Charlie Loram* ISBN 978-1-905864-13-3, £9.99
3rd edition, 192pp, 53 maps, 10 town plans, 40 colour photos

Pennine Way *Keith Carter & Chris Scott* ISBN 978-1-905864-02-7, £11.99
2nd edition, 272pp, 135 maps & town plans, 40 colour photos

Coast to Coast *Henry Stedman* ISBN 978-1-905864-09-6, £9.99
3rd edition, 240pp, 109 maps & town plans, 40 colour photos

Pembrokeshire Coast Path *Jim Manthorpe* ISBN 978-1-905864-03-4, £9.99
2nd edition, 208pp, 96 maps & town plans, 40 colour photos

Offa's Dyke Path *Keith Carter* ISBN 978-1-905864-06-5, £9.99
2nd edition, 208pp, 88 maps & town plans, 40 colour photos

South Downs Way *Jim Manthorpe* ISBN 978-1-873756-95-9, £9.99
2nd edition, 192pp, 60 maps & town plans, 40 colour photos

Hadrian's Wall Path *Henry Stedman* ISBN 978-1-905864-14-0, £9.99
2nd edition, 208pp, 60 maps & town plans, 40 colour photos

North Downs Way *John Curtin* ISBN 978-1-873756-96-6, £9.99
1st edition, 192pp, 60 maps & town plans, 40 colour photos

The Ridgeway *Nick Hill* ISBN 978-1-905864-17-1, £9.99
2nd edition, 192pp, 53 maps & town plans, 40 colour photos

Cotswold Way *Tricia & Bob Hayne* ISBN 978-1-905864-16-4, £9.99
1st edition, 192pp, 60 maps & town plans, 40 colour photos

Cornwall Coast Path *Edith Schofield* ISBN 978-1-873756-93-5, £9.99
2nd edition, 224pp, 112 maps & town plans, 40 colour photos

'The same attention to detail that distinguishes its other guides has been brought to bear here'. **The Sunday Times**